THE SOCIOLOGY OF ADULT AND CONTINUING EDUCATION

THE SOCIOLOGY OF ADULT & CONTINUING EDUCATION

PETER JARVIS

ROUTLEDGE
London & New York

First published 1985 by Croom Helm Ltd
Reprinted by Routledge 1989
11 New Fetter Lane, London EC4P 4EE
29 West 35th Street, New York, NY 10001

© 1985 Peter Jarvis

Printed and bound in Great Britain
by Billing & Sons Limited, Worcester

British Library Cataloguing in Publication Data

Jarvis, Peter, *1937–*
    The sociology of adult & continuing education.
    1. Adult education & lifelong education. Sociological
    perspectives
    I. Title
    374
    ISBN 0-415-03977-0

CONTENTS

Contents

Contents

Contents

LIST OF TABLES

FIGURES

ACKNOWLEDGEMENTS

The origins of most books are complex and often
hard to unravel, but this is not always the case.
This book emerged from the encouragement of
students following the sociology of the education
of adults course in the Post Graduate Certificate
in the Education of Adults at the University of
Surrey. Additional support was forthcoming from
those following the Adult Education option in the
M Sc in Educational Studies and I would like to
thank all of them for the constant stimulation
that they have provided during the book's
preparation.
     Colleagues in the Department of Educational
Studies have also contributed through the
provision of a stimulating climate within which to
teach. Friends, such as Colin Griffin, have
pointed me in the direction of books and ideas
which have considerably enriched this analysis.
Kay Thomas transformed a handwritten script into
a typescript with accuracy and efficiency.
Finally, and above all, my family have once again
tolerated a husband and father who seemed to spend
more time in his study than he should: to
Maureen, Frazer and Kierra I offer my sincere
gratitude for all their help and support.
     A part of the fourth chapter of this book has
already been published in Studies in the Education
of Adults as a separate paper 'Andragogy - a sign
of the times' and I am grateful for the opportunity
to use some of that material here.
     Despite all the support and stimulation that
I have received in the preparation of this book,
in the final instance it must be seen as my
responsibility.

INTRODUCTION

The early 1970s saw a growth in the interest in
the sociology of education but nearly everything
that was produced in that field was about initial
education. Adult and continuing education was not
really analysed from this perspective at all,
although a decade later there were indications that
this was beginning to occur in the United Kingdom
although this was perhaps less true of the United
States. This book, therefore, may be seen as a
part of the continuing sociological interest in
education. It is written to provide both those
who study the field and those who work in it with
a sociological overview. It seeks to draw on all
branches of sociology rather than to adopt merely
one approach; it does not seek to argue any case;
it espouses no ideological viewpoint - but that is
not to deny that the author's perspective may not
be discovered within the study. However, it is
hoped that this text will stimulate those who read
it to set adult and continuing education in a wide
sociological context.

PART I

SOCIOLOGICAL PERSPECTIVES

Chapter One

SOCIOLOGICAL INTRODUCTION

The education of adults is no new phenomenon: it
has existed for centuries in one form or another.
The Greeks separated education from training and
trained their children for their place in the
wider society but enabled their adults, who were
leisured enough, to be educated.   Hence, the
education of adults was not new in that society and
education itself was a phenomenon that would have
been open to the considerations of the social
analyst.   Indeed, there is a sense in which Plato
actually performed that function, although obviously
his analysis formed the basis of the philosophy of
education rather than a sociology of education.
Many centuries were to elapse before that was to
appear.   However, over that period the education
of adults has continued and as more studies in this
discipline appeared they have been embedded in
psychology, in adult learning and in designing
programmes for adult learners.   Clearly there are
many reasons why emphasis has been placed upon these
areas, such as the fact that it had traditionally
been assumed that intelligence declined in adulthood.   Hence myths of this nature had to be laid
to rest.
     More recently, it has been recognised that the
education of adults might be an instrument in
social change;   Gramsci (see Entwistle 1979), for
instance, thought that worker education could help
destroy the cultural hegemony of the dominant
social classes in Italy and, since the Second World
War, the education of adults has been viewed as
an instrument for the development of Third World
countries, by organizations such as UNESCO.
Additionally, it has been recognised that adult
education serves other functions in society, such
as a leisure function (Parker 1976).

Sociological Introduction

Despite its long history, no sociology of the education of adults exists in the same manner as there are sociological studies of initial education. Indeed, throughout this study recourse will be made to some of the insights in these analyses and their findings will be examined in the context of the education of adults. Thompson's (1980) symposium was one of the first attempts to produce a genuine sociological analysis of adult education but for a variety of reasons it was not received with tremendous enthusiasm by adult educators in the United Kingdom. Reviewers (Legge 1980, Stock 1981), while welcoming it, were critical for a variety of reasons including the fact that many of its contributors were university academics, it had a limited perception of adult education and the papers were of variable quality. However, one other major reason exists and this may be because it adopted a critical sociological perspective with a radical ideological approach. By contrast, Cunningham (1983:257) in America welcomed it as a 'breath of fresh air'. She was also aware of the book's deficiencies which exhibited no suspicion about the writers nor their perspectives.

Since the publication of that symposium there has been no systematic attempt to analyse the education of adults from the perspective of the social theorist, although there have been a number of studies published, some of which continues the debate that Thompson's book started. Thomas (1982), for instance, examines radical adult educators and shows the strategies that have been adopted to ensure that their ideas have not found wider audiences than they have. Since he is also interested in comparative adult education he has included in his study reference to what he regards as an institutionalised form of radical adult education, the Danish Folk High School, but in this sense Thomas ceased to deal with a politically radical form of education, so that while his study adds to the sociological literature it does not fall into the category of a systematic sociological analysis of the education of adults. Indeed, that was not the author's intention. Consequently, a gap still exists in the literature about adult and continuing education and the intention of this present study is to attempt to fill the void.

One of the reasons why no study of the education of adults has been undertaken from this perspective is the difficulty in deciding precisely what is the phenomenon under consideration.

McCullough (1980:158) nicely summarises this
problem:

> Extracting adult education from its
> surrounding social milieu - or at least
> differentiating adult education from its
> social milieu - is as difficult as a
> determining how many angels can dance on
> the head of a pin. Is adult education a
> practice or a program? A methodology or
> an organization? A "science" or a
> system? A process or a profession? Is
> adult education different from continuing
> education, vocational education, higher
> education? Does adult education have form
> and substance, or does it merely permeate
> the environment like air? Is adult
> education, therefore, everywhere yet
> nowhere in particular? Does adult
> education even exist?

He concludes in the affirmative in response to
this last question but many of the others remain
unanswered. However, two things he (1980:159) is
sure about, that adult education has an 'organization and a purpose that can be structurally
analyzed'. However, these conclusions and the
questions raised in the long quotation merely
reflect the complex issues that Peters and his
associates (1980) were grappling with in this
American study of adult education. The various
contributors to this study clearly differed in their
views about whether their lack of coherent structure
was a good or a bad thing for adult education:
Knowles (1980 a:39) appears to consider that it gives
flexibility to it to respond to whatever social
needs arose while Griffith (1980:74) considers that
this is a weakness because it inhibits planned
co-ordination. However, the fact remains that
the rich diversity of adult education makes it a
difficult subject to study sociologically and this
will be a recurrent theme throughout this text.
    That something exists for the education of
adults in a multitude of forms and organizations is
undeniable, and as such constitutes a 'social fact',
in Durkheim's sense, that may be studied by the
social analyst. However, sociological study of
this diverse phenomenon is complicated by another
factor; sociology itself is not a united
discipline. Hence, no single sociological per-
pective exists which encourages a systematic study

to be undertaken.   Herein lies another major
difficulty, since even if it were possible to
determine the parameters of the education of adults,
it is still necessary to recognise that any
sociological perspective adopted may reflect only
one element of the discipline.   Yet this does not
mean that it is impossible to examine adult
education from the social theorist's perspective
since, as McCullough points out, that it has both
structures and processes.   Significantly, but
unsurprisingly, the differences between structures
and processes reflect the differences between the
major perspectives in social theory, so that
before adult education is actually discussed it is
necessary to clarify these different sociological
schools of thought.   Hence this chapter focuses
both on the two different perspectives and, thereafter, on schools of thought and ideologies, and
concludes with a brief discussion of the implications
of the previous analysis for the study of adult and
continuing education.

The Two Sociologies
The phrase 'the two sociologies' is the title of a
well known paper by Dawe (1970) in which he argued
that since sociology is concerned with both order
and control in society two quite fundamentally
different perspectives might be adopted.   The first
of these commences with the assumption that
sociology is basically concerned with the problem
of order and for society to exist at all social
order must be imposed on individuals.   Only when
there is conformity to the rules of society can it
actually exist and survive in time.   The underlying
point is that social order precedes the individual
and if constraints are not imposed on persons then
'man would run wild' and chaos would reign.   Social
order consists of the boundary maintaining system,
supported by and supporting the power structure of
that society, so that its various elements are
clearly demarcated.   Boundary maintenance itself
presupposes that the social system has some form of
structure, i.e. certain properties that are
independent of individuals (Giddens 1979:66).
     One of the main criticisms of this approach is
that man is regarded as nothing more than a
reflection of the social order in which he has been
socialized.   He is no more than an automaton who
has been enculturated into the social system, its
values, meaning system, etc. and that all of his
actions merely reflect that which has been

imprinted upon him. If this were totally the
case then 'Brave New World' would be a reality but,
as it may be recalled, one of the concerns of that
novel was with the non-conformist. This is a
significant point since, as Wrong (1976:61-2) notes,
there has been an intense concern among sociologists to construct an adequate theory of deviant
behaviour. It was also Wrong (1961) who was
among the first sociologists to criticise this
approach to sociological analysis, suggesting that
it resulted in an oversocialized conception of
man. He recognised the validity of Freud's
insight, that man does not necessarily experience
guilt when he does not conform to society's norms,
although he should if man were merely a reflex of
the social system, but he often experiences it when
he does conform. Hence, man must be more than
merely a reflection of the social system. This
does not, however, rule out the idea that man is
socialized into the culture of his society, or
else there would be little basis for social interaction but it does point to a much more sophisticated interpretation of that process. This will
be referred to again in the section where human
learning is analysed later in this text.

The notion of individuality is, therefore, one
that is at the basis of the criticism of this
approach to sociological analysis, so that it is
the point at which Dawe's other sociology' may
be examined. He suggests that the Enlightenment
produced an intellectual realization that social
institutions were man-made rather than divinely
created. Hence, the key issue for other theorists
has become that of autonomous man seeking to gain
control over essentially man-made institutions.
From this perspective, action constitutes attempts
'to exert control over existing situations,
relationships and institutions in such a way as to
bring them into line with human constructions of
their ideal meaning'. (Dawe, cited from Thompson
and Tunstall 1972:547). It should be noted
immediately that the phrase 'ideal meaning' opens
up the whole issue of ideology, a point which will
be discussed in the following section of this
chapter and elsewhere in this book. In this
approach the individual is regarded as an agent
capable of making 'casual interventions... in the
on-going process of events-in-the-world.'
(Giddens 1979:55). The social system is now
regarded as the outcome of human action. The
individual is free to act in this way although, as

Goffman (1959) noted, the person usually manages to present himself in a way that he perceives to be acceptable to his fellow human beings. Hence, while he feels that he is free he is still constrained by his perception of others' expectations of him, so that his approach is still open to the criticism that man is over-socialized (Wrong 1976:67), since man seeks conformity. The difference in the two approaches, according to Wrong, is that the former makes man appear to be all super-ego while the latter places the emphasis on the ego. Additionally, this approach tends to avoid the issues of power and structure.

Neither perspective, therefore, is beyond criticism: the strengths of the one tend to be the weaknesses of the other. Both approaches highlight some valid issues and yet in other ways they are in opposition to each other. Dawe summarises these differences thus:

> There are, then, two sociologies: a sociology of the social system and a sociology of social action. They are grounded in diametrically opposed concerns about two central problems, those of order and control. And, at every level, they are in conflict. They posit antithetical views of human nature, of society and of the relationships between the social and the individual. The first asserts the paramount necessity, for societal and individual well-being, of external constraint; hence the notion of a social system ontologically and methodologically prior to its participants. The key to the second is that of autonomous man, able to realize his full potential and to create a truly human social order only when freed from external constraint. Society is thus the creation of its members: the product of their construction of meaning, and of the action and relationships through which they attempt to impose that meaning on their historical situations.
> (cited from Thompson and Tunstall 1972:550-1)

Obviously man cannot escape from the fact that he exists in a society so that structure and agency must co-exist and they must necessarily be interdependent if the social system is to survive in time.   Social theory, however, is confronted with the dilemma of synthesizing apparently opposing

perspectives in order to account for social
reality. Whatever approach is adopted, its
weaknesses may be seen in the strengths of the
opposing viewpoint, so that synthesis is important
in the development of social theory (see Giddens
1979) but since both approaches highlight
different aspects of society and different facets
of the education of adults both will be utilised
in the following pages. Yet these two broadly
different perspectives do not exhaust the
differences within social theory and it is now
necessary to focus upon some of the other
variations before proceeding to an analysis of
adult and continuing education.

Sociological Schools of Thought and Ideologies

Not only has social theory two main approaches,
each of these may be sub-divided into a number of
different schools of thought which, in turn, may
relate to varying ideological perspectives. It
is necessary to understand these before analysing
the education of adults and this section follows
the structure of the previous one.
    Structural approaches to analysis have emerged
in a number of the social sciences. Levi-Strauss
(1968:279) suggested that social structures are
models of the patterns of social relationships that
exist within a given social system. The system
may be treated as the actual functioning of those
relationships. Two major schools of thought
have emerged from this; that which analyses
society 'as it is' and that which regards what is
as morally repugnant and in need of change. The
former is structural functionalism, often simply
termed functionalism, and the latter is marxism:
functionalism is inherently conservative in its
ideological perspective simply because the
starting point of the analysis is society as it is
perceived to be while the other offers an idealistic alternative to what is and so condemns it.
    Functionalism, associated with the work of
Talcott Parsons (1951), views society as a
complex social system, one that has become even
more complex since the level of technology has
become more sophisticated. Change, when it
occurs, is of a gradual, evolutionary nature but as
the system is regarded as cohesive, with each
of the elements in functional harmony with every
other, any change in one variable will automatically
cause the remainder of the system to re-adjust
in order to re-establish the social equilibrium.

Man is the product of this social system and its culture is transmitted to him so that new generations are integrated into the existing social system without too great a disruption to its functioning; in this way it ensures its survival and maintenance through time.

Clearly there are major weaknesses in the functionalist perspective and Cohen (1968:47-64) summarised these as logical, substantive and ideological. Logically, he points out that functionalism is teleological (a phenomenon's existence is explained by asserting 'that' it is necessary to bring about some other consequence) and this is inherently unacceptable since it treats an effect as a cause. Additionally, it is an untestable theory which also inhibits comparison and generalization. Substantively, it over-emphasizes the harmonious interrelationship of parts of the social system and it is unable to explain either persistence or change. Finally, functionalism is inherently conservative ideologically. However, Cohen (1968:64-65), while agreeing that some of these criticisms are justly founded, points out that functional analysis may be part of a genuine sociological explanation.

These criticisms have resulted in structural functionalism losing its dominant place in socio-logical theory in recent years and two major sets of responses have emerged, both suggest different structures to society and one of them concentrates upon an ideological perspective as well. They are discussed separately here in order to illustra-te the differences in their response.

The social system as elaborated by the functionalists tended to play down the significance of power and class. The marxist analysis of the social structure concentrates upon these neglected issues and has received considerable attention. From this viewpoint society is regarded as having a substructure, the economic institution, and a superstructure; the shape and direction of change of the former determining the shape and direction of change of the latter. Hence, those who own (or control?) the substructure (the bourgeoisie) are in a position to exercise power over the remainder of society (the proletariat); the former do so for their own ends and to their own economic gain. This power need not be exercised overtly for much of the influence of the bourgeoisie is built into the social system and consequently exercised covertly, e.g. Gramsci's

notion of hegemony (Entwistle 1979:12-23).
However, since there is a conflict of interests
between these two sections there will ultimately be,
so it is claimed, a conflict between them.
Social change is regarded as something that results
from class conflict. As a result of the next
period of conflict the capitalist structure of
society will be destroyed, so marxism claims, and
a classless society will be established.
     Obviously such a theory has many critics.
For instance, social change may and does occur as
a result of factors other than class conflict but
whether such change actually affects the power
structure of society is a more questionable point.
Theorist also regard the idea of classlessness as
idealistic and impractical. The elite theorists
(see Bottomore 1966) argued that no society could
survive without a ruling elite. Some have
criticised marxism on the grounds that it is too
deterministic. Weber (1930) suggested that
capitalism itself emerged as a result of the
Calvinist ethic, while elsewhere he (1948) claimed
that power resided in class, status and party, so
that Marx's analysis of power was too narrow.
This latter point clearly suggests that there might
not be one elite in society but several and that
society's several institutions all have their own
elite. C. Wright Mills(1959), for instance,
was unwilling to claim that American society had a
ruling class as a result of his analysis of the
power elite of three institutions. Hence, there
has been some suggestion that society comprises a
plurality of institutions, each pursuing its own
interest and a delicate balance being achieved
within a social equilibrium. Thus the claim is
made that this type of society is more democratic
than that implied by the marxist analysis.
     Marxist analysis regards the social structure
as constraining man in an unequal manner as a
result of his position in the social structure.
Since the structures favour the rich and powerful
they deprive the underprivileged proletariat who
are prevented from achieving their full human
potential. Man is therefore a reflection of his
position in the social structure and yet he has
within him the potential to transcend that and
realize that his consciousness of reality is false
and determined by his class position. Pluralists
also regard man as a result of the social
processes that operate in society and see him as
subject to certain constraints but in this instance

these are less restrictive than those implied by
the other structural analyses discussed in this
section.

Functionalism, marxism and some form of
pluralism are the three major structural forms that
have been suggested by theorists of contemporary
society. The first of these is regarded as being
inherently conservative in its ideological
orientation because it cannot account fully for
social change. Ideology itself is a difficult
term with a variety of meanings: Althusser
(1972:262) suggests that it is 'the system of
ideas and representations which dominate the mind
of a man or a social group' while Harris (1968:22)
uses it to imply a description of the world from
a particular viewpoint. Hence, despite the
connotation of the term it has a rather general
meaning relating to the way that individuals or
groups interpret aspects of social reality. A
conservative ideology, therefore, is one that
favours the retention of the status quo in society
and resists change. By contrast, radicalism is a
perspective that views the social structures as
unjust and in need of change. Radicalism should
not be equated with marxism, although marxism is
undoubtedly radical, since it preceded marxism
and embodies ideological perspectives of many other
activist groups in the history of society.
Radicalism is, however, an ideology of change and
the means by which that change is achieved may
vary but that is not particularly relevant to the
present discussion. Marxism obviously embodies
radical perspectives and suggests that conflict
situation is necessary for its ends to be realized.
Clearly radical perspectives are more likely to be
embraced by those social groups whom Marx would have
categroized as being members of the proletariat.
By contrast, those who exercise power and are
relatively free of the constraints of the structure
that they impose upon others are unlikely to espouse
such a position themselves. They are more likely
to embrace a classical liberal ideology which
views individuals as independent, free to pursue
their own interests and consider that they are
able to do this through the exercise of their own
rational judgements. They are, therefore,
unlikely to advocate radical changes in the social
structure so that their liberalism may be viewed
as having conservative outcomes in terms of
political ideology. Liberalism is, coincidently,
the ideological perspective that is likely to be

associated with some of the non-structuralist
perspectives in sociological analysis, so that
further reference will be made to it.   An
approach similar to radicalism in that it embraces
the idea that change might be beneficial is
reformism: this is an ideology that may be
associated in part with pluralism.   Reformists
see the individual as restrained by the social
structures but relatively more free to pursue
interests within the limits that the more open
social structures allow.   At the same time,
individuals are not regarded as being totally
independent, so that they may need help in
identifying and articulating their interests.
    Thus far in this section three interpretations
of the social structure have resulted in the
specification of four ideological perspectives
and the following table summarises a possible
relationship between them.

Table 1.1:   Structure and Ideology

Structural Analysis	Ideological Perspectives (implicit and explicit)
Functionalist- society as a social system	Conservative - individual constrained by the social system and no change envisaged
	Liberal - man is free , independent and rational. Man is free to change things if they are in his interests and, if so, reformist
Pluralist - plurality of institutions with own elite groups	Reformism - individual partially free and independent although structures still constrain. Change should occur gradually
Marxist - single elite control of infra- structure	Radical - individual constrained by social structures imposed by elites

    Having examined the structural analysis of
society, it is now necessary to turn to Dawe's

'other sociology' and to investigate those schools of thought that reflect social action theories. Three sets of perspectives are scrutinized here: symbolic interactionism, phenomenology and ethnomethodology.

Symbolic interactionism has, it is claimed (Meltzer et al 1975:1), three basic premises: human beings act towards things on the basis of the meanings that the things have for them; these meanings are a product of social action in human society; these meanings are handled and modified through an interpretative process that is used by each individual in dealing with the signs that are encountered. This approach owes its origins to Mead (1934) whose central concern was the individual self which emerges as a result of interaction with significant others and is maintained by continued interaction with other people in a more generalised sense thereafter. Consequently the self is able to communicate with itself, reflect and even act against itself. Mead has provided a valuable set of ideas that help explain the human being and human action but it is ahistorical and not greatly concerned with the issues of structural analysis, which may be conceived as major weaknesses. Additionally, despite its emphasis on the self it tends to neglect psychological insights.

Mainly as a result of the work of Schutz (1972) and Berger and Luckmann (1967), phenomenology has played a significant part in sociological theory in recent years. Phenomenology derives from the work of Husserl, although its current concerns are a little removed from his original interests. Now it focuses upon how individuals construct reality for themselves and the social processes that enable that reality construction to be maintained. While each person has his own stock of knowledge and his own construction of reality, interaction is possible because there are sufficient aspects in common to enable communication to occur. It is this common element that enables taken-for-granted commonality to exist, as if it were objective. This viewpoint is criticised by Flew (1976) who claims that not only does it lead to a relativistic perspective but that it denies objective knowledge. Clearly, phenomenological perspectives may lead to relativism but only in regard to certain forms of knowledge, since it does not deny logical nor empirical knowledge. However, this approach does imply that social structures may be experienced and interpreted by individuals in different ways, and this allows for differing ideological perspectives to be combined with it. Hence, in the 'new' sociology of education there are scholars who combine both the insights of phenomenology with the ideology of radical Marxism and their works will be referred to later in this text.

Ethnomethodology is, according to its founder Garfinkel (1974:18), concerned with studying practical activities, commonsense knowledge and the practical organizations of reasoning. Since it is concerned with interaction as well, it is more than a sub-discipline of phenomenology, although Schultz's work was also a major influence on Garfinkel. Douglas (1971:15) distinguishes between situational ethnomethodologists whose main concern is the negotiation of social order, often studied by the experimenter disrupting the social situation in order to expose the background assumptions and expectations of the actors, and linguistic ethnomethodologists who concentrate on the conventions of everyday speech. The aim of these forms of research appear to be to discover the universal practices which make possible the creation and maintenance of social order and social structure. However, their research findings have not added greatly to the body of sociological knowledge and ethnomethodology appears less significant currently than it did a few years earlier.

However, it may be seen that these schools of sociological thought start from a totally different perspective to the structuralist approaches. Unlike them, there is less concern with ideology since it is implicit that the individual is free to interact and to respond to his experiences, so that there is a similarity to liberalism in some ways. Even so, it must be noted that some phenomenologists have also incorporated a marxist radicalism within their analyses. Dawe's two sociologies are, therefore, manifest in a number of different theoretical schools of thought, all of which have been utilised in the analysis of initial education and some of which have been employed in investigating adult and continuing education.

Concluding Discussion
If the foregoing analysis is substantially correct than it may be concluded that no single sociological

perspective actually exists but that various
branches focus upon specific facets of social life.
Since education is also a social phenomenon it is
open to analysis from these different perspectives
and that each analysis may contain some of the
strengths and weakness of the theoretical perspective itself.   And, indeed, education, since it is
an element within the wider society, may itself be
viewed from the same dual perspective as society
itself - as structure and action.   Initial
education which is much more institutionalised than
the education of adults may most clearly be
analysed from the holistic perspective and be
located within the structures of the wider society
while the actual process of teaching and learning
may be viewed from the social action perspective.
By contrast, adult and continuing education is not
as highly institutionalised and systematised as
initial education, as the quotation from McCullough
(1980:158), cited earlier in this chapter,
demonstrated.   Indeed, it may be argued that it
is actually because the structures of the education
of adults have not been so clearly demarcated in
the past that greater emphasis has been placed
upon the process of learning than has occurred in
some other branches of education, i.e. greater
emphasis on action than upon structure.   Until
recently there has been little co-ordination of
the education of adults, but as it is assuming a
more significant place in society it may become
more institutionalised and play a more notable
role so that more control may be exercised over it.
Indeed, there have already been publications to
this effect in several countries and the Ministry
of Education in Ontario, Canada, has published a
discussion paper 'Continuing Education - The
Third System' (no date) in which it is suggested
that there are advantages to co-ordinating
continuing education.   Hence, more emphasis may
be placed upon the structures than upon the action
within the education of adults, at least in some
sections of it, in the future.
     This dichotomy between structure and action
may also be reflected in the origins of the word
'education' itself.   It is generally recognised
that it may be derived from either one of two
Latin words, 'educare' or 'educere': the first
means 'to train' which implies to prepare a
person to take their place within the structures
of society while the second means 'to draw out',
which places more emphasis upon the person and the

process.
However, it may be seen that there are broadly
'two sociologies' which relate to structure and
action and that there are clear parallels to this
in the analysis of education.   It is not
surprising, therefore, that there are many possible
approaches to the sociological analysis of adult
and continuing education.   This study will employ
different sociological perspectives to analyse a
variety of concepts and social phenomena within the
education of adults.   However, it must be
recognised that any analyses of social phenomena
do so both from a specific sociological perspective
and also they will invariably incorporate an
ideological perspective, either overtly or
covertly.   This distinction has already become
apparent from Lawson's (1982) response to the
more radical marxist analyses contained in
Thompson (1980), where he (1982:10-18) appears to
assume that liberal adult education is based upon
rationality and, therefore, not ideological
whilst the radical analyses are ideological.   Such
a conclusion is open to considerable discussion
and this will occur later in this text.   However,
before this can be embarked upon it is important to
examine the education system itself and place
adult and continuing education within that wider
social context.

Chapter Two

EDUCATION AND SOCIAL CHANGE

Having examined the different sociological
perspectives it is now necessary to place education
within a wider social context and to see precisely
how it has been affected by social change.   It
is important to note two factors here: firstly,
that education is probably more likely to be
affected by social forces than it is to be a force
for change, although this does not preclude
education from being an agent in structural change;
secondly, that change is the norm in society and
stasis is no more than a heuristic model in the
study of society.   Hence, one of the major
criticisms of the structural functional model of
society is that it is orientated towards an
analysis of the status quo and that it gives
little heed to the dynamic elements.   Having
located education within a theoretical context of
social change, the chapter will conclude with an
examination of adult and continuing education
from this perspective.

Change in Society
It may be recalled from the previous chapter that
Marx, employing his own version of the Hegelian
dialectic, claimed that change emerged from
conflict, especially class conflict.   However,
Weber and other theorists disputed this and,
indeed, a number have argued that change is of an
evolutionary nature.   Auguste Comte, writing
before Marx, suggested an evolutionary perspective
in which society etc. passed through three stages
and these may be seen in various aspects of
society.

Table   2.1:   Comte's Evolutionary Stages of
                Development

Intellectual Phase	Material Phase	Type of Social Unit	Type of Order	Prevailing Sentiment
Theological	Military	Family	Domestic	Attachment
Metaphysical	Legalistic	State	Collective	Veneration
Positive	Industrial	Humanity	Universal	Benevolence

(Timasheff 1957:26)

Comte's idea that man is in the process of
development is a value judgement that is in the
least disputable and his stages today appear to
be rather simplistic, so that many of his ideas
have little currency in social theory at present.
Even so, the significance of the idea of social
evolution should not be lost.   Another of the
early sociologists, Herbert Spencer, also placed
great emphasis on the idea of social evolution: he
regarded society as being rather like a biological
organism which, as it evolves, becomes more
complex and differentiated.
      In 1887, Toennies (1957) showed how society
was evolving by depicting two ideal types at
different stages in the evolutionary continuum:
Gemeinschaft and Gesellschaft, which may be
translated as 'community' and 'association'.
Communities occur when individuals tend to be
static both geographically and socially, so that
status may be ascribed to them as a result of their
birth rather than their achievement.   Gemeinschaft-
type societies tend to be homogeneous and their
cultures enforced quite rigidly, so that deviants
have either to be cast out or forced to conform.
By contrast, Gesellschaft societies are the exact
opposite;   relationships tend to be impersonal,
more rational and regulated by contrast.   Status
is achieved rather than ascribed.   Toennies,
incidentally, regarded the appearance of this
latter type of society as an essential prerequisite
for the rise of contemporary capitalist society.
His emphasis on rationality was reiterated by
Simmel (1903 - translated 1950), who claimed that
among the most profound problems of modern living
is that of the individual retaining his autonomy
and individuality in the face of the overwhelming
social forces.   Hence, the varieties of

metropolitan man develop intellectuality and
rationality in order to protect them. Simmel
claims that:

> The matter of fact attitude is
> obviously so intimately interrelated
> with the money economy, which is dominant
> in the metropolis, that nobody can say
> whether the intellectualistic mentality
> first promoted the money economy or the
> latter determined the former.
> (cited from Thompson and Tunstall 1971:85)

Two significant points arise here: firstly,
Simmel suggests that both rationality and
intellectualism are related to metropolitan living
and, if he is correct, then the basis of
rationality itself may require further examination
since it may not be absolute nor objective;
secondly, he is not sure whether intellectualism is
the product of the system or the system the product
of the mind. This, then is the dilemma
highlighted in the opening chapter.
    In a similar manner to Toennies, in 1893
Durkheim (1964) suggested that social change may be
seen in two types of society, those having either
mechanical or organic solidarity. Like Spencer,
Durkheim regarded society as being like an organism
or a system. For him, mechanical solidarity
occurs in a society in which:

> The totality of beliefs and sentiments
> common to average citizens of the same
> society forms a determinate system which
> has its own life; one may call it the
> collective or common conscience, ... it
> has specific characteristics which make
> it a distinct reality. It is, in effect,
> independent of the particular conditions
> in which individuals are placed; they
> pass on and it remains.
> (Durkheim 1964:79-80)

Hence, Durkheim regarded individuals as being
moulded by a society which exists before them and
which will exist after them, a society which in a
sense transcends them. Like Toennies, Durkheim
regarded the more modern form of society as being
totally different. In organic solidarity,
society has become more differentiated through the
division of labour so that individualism is

possible, but society is not so individuated that
there are no relationships between its members.
Rather, one of the major characteristics of
societies having organic solidarity is that of a
functional interdependence in the division of
labour. Unlike Toennies, however, Durkheim
did not regard the emergence of organic solidarity
as a prerequisite of capitalism but he did suggest
that as the division of labour becomes more
intensive and specialised, then the type of
relationship between the society's members changes
and the collective conscience begins to decline,
so that individuality and functional interdependence emerge.

All of these analyses reflect the idea that
social change is of an evolutionary nature and a
more recent sociologist, Robert Bellah, has
provided a definition of social evolution that
incorporates many of the ideas included in this
discussion. Bellah (1970:21) suggests that
social evolution is:

> a process of increasing differentiation
> and complexity of organization that endows
> the organism, social system, or whatever
> the unit in question may be with a greater
> capacity to adapt to its environment,
> so that it is in some sense more autonomous
> relative to its environment than were its
> less complex ancestors.

Thus it may be seen that Bellah regards social
evolution as a process whereby individual institutions become more distinct and each becomes more
autonomous and complex. However, for society
to cohere, each of these differentiated social
institutions must relate to every other one, so
that functional interdependence is created.
Without interdependence society cannot survive.
Hence it is possible to detect from this type of
analysis the manner in which education emerged
as an institution, separate from religion and grew
into the complex social institution that it now is.

Emergence and Growth of Education
This section does not purport to present a social
history of education, merely to illustrate the way
that society has evolved and how education has
emerged in that process.

In most primitive societies in the world the
education of the young occurs informally in the

family, the clan or the tribe. Additionally, some
instruction is often given to the initiates just
prior to, or during, the 'rite de passage' into
adulthood (Turnbull:1984). However, formal
instruction is of a limited nature although
learning and non-formal education are common.
While it is unwise to transport contemporary
practices of primitive peoples back into the
history of industrial societies, it may be safe
to assume that formal education and learning from
the everyday business of living were both early
forms of education because they appear essential
for the survival and continuity of the social unit.
Formal education and schooling appear late on the
educational scene.

Indeed, in England, formal education was a very
rudimentary affair before the Industrial Revolution
and what there was tended to be vocational and
ecclesiastically based (Williams 1961:148). For
the remainder of the children, they were sometimes
afforded the opportunity to learn the catechism but
they were apprenticed to learn a trade. Few
opportunities existed for the majority to be
educated and of those who were, entry to the
ecclesiastical institution seemed to be one of the
only ways of using that education. Even so, many
who entered remained very poor and social mobility
was rare. By contrast, the upper classes had
their private tutors, public schools and the
ancient universities. One of the first major
expansions in education occurred when the merchants
and the wealthier middle classes wished to provide
an education for their children, which led to some
of the other public schools being established.

However, the main impetus for the expansion of
education came with the Industrial Revolution.
Industrialization created a greater range of
occupations, many of which required more education
and training, so that additional educational
institutions were established in order to assist
both adults and children learn how to read and
write and to acquire some of the new knowledge that
had been discovered: there were Sunday Schools,
church schools, Mechanic Institutes, scientific
societies for the working classes and a variety of
other providers (see Kelly 1970).

In 1870, the Forster Education Act was passed
and this made education compulsory; board schools
were created to ensure that there were no gaps in
the provision which had until that time been
entirely provided by voluntary effort. This

expansion in education was claimed to be
concerned with extending literacy and numeracy
(Worsley et al 1970: 160) but Kumar (1978:24) claims
that the 'educational consequences of the 1870 Act
are nearly always exaggerated. Most English
people could read and write, most indeed went to
school before the Act made it compulsory'.
Indeed, Williams (1961:157) estimates that by 1861
ten out of every eleven children attended school,
so that the Act only reflected what was already
occurring in society. Many more Acts of Parlia-
ment were to follow, many of which extended
children's compulsory schooling but there now
appears to be an inverse relationship between the
amount, or duration of schooling offered and the
needs of society for child labour. Even so, a
feature of modern industrial societies is the
amount of compulsory schooling offered to the
young.
     At about the same time as the 1870 Education
Act was passed, there were other elements in the
expansion of education. In 1867, James Stuart who
was a Fellow of Trinity College, Cambridge,
delivered a course of lectures in various cities
organized by the North of England Council for
Providing Higher Education for Women and this is
generally regarded as the start of the university
extension movement. Within a few years there
were extension colleges established in a number
of towns and cities and these were to gain their
own independence and become separate universities.
Since then even more universities have been
established and in the 1960's there was a major
expansion of higher education with the foundation
of the polytechnics. In addition, there has
been a great increase in the provision of less
advanced further education through the colleges of
technology and colleges of further education.
Cantor and Roberts (1972) call this expansion a
post-war 'explosion' in the provision of further
education.
     In addition to all the formal educational
provision, the professions have expanded and in
the process of their own professionalization they
have each increased the amount of training that
they expect from their recruits. But as knowledge
has been changing so rapidly in recent years it is
now recognised that initial preparation for
professional practice is not sufficient. The
Advisory Council for Adult and Continuing Education
(1982:9) reported that:

In recent years the obsolescence of
knowledge has been most marked in the
professions. Many professional bodies now
encourage, and sometimes require, their
members to undertake regular courses in
continuing education and professional
development. This need for regular
updating will broaden across much of the
working population. There is also going
to be an increasing demand for retraining
as structural shifts in the economy make
some jobs redundant and create new ones.

Hence, the ever-increasing sophistication of
technology has led to the expansion of education
in the professions from initial preparation to
post-basic continuing education. Despite this
rapid growth, Evans (1981:31) accuses the
institutions of higher education of failing to
respond to the demand that now exists for higher
education. Nevertheless, it is very clear that
formal education has become an essential component
of technological society.
    However, as women have wished to pursue their
careers so there has been a need to provide some
form of care for their offspring before they reach
school age, so that there has been an increase in
the provision of nursery education and Kumar
(1978:248) records an increase of those receiving
some form of pre-school education 'from less than
10 per cent in 1961 to over 20 per cent by 1975'.
At the other end of the age span there has been a
growth in pre-retirement education (Coleman 1982)
and the growth of educational gerontology (Sherron
and Lumsden 1978).
    Thus it may be seen from this brief overview of
some of the areas of education that, from the
limited amount of non-formal education in the
non-technological society, education has evolved
into lifelong education in industrial society.
As society has become more differentiated and
complex so education has done likewise. The
growth and change in education reflects the changes
from society having mechanical solidarity to one
having organic solidarity. But not only have the
structures of education changed, the concept itself
has changed.

The Changing Concept of Education
Unless a definition reflects the reality of the
phenomenon that it is defining it is of no value,

23

Hence as education has changed, so the concept itself has changed and this might be said to indicate some of the conceptual weaknesses in the original definition but this is a point to which further reference will be made below.

Durkheim (1956:71) has a rather simple definition that suggested that education was a single, homogeneous phenomenon since he claims that it is 'the influence exercised by adult generations on those who are not yet ready for social life'. In a similar manner the philosopher John Stuart Mill claimed that the content of education was to be found in 'the culture which each generation purposely gives to those who are to be their successors' (cited in Lester-Smith 1966:9). Education, then, was regarded as no more than the selection of culture that one generation sought to transmit to the next and this reflects a type of education that may have occurred prior to the Industrial Revolution. By the time that Durkheim actually wrote his definition in 1902-3, changes had occurred that had made it substantially incorrect. Within a few years of his writing this Dewey (1916:2-8) was having to prefix the term 'education' with 'formal' in the order to convey the same meaning for he recognised that this differed considerably from non-formal education. This discussion implies that he recognised the growing complexity of the educational institution.

Much more recently the philosopher R. S. Peters (1966:23-5) has adopted Wittgenstein's argument that there are now some phenomena that are too complex to be defined and that education comes into this category. The significant point about this observation is simply that the phenomenon of education has now evolved to such a degree that some thinkers consider it too complex to be defined. That the phenomenon of education is very complex is now not in doubt, but that it is indefinable is unacceptable since any use of the term implies a covert meaning so that it is important to have a working definition. Hence, it is necessary to explore this complex phenomenon a little further.

In order to try to overcome this problem, Peters actually proposed three criteria to which a learning process should conform if it is to be regarded as educational. He (1966:45) claims that education

   - implies the transmission of what is worth-
     while to those who become committed to it;

- must involve knowledge or understanding
  and some kind of cognitive perspective
  which is not inert;
- at least rules out some procedures of
  transmission on the grounds that they lack
  willingness and voluntariness on the part
  of the learner.

Clearly these are the foundation stones of one
definition of education which reflects the criterion
of worthwhileness, which is itself relative and
probably class biased.   Even so, it does suggest
that Peters is actually trying to draw parameters
around that part of learning which he regards as
education.   In a similar manner Jarvis (1983a:5)
sought to produce a definition which overcame the
problems of worthwhileness and the social class .
sub-cultural implications by arguing that
education is about aims and methods rather than
content.   Education is regarded as 'any planned
series of incidents, having a humanistic basis,
directed towards the participant(s) learning and
understanding'.   This definition can incorporate
a multitude of different teaching and learning
situations and is applicable to a variety of
educational forms and provision in contemporary
industrial society.
     However, the significant point of this
discussion is to indicate that the definition of
education itself is one which has changed with
social evolution: it has necessarily become more
abstract, less functional and applicable to a wider
variety of educational situations.   It is in the
nature of knowledge itself that this should occur,
so that it might be asked whether there is an
absolute, objective definition of education.
Clearly learning, which is a basic human capacity
may be seen as a universal process, even though
its definition has not been universally agreed ,
changing from behavioural to a broader perspective.
However, any attempt to differentiate education from
learning will be relative to the norms of the
process considered acceptable at the time when
the definition is framed.   Therefore, it must be
recognised that the concept of education will always
be relative and reflect the social conditions of
the time of its definition.

Adult and Continuing Education
In the opening chapter of this study a quotation
from McCullough (1980) was used to illustrate how

diffuse adult education has become, so that he despaired to being able to discover adult education at all. This quotation is itself evidence for the social evolution of adult education, or more specifically, in the United Kingdom, the education of adults (see Jarvis 1983b:29-32 for a further discussion on this distinction). This diversity of the education of adults has resulted in some scholars trying to capture its essential nature in a complete model. Boyd and Apps (1980:1-13) have attempted to produce such a model, claiming that it is not based on 'disciplines such as philosophy, psychology or sociology.' Their model is depicted in Table 2.2 below:

Table 2.2   The Boyd-Apps Model in Tabular Form

Transactional	Independent/Individual, Group/Class, Community
Client Focus	Individual, Group, Community
System	Personal, Social, Cultural

This model, they believe, encapsulates all the diverse froms of adult education since it demarcates 'a conceptual structure of the nature and parameters of adult education'. However, this model is open to many criticisms. Firstly, since education involves people in human interaction and is an institution within society it seems to be a most retrogressive step even to attempt to construct a model that does not incorporate the insights of other disciplines. But, ultimately, they actually did adopt these perspectives and their model is fundamentally a structural functional one, based upon Parsons' (1951) analysis of the social system. Hence, as a sociological model it is open to all the same criticisms as functionalism, namely it omits to consider power, social change or social class. In addition, the model seems to assume that it need not consider the multitude of providers of adult education. Criticisms of the model are many and recently Cookson (1983:51-2) has claimed:

that the coordinates named in the model are not mutually exclusive, that the criteria

for their determination need more
explanation, and that further elaboration
will be necessary before the conceptual
model can become more than a heuristic
device for subsequent theoretical and
research contributions to adult education
literature.

Boyd and Apps do publish a criticism of their
model in their own book by Carlson, to which they
do not respond, in which he accuses the authors
of basing their model upon a utopian philosophy
and, he (cited in Boyd and Apps 1981:179) claims
that the 'vast majority of adult education lies
beyond the scope of the Boyd-Apps model'. The
significant point of Carlson's criticism, for the
purposes of this argument, is that despite a
very genuine attempt to capture the diversity
of adult education within a conceptual framework,
they have not managed to do so. The education of
adults is even more diffuse than this model,
indeed it is so diverse that it may be that, in
Wittgenstein's sense, they were attempting the
impossible task of drawing parameters around a
diverse phenomenon. Hence, it is not surprising
that some of the recent attempts to define
education, and the education of adults, have sought
to focus upon the common features of the diverse
phenomena and to reach a definition from these.
Consequently, the education of adults is regarded
here as 'any planned series of incidents, having
a humanistic basis, directed towards learning and
understanding in those participants who are
accorded the social status of adults'. But it will
be noted immediately that there is no clear
boundary between child/youth and adult, so that
the definition is blurred at this edge. Despite
the deliberations of Knowles (1980), this is
regarded as inevitable since there is no distinct
boundary between these statuses in industrial
society, so that adolescence has almost become a
'rite de passage' in itself and the completion of
this ritual varies with different people, i.e. they
may be intellectually mature but still in initial
education, they may have completed their initial
education but still not be regarded as adult.
Hence, the education of adults may itself be
regarded as one of the elements of lifelong
education which Gelpi (1979, Vol 2) regards as
having two fundamental elements - general education
and vocational education. This distinction was

accepted by the Advisory Council for Adult and
Continuing Education (1979:9-9):

> A 'vocational course' has a specific and
> defined occupational purpose: to make
> the student a competent automobile engineer,
> for example.   A 'general' course is
> designed for wider purposes.   It may provide
> a basic grounding for a career or help
> illuminate a student's job; but it may also
> develop creative activities or be studied
> simply for its own sake, as intellectual
> stimulation or enlightenment, or to enable
> people to make a more effective contribution
> to society.

A subsequent report (ACACE 1981) made it clear that
general education refers to that form of education
traditionally regarded as liberal adult education,
while vocational education is that orientated to
occupational ends.   Both may form part of the
wider concept of continuing education, although the
term 'continuing education' is being used by some
with reference to post-initial vocational education.
This form of education is, consequently, concerned
with transmitting to the workers that knowledge
or skill which should enable them to become more
effective workers in modern technological society.
Hence, knowledge and skill are assumed to exist
externally to and independent of the individual;
it assumes that the social system exists, that its
structures are undergoing rapid social change and
that the individual has to acquire the relevant
knowledge or skill in order to fit into the system.
In short, the system and its structures exist
independently of the individual and that the person
has to be educated to respond to the structural
needs of society or industry.
       By contrast to this, general adult education
may be based upon the individual learner and his
needs, interests or demands at any time.   Hence,
Hostler argues that the most significant longterm
goals of adult education should be the student's
autonomy, individuality and his equality with the
tutor.   He (1981:56) states quite explicitly that:

> These three values deserve special emphasis
> ...because they are the ones which make
> adult education a distinctive enterprise.
> They constitute the basis of the whole
> ideology, and thus they ultimately account

For most of the characteristic features of
its procedures and organization. And
they contradict absolutely the current
theory and practice of most English Education.

The reason for this is clear, most formal
education and most vocational adult education is
designed to assist the individual find a niche
within the structures of the social system. Even so,
it must be recognised that the distinction between
vocational and general education discussed here may
only reflect this division at the level of the
educational aims but it may also occur at the level
of educational methods. Hence, it would be
possible to utilise certain methods of teaching
in vocational education that might **reflect** the
ideological position of Hostler's adult education
and, by contrast, it may be possible to employ
teaching methods in liberal adult education classes
that might appear more appropriate for vocational
education. Therefore, it must be recognised that
the general vocational types of education are not
distinctive in every respect. Hence, what emerges
from this discussion is that there are major
curriculum issues that revolve around two broad
types of education, which may be classified, as
'education from above' and 'education of equals',
these reflect the sociology of the social system
and the sociology of the social action. Like the
two sociologies, these two types of education are
neither discrete or always easily distinguishable
but, for heuristic purposes, these polar types
will be used throughout this text. Gelpi
(1984:79) summarises the two educations thus:

> On the one hand, there is education for
> development, creativity, invention,
> cooperation, democracy, participation,
> self-development, and the second for
> significant values, freedom of expression
> for individuals and groups, the right of
> everyone to aesthetic experience, the
> satisfaction of needs both essential and
> 'non-essential'. On the other, education
> is an instrument of oppression, control,
> segregation, intolerance, to a greater
> or lesser extent covert racism, boredom,
> bureaucratization, social reproduction, the
> triumph of platitudes, moralism, the
> reification of significant values.

This analysis of the two types of education
reflects the ideas contained in the writing of
Freire (1972a:45-59) where he distinguishes
between the banking concept of education and
education for liberation.   Elsewhere he (1972b)
explicitly discusses these two approaches in terms
of his understanding of man and the structures of
the world in which he clearly recognises that the
structures can oppress the individual and mould
him so that he is silent and fatalistic about the
world but, by contrast, Freire (1972b:40) also
argues that education should be liberating and
utopian, enabling the individual to act both upon
the structures of the world and change it.   Hence,
he rejects the one education and favours that
which he believes will enable man to build his world
afresh.   For him if education is not utopian it is
because 'either the future has no meaning for
individuals or because man is afraid to living the
future'.   (Freire 1972b:40)

Conclusion
The two sociologies are, thus, correlated to the
two educations, each having similar sets of presuppositions of man in society.   Each sees man
either as the product of society or society as the
product of man.   Since Freire's analysis is
political and about a society that many would have
recognised as oppressive, it may be hardly
surprising that he reaches revolutionary conclusions
about the role of education in society.   However,
in societies that are less overtly oppressive the
'banking' approach to education may not appear to
be such an instrument of social control, so that
radical interpretation of education may be less
likely to be embraced or even acceptable and
education regarded as much more a mechanism of
transmission of knowledge than as an instrument
of social control.   In these societies discussion
about different methodologies may appear more
realistic and yet the different methodologies
themselves presume different ideological perspectives of man in society.   Hence, there is no way
in which education may be regarded as value free, so
that it is now necessary to examine briefly the
issue of ideology.

Chapter Three

INTERPRETING ADULT AND CONTINUING EDUCATION

Before analysing the 'two educations' any further
it is necessary to understand one other aspect
of any analysis; that theories, values, beliefs
and ideologies all intrude into any analysis of
social phenomena. Since adult and continuing
education may be construed as a social phenomenon,
a separate social phenomenon, it is consequently
open to such a process of interpretation and
explanation. Hence, it is maintained here that
when writers employ such phrases as 'liberal adult
education' or 'radical adult education' they are
not actually specifying a social phenomenon but
employing a term to describe the end-product of
such a process of analysis and explanation. The
social phenomenon is the education of adults but
the terms employed are explanations or intentions
of the educational process. Discussion on the
intentions of the process will be deferred to a
subsequent chapter and this one will concentrate
upon an analysis of the process of explanation.
However, before such concepts as 'liberal' and
'radical' are discussed, it is essential to
analyse the process by which interpretations of a
phenomenon are reached. Thereafter, there will be
a discussion about liberal and radical adult
education and the chapter concludes with an
examination of how and why apparently incompatible
theories can relate to the same social reality in
a valid manner.

Interpreting Social Phenomena
The education of adults is a social phenomenon - it
occurs in society. However, that fact tells the
social analyst nothing about it, except that it
occurs. Even a statement such as 'it is the
government's policy to support continuing education

but to leave adult liberal education to be self-supporting' tells the analyst nothing about the policy. No explanation of why the government is pursuing such a policy or of the process by which the decision is made is provided. The social fact is that the government is pursuing such a policy, or might be. Hence, it may be seen that social facts do not speak for themselves: interpretations and explanations have to be placed upon a phenomenon before it can be understood, but since those interpretations and explanations are social processes they themselves can be understood.

However, it might be claimed that it is not the government's policy to support continuing education and to leave liberal adult education to be self-supporting. This claim may be perfectly correct and the illustration was deliberately chosen to make this point - that social facts are not themselves always easy to determine. It is, therefore, necessary to substantiate the existence of a social fact before it can be analysed.

Once the existence of a social fact has been established, it is necessary that it should be interpreted. But if the fact was hard to substantiate, it may be even more difficult to interpret it. Analysts bring to the interpretation their own theories, their own values, beliefs and ideologies and any interpretation will depend upon a synthesis of these with a perception of the social phenomenon under consideration. But is it not possible for the analyst to divorce himself from his subjectivity in order to offer an objective explanation in the same way as pure scientists do? Nagel (1961) claims that there are no intrinsic reasons why this should not occur although he does show how difficult it is for this to happen. However, Nagel's position is difficult to sustain because there is at least some agreement among 'pure' scientists about the nature of the elements that they are studying but, as was shown in the first chapter of this text, there is little agreement by social scientists about the structure of the society in which the phenomena they are studying occur. Hence, it is necessary to bring to the analysis a theoretical perspective about the nature of society, even when studying adult and continuing education.

But it might be claimed that theories depend upon facts! To a certain extent such a claim might be upheld, but not all theories depend upon

social facts that have been established or even
are able to be substantiated. For instance, the
fact of the nature of society has not been
established, so that the analyst brings his
interpretation of it to his analysis. Hence, an
analyst may bring a structural-functional, a
marxist infrastructure-superstructure or a
pluralist theory of society to his interpretation
of why the government had, or had not, espoused a
certain policy on adult and continuing education.
In a similar manner the social analyst may bring
his own values to his analysis. Supporters of
Nagel's position may claim that the social scientist
should divorce himself from these but he himself
recognises that for the most part people are unaware
of many of the assumptions that enter human analyses
and actions. Hence, the third element of values,
beliefs and ideologies must be taken into
consideration when interpreting social phenomena.
     From the above discussion, it may be concluded
that it would be quite strange if any single
explanation about facts in adult and continuing
education actually achieved an agreed interpretation
by all the theorists who examine it. However, it
might be asked whether such a diversity of
explanations about social phenomena is a "good
thing". Clearly in more primitive societies,
where mechanical solidarity existed, such diversity
of explanations would not be possible. Indeed,
in such societies deviance from the norm was
severely punished, with the deviant often being
cast out, in order for the society to survive.
Yet as societies have evolved and have grown more
complex, so they are able to survive without the
need for complete agreement between their members.
Pluralism of interpretations emerged after the
Reformation in Western Europe and this diversity
has become a feature of societies having organic
solidarity. If such a diversity did not exist,
it would be a sign either of the self-evidence of
the meaning of the social fact, or of society
being structured in a totalitarian manner for one
reason or another. In a socially evolved, open
society, where some measure of democracy exists, a
variety of explanations and interpretations of
social phenomena should occur for no other reasons
than the fact that such diversity reflects the
nature of society.
     Even so, many of the explanations about
education, especially in the literature of adult
and continuing education in recent years, have been

focused upon two quite explicit types of
explanation: liberal and radical education.
Hence it is now necessary to examine these two
interpretations of the social phenomena of the
education of adults.

Liberal Adult Education

The concept of liberal education has a long history
within education but because of the ideological
implications of the term 'liberal' the concept
requires some discussion here. It appears that
there are three possible interpretations of this
term in its historical context in education:
education in the liberal arts, education of the
free man and education to free the mind. These
three interpretations are each discussed
separately in order to clarify the issues involved.
Hirst (1965:115) notes that the Greeks
regarded liberal education as that form of
'education in the seven liberal arts, as introduction to and a pursuit of the forms of knowledge
as they may be conceived'. He goes on to argue
that these forms of knowledge may now be
considered to be: mathematics, physical sciences,
human sciences, history, religion, literature and
the fine arts and philosophy. He claims that
since liberal education, in this sense, is about
the comprehensive development of the mind it is
necessary to study some aspects of these
disciplines. Without discussing the validity of
Hirst's forms of knowledge, it may thus be seen
that in this sense of the concept, liberal
education is similar to general education and the
debate about whether the educated person is one who
has breadth or depth of knowledge becomes more
significant. In addition, it must be recognised
that the structure of knowledge itself may be
related to the structures of society which may in
turn relate to other social factors, including the
level of technology in a society and the ideology
of the elite. Nevertheless, discussion will be
deferred on the social nature of knowledge, but it
will been seen that one other issue is significant
here. The knowledge to be learned is not
prescribed necessarily, so that the selection may be
made by the learners in order for them to pursue
their own interests or it may be prescribed by
the teacher, the syllabus, etc. Hence, liberal
education may be 'education of equals' or
'from above' and in this sense it may be regarded
as a relatively value-free concept, but one that

is similar to general education.

Liberal education may also refer to education of the free man rather than education of the slave. In this sense, the meaning of the work 'liberal' is clearly made by Paterson (1979:37) when he claims the postulate of liberal education is that man is 'free to become everything that it is intrinsically good for man to be.' This claim reflects the ideology of liberalism referred to in the opening chapter, that the individual is free and able to act rationally in order to pursue his own interests in life. Two issues require discussion here: the extent to which people are free and whether rationality is itself a non-ideological concept. The fact that the concept of liberal education, as a concept, emerged in a society in which there were free men and slaves and that it was the education of the free indicates that it is a concept that has certain biases within it. But it might be argued that there are now no slaves, so that this argument has no validity. However, no complex industrial society can exist without a ruling elite who have considerably more freedom within the social structures than those who do not have their wealth or power. Yet freedom is not only the prerogative of the elite, the middle classes certainly have more control over their lives than did the slaves of Greece. Indeed, it might be claimed with justification that all people in a 'free' society have more freedom than that and while this would not be disputed, it would be true that those at the upper end of the social hierarchy probably have more control over their lives than do those at the lower end. Hence, the phenomenon of liberal adult education may have a conceptual bias towards those who are more free. In addition, the idea that people are rational and free to pursue their own interests raises a number of problems. The logic of this position is that if liberalism is to be an ideology that can be embraced by all, then all people can be free to pursue their own interests and that it is rational for them to embark upon such a course. However, in common with a position argued by Marcuse (1971), it will be suggested here that the rationality of this statement is itself ideological. If everybody were free to follow their own interests and that it appeared rational so to do, then the social result would be chaos, as Hobbes recognised many centuries ago. Hence, it is rational to impose a rule of order which

seeks to ensure that chaos does not reign but that
society's scarce resources are distributed amongst
the populace.   It thus appears rational to have a
rule of order and indeed Lawson (1982:16) claims
that 'it is logically impossible to have any kind
of society which does not depend for most of the
time on rational principles because they underlie
any form of organization'.   Yet if it is rational
for free men to pursue their own interests and
rational to impose a rule of order that prevents
free men pursuing their own interests, then the
'rationality' that prevails must itself be ideology
or else one of the preceding claims is irrational.
Before the argument is pursued any further, it is
important to note what actually happens in society
when this apparent conflict occurs.   Harris (1968:
136) indicates this clearly when he writes about
the evolution of liberalism in Italy:

> More significant perhaps than the Right
> proper was the evolution of Liberalism
> itself in the late nineteenth and early
> twentieth centuries.   For both intellectuals
> and businessmen were moving away from
> the conception of freedom in society that
> had been the essence of Liberalism.   Pareto,
> economist and social theorist, is a
> representative figure in that he was both
> a Liberal and an anti-democrat, someone
> who more vividly felt the threat to his
> own freedom than the oppression of others
> his freedom might entail, and who saw in
> Mussolini a saviour of his freedom.

Ultimately, then, for some people to have freedom,
others must have their freedom curtailed.   For
some people to be free to pursue their own
interests, others must be prevented from
pursuing theirs.   Hence, if liberal education is
an essential element in the good life (Hirst 1965),
then it is for the good life of the few rather than
for the many.   Hence, if liberal education implies
that man is free and rational i.e. able to pursue his
own interests then the concept is more applicable
to those who have more than it is to those who
have less freedom.

   The third approach to liberal education is that
it 'frees the mind to function according to its
true nature, freeing reason from error and
illusion..'(Hirst 1965:115).   In the sense that
education is designed to produce in learners a

critical awareness is a claim that few people would
dispute.   As such Paterson's (1979:38) claim that
in "characterizing certain activities as 'liberal'
we are proclaiming that they really are educational
activities" is almost indisputable.   Indeed, if
education is any planned series of incidents that
are directed towards learning and understanding
(Jarvis 1983:5) and understanding includes
critical awareness, then the prefix 'liberal'
becomes superfluous since a learning episode is not
educational unless it results in 'freeing reason
from error...!   One of the results in liberating
the mind in this way is that the individual may
develop a profound dissatisfaction with the
society in which he lives and wish to reform it
either gradually or dramatically in a revolutionary
form.   In this instance, the result of an
educational activity, that may have been regarded
as liberal, may only be interpreted as radical.
Hence, the debate between liberal adult education
and radical education as viewed by Lawson (1982)
is unrealistic since they are not always opposing
concepts.
      Thus it may be seen from the above discussion
that the confusion with the concept of 'liberal'
had to be clarified.   Where 'liberal' refers to
free and rational individuals, then there are
implications of power and liberal adult education
may be seen to be embracing individualistic and
elitist ideologies.   The significant point is
that the phenomenon of adult education is being
interpreted from a specific ideological perspective:
that man is free and able to pursue his own
interests in a rational manner.   This approach
also seems to favour a form of 'education from
above' since Lawson (1982:16) appears to imply that
'an imperative exists which says that members of
the working class ought... to be encouraged to
accept the traditional forms of education', even
though he does pose this as a question in the
context of the quotation.   Paterson (1984) also
seems to suggest that this form of education must
be 'education from above' since he claims for the
educator the duty to teach what is objective
reality, while omitting consideration of some of
the broader curriculum issues.   Whilst these are
the implications of this position, it would be
wrong to claim that either of these writers would
claim that it is imperative that education is
always from above.   However, not all versions of
liberal adult education were interpretations of

the educational phenomenon from a liberal
ideological perspective. The other two interpretations of the term refer either to education
per se or to general, non-vocational education.
Since, in neither instance do they incorporate
the ideology of liberalism, the term liberal adult
education will be restricted here to that form
of adult education that incorporates within it
the liberal ideology.

Radical Adult Education

If liberal adult education is about a theory of
adult education which presupposes the freedom of
the individual to pursue his own interests, radical
adult education starts from the presupposition
that the individual is constrained by social
structures that prevent him pursuing his own
interests. Since the social structures constrain
individuals unequally, they need to be replaced
and adult education should liberate the people
so that they can act back upon those structures
and so build a more equal society. However,
radical adult educators, and other social analysts,
regard one of the functions of formal adult
education as perpetuating and legitimating the
status quo (Thompson 1980). Hence it may be seen
from the outset that radicals bring to their
analysis an opposing ideology of man in society –
that he is not free but that he should be
liberated and become conscious (Freire 1972b)of how
how he can act upon society and change it for his
own and others' benefit. In some ways there are
similar perspectives upon the initial results of
the educational process: that man should be
freed intellectually but what he does thereafter is
not necessarily the concern of the educator.
However, the proposals that some radical analysts
make are in fact curriculum issues. Jackson
(1980:17-18) summarises these under the following
five points: resource allocation, institutional
forms, content of education, relationship between
content and process and the relationship between
the adult tutor and the adult student. He notes
that these are all political choices but since they
are also significant curriculum issues discussion
upon them will be deferred until a later chapter.
    Naturally the position that radical adult
educators adopt comes in for criticism but this is
not levelled at the five basic points that
Jackson raises but because some of the radicals
adopt phenomenological perspectives. This is not

true for the authors in Thompson (1980) but also for those in Young (1971). Among those who seek to refute this position are Flew (1976), Lawson (1982) and Paterson (1984). For instance, Paterson (1984:27) writes:

> The allegation that teachers of liberal education fail to be objective, that they offer middle class 'versions of reality' is by no means an intrinsically nonsensical allegation, although as an empirical generalization it is highly exaggerated and itself vulnerable to accusations of subjective bias. What is nonsensical is to claim that there is a middle class reality.

But radical adult educators might not claim that there is a middle class reality although they might claim that there is a middle class construction, or perception, of reality and they certainly assert that liberal adult education has a middle class bias 'in terms to cultural capital and cultural competence' (Westwood 1980:41). Radicals would claim, as indeed would non-radical sociologists (see Mackenzie 1975) that constructions of reality are social. However, this does not deny that there is a reality beyond its perception or construction, that is not a sociological concern but a philosophical one; it only indicates that individuals are prone to equate their constructions of reality with objective truth. Thus the philosophers' failure to comprehend the sociological argument has resulted in them seeking to destroy their image of the radical position, rather than the radical position itself. Unfortunately, the philosophical refutations of the radicals hardly touch the points that Jackson raises, issues that will be discussed more fully in the ensuing chapters. Suffice it to note here that the radical adult educator brings to his theory of adult education his own ideologies and values and these differ from those of the most conservative, or liberal, philosophers who have attacked them. But since both sets of scholars bring differing values and beliefs to their interpretations of adult education they are bound to produce different conclusions and this is not a bad thing since the overall debate continues to enrich the body of theory about adult and continuing education.

Radical adult education certainly demands a form of education that may be typified as 'education of equals' since it is concerned with the perception of reality of the participants and with ideological perspectives of equality between all the participants in the teaching and learning process. These are some of the curriculum issues that require further discussion but before this is embarked upon it is necessary to examine why the same phenomenon - traditional adult education - may be conceived so differently.

Underdetermination in Adult Education

Both liberal and radical adult educators have opposing theories of the phenomenon of adult education, so that it may be wondered why it is that two apparently opposing theories may both have relevance in explaining the same phenomenon. Surely one must be correct and the other false? However, this need not be so, since both theories explain certain aspects of the phenomenon although they are incompatible with each other. It is situations such as this which Lukes (1981:396-405) regards as underdetermination. He (1981:396) suggests that theories 'may conflict yet be empirically equivalent, that is compatible with all the observations that not merely are but could be made'. Lukes claims that this is more likely to occur in the social sciences than in the natural sciences for a number of reasons including:

> Social theories are themselves partly constitutive of the very reality being theorized about, so that the actors' beliefs and actions are themselves already going to embody theories, other actors' theories and the observer's theory and indeed other observers' theories may well conflict ...
> ... Social theories come in overall packages, involving methodological and epistemological but also moral and political positions, which are therefore also at issue in theoretical disputes.
> (Lukes 1981:397)

Therefore, it may be expected that no one theory will explain the phenomenon of adult education even though all the observations about it seem to fit it perfectly, from whatever theoretical perspective it is viewed. No attempt is made

here to synthesise the positions discussed although
some of the weaknesses in the broad claims of the
liberal position have been highlighted.

Conclusion
This chapter has sought to highlight the constituent elements of theories of adult education and it
has sought to show that a variety of theories
may fit the observed facts about the phenomenon.
However, another issue has become quite clear
throughout this discussion and that is not that
liberal and radical adult education necessarily
describe different types but that they may
reflect different forms of curriculum and that these
may relate to the curricula of 'education from
above' and 'education of equals', so that the
following chapters examine some of these curricular
issues from a sociological perspective.

PART II

A SOCIOLOGY OF A TEACHING AND LEARNING CURRICULUM

Chapter Four

THE TWO EDUCATIONS

In an earlier chapter it was suggested that there
are two models of education in the same way as
there are two sociologies: 'education from above'
is a model that demonstrated that education is
functional to the social system so that the
individual is moulded to fit his niche in society
through the educational process, whereas
'education of equals' assumes that the individual
is free, able to develop and fulfil his own
potential and able to create a truly human social
order as a result of his new-found knowledge,
skills and ability.   These two educations
presuppose two distinctive types of curriculum
which are perhaps best represented by the discussions about classical and romantic curricula in
initial education.   Therefore the first section
of this chapter is devoted to a discussion of these
two types of curricula and of their application to
the curriculum theory of adult education.   The
second part continues this discussion and relates
it quite specifically to the two educations.   The
penultimate section relates this theory to the
writings of Knowles (1970, 1980) and especially to
his discussion about andragogy and pedagogy.
The final section analyzes why andragogy and the
romantic curriculum appeared when they did.

Classical and Romantic Curricula
Lawton (1973:22-24) produced three formulations of
the distinction between these two types of
curriculum and these are summarised below in order
to demonstrate the relation between the earlier
discussion and these two traditional models of
the curriculum.

Table 4.1:   Classical and Romantic Curricula
             following Lawton (1973)

Classical	Romantic
Subject centred	Child centred
Skills	Creativity
Instruction	Experience
Information	Discovery
Obedience	Awareness
Conformity	Originality
Discipline	Freedom
Acquiring Knowledge	'Living' attitude and values
Subjects	Real Life topics and projects
Didactic	Involvement
Competition	Co-operation
Tests(teacher-set) and Examination (public and competitive	Self-assessment (in terms of self-improvement)
Standards	Expression
Structure	Style
Unity	Diversity
Excellence	Excellences
Rationality	Experience
Culture	Sub-cultures

(adapted from Skilbeck 1969)

Few, if any educationalists, would claim that
children's education actually occurs at one end
of the continuum or the other; it would be
generally agreed that these do form polar types
and that it would be quite possible to locate
schools/colleges/classes somewhere along each
continuum, with a certain degree of consistency
occurring. It may be noted from the above that
Lawton's work refers totally to initial education
and to the education of children. At the same
time, it is not too difficult to see how these two
models of curriculum relate to the two forms of
education that have been discussed previously.
Before this perspective is applied specifically to
the 'two educations', it is important to recognise
that Griffin (1978) undertook an analysis of
continuing and recurrent education from the

perspective of classical and romantic curricula. A summary of his argument was reproduced by Jarvis (1983b:226-228) and this is reproduced below.

Table 4.2 A Curriculum Analysis of Continuing and Recurrent Education - following Griffin

	Continuing Education	Recurrent Education
Aims	Professional standards of provision Flexible and accessible structures of provision Unity of response to diversity of need Institutionalised standards of achievement and excellence Means/ends rationality model of institutional response Access to common culture	Autonomous learning Personal authenticity Diversity of learning experiences De-institutionalised criteria of performance Assimilation of education to life-experience of individual learners Production of cultural diversity in the context of meaning and goals
Content	Public criteria of learning performances Subject structures reflecting forms of knowledge Mutual evaluation of subject demand Mastery of, or initiation into, forms of knowledge and skill Knowledge of rational control and social mobility Culturally appropriate institutional systems	Expressive criteria of learning performances Structures of knowledge contingent upon learning experience Problem solving response to conditions of alienation Standards of learning performance relative to learning experience Understanding of transformation through social solidarity Relevance for maintenance of subcultural identity

Table Continued ....

Table 4.2: Continued

	Continuing Education	Recurrent Education
Methods	Effectiveness and evaluation Professional criteria of relevance Professional standards based on adult learning theory Standards of teaching methods as a function of institutional provision Methods reflecting the rationality of provision Teaching roles distinguish educational from social authority	Methods stressing individual expression Learners decide learning methods Methods reflecting diverse characteristics of learning situation Standards as a function of personal authenticity Methods for transforming life-experience Methods reflecting culturally significant aspects of learning

While this analysis is insightful in many ways
there is occasional confusion of categories that
make it less useful than it might otherwise have
been.   In addition, his restriction to the
distinctions between continuing and recurrent
education without reference to other forms of the
education of adults also restricts it.   However,
Griffin (1978:7) himself only regarded his work
as a tentative exercise and as such it was a
significant step in the development of curriculum
theory in the education of adults.   His analysis,
consequently, forms the bridge between Lawton's
work and the following analysis of the two
educations.

The 'Two Educations'
The two educations are models of education having
entirely different ideological perspectives and
as Lawton (1973:23) points out since the list of
distinctions between the classical and romantic
curricula 'could be added to almost indefinitely'
the following list endeavours to capture some of
these ideological differences.

Table 4.3:   The Two Educations as Curricular Models

	Education from Above	Education of Equals
Aims	Individual should be initiated or maintained in the social system and its culture System needs must be met	Individual should be encouraged to achieve his human potential Individual needs should be met
Objec-tives	Specific and behaviou-ral objectives employed	Expressive objectives utilised
Content	Selected from culture of the social group by those delegated by society Initiates individuals into publicly accepted knowledge, its forms and structure	Selected from culture of the social group(s) by learners, often in nego-tiation with teachers, according to interests and relevance Problem based on knowledge integrated rather than structured
Methods	Didactic Socratic, when directed towards specific learn-ing outcomes Teacher seeks to control learning outcomes Teacher's role clearly demarcated and regarded as essential to learning	Facilitative Socratic, when seeking to stimulate learning Teacher seeks no control over the learning outcomes Teacher's role less clear-ly demarcated and not regarded as essential to learning
Assess-ment	Public examination, competitive. Teacher set tests Emphasis upon standards	Self assessment by learner Peer assessment Emphasis upon learning

Thus it may be seen from the above table that the two educations are diametrically opposed: 'education from above' assumes a classical curriculum form whereas 'education of equals' reflects the romantic curriculum.   In the former, the emphasis is upon the social system and the individual is prepared to fit into it;   education is a kind of initiation into society, rather than an extension of socialization: in the latter, the emphasis is placed upon the individual and his ability to achieve his potential so that he can act as an agent in society. Many of these points will be elaborated upon in subsequent chapters in this section so that further discussion will be deferred. Even so, it may be seen that 'education from above' is functional to the social system so that there is an inherent conservatism within it that allows for it to be criticised by radical educationalists. By contract, 'education of equals' has a more liberal perspective in as much as the individual is regarded as free and able to achieve his full potential. However, many liberals (e.g. Lawson 1982, Paterson 1984) would want to argue that liberal adult education can embrace the content and, perhaps, the methods of 'education from above' which produces a more conservative perspective to liberal adult education than that assumed by those who would ascribe to the majority of the tenets in the 'education of equals' column.

The methods and content elements of the 'education of equals' has been espoused by many adult educators, especially those having a humanistic perspective (e.g. Rogers 1969). Knowles' (1983) discussion of andragogy also reflects the perspective and it has been embraced by many adult educators as a valid theory of adult education. Nonetheless, a number of its weaknesses have been highlighted by a variety of writers in the United Kingdom and the United States (see, for instance, Elias 1979, Day and Baskett 1982, Hartree 1984). Day and Baskett (1982:150), for instance, claim that it is an educational ideology rooted in an enquiry-based learning and teaching paradigm - and should be recognised as such'. Whatever the weaknesses of the formulation, the significance of the concept is such that it cannot be neglected. However, theorists frequently discuss Knowles' analysis of andragogy apart from his description of pedagogy, which is a mistake since only when the two are discussed together may it be seen that Knowles was actually formulating a curriculum theory for adult education.

Andragogy and Pedagogy
Knowles (1980:43-4) focuses upon four assumptions when he compares andragogy and pedagogy and these are summarised in Table 4.4.

Table 4.4: A comparison of the Assumptions of
            Pedagogy and Andragogy - following
            Knowles

	PEDAGOGY	ANDRAGOGY
The Learner	- dependent Teacher directs what, when, how a subject is learned and tests that it has been learned	- moves towards inde- pendence - self-directing Teacher encourages and nurtures this movement
The Learner's Experience	Of little worth. Hence teaching methods are didactic	A rich resource for learning. Hence tea- ching methods include discussion, problem- solving etc.
Readiness to Learn	People learn what society expects them to, so that the curriculum is standardized	People learn what they need to know, so that learning programmes organised around life application
Orientation to Learning	Acquisition of subject matter. Curriculum organised by subjects	Learning experience should be based around problems, since people are performance centred in their learning

By comparing these two tables, it is possible
to see that Knowles is actually using the term
'pedagogy'to refer to the classical curriculum
and 'andragogy' to refer to the romantic
curriculum. Perhaps, even more significantly, in
the light of the position adopted in the text,
for Knowles 'education from above' is pedagogy,
while 'education of equals' is andragogy. There
may be many reasons why Knowles failed to formulate
this distinction in curriculum terms, including
the fact that this own ideological perspective
would lead him to focus upon the learner and this
may be indicated from his use of the term
'assumption' but, also, because curriculum theory
has not been widely developed in adult education.
    Like many expressions of the romantic
curriculum, andragogy emerged in the 1960s, although
its history is far longer. Knowles (1978:51),

himself, notes that he became aware of the term
andragogy in the mid 1960s even though attempts
'to bring isolated concepts, insights and research
findings regarding adult learning together into an
integrated framework began as early as 1949'
(Knowles 1978:48).   Why then was it successful in
the 1960s?   It would be facile to suggest that
the answer to this lay in the emergence of Knowles'
writings alone.   Other expressions of the romantic
curriculum were also being widely accepted in the
1960s, so that it must be recognised that both the
agent and the social structures played their
respective parts.

Romanticism and the 1960s

The 1960s, argues Martin (1981:15), were a
manifestation of an 'Expressive Revolution', a
period in which the structures of society were
stretched and changed and for a brief period
romanticism reigned.   By the mid 1970s, the
structures of society, changed as a result of the
1960s, reasserted themselves and society appeared
more stable.   Martin's argument was originally
formulated by Mary Douglas (1970) in which she
claimed that all social systems have both
external boundaries, which she calls group
boundaries, and internal ones which she calls grid.
Where both sets of boundaries are strong an
individual is involved with other people but
separated from them by numerous social customs
and conventions.   Each role is clearly defined and
the role player is expected to play it precisely.
But there are societies where both group and grid
are weak and then she (1970:59) argues 'man is
neither bound by grid nor group.   He is free of
all constraints of a social kind'.   It is this
argument that Martin pursues when she argues that
there are periods of history when zero structures
may be approached.   These are periods of
expressiveness and romanticism.   It is during
these periods, when the structures of society are
malleable, that innovations emerge and social
change is possible.   Witness the changes in the
arts, youth culture, music, etc. in the 1960s.
Once the period drew to a close in the mid 1970s,
'many things which had seemed traumatic,
revolutionary in the previous decade had been
incorporated into mainstream culture' (Martin
1981:16).   But this also happened in the
professions, education being one of those which
responded to this social situation and one of the

ways in which this occurred was through changes in the curriculum.

Basil Bernstein (1971), from whom Mary Douglas acknowledges she gained some of her main ideas, has shown precisely how this operates within the curriculum. He uses two different terms to contrast what are essentially the same two curriculum forms: the collection-type curriculum and the integrated type. A collection-type curriculum is essentially a subject based one in which each subject is clearly bounded and insulated from every other one - it is, in effect, a classical curriculum. Whereas the integrated-type curriculum is one where the subjects are not isolated from each other but are open to each other and this is a form of the romantic curriculum. Bernstein recognises that the boundaries between the subjects are significant and notes that collection-type curricula have a strong classification of disciplines but integrated curricula have a weak classification. For Bernstein the concept of classification is similar to Douglas' grid boundaries, since they are boundaries internal to the curriculum.

However, the total curriculum is also framed: frame refers to the form of the context in which knowledge is transmitted and received. Hence where framing is strong: there is a clear demarcation of role between teacher and taught; a strong boundary separating that which should be taught from that which may not be included in the curriculum; the choice that the teacher and student have in what to teach/learn and how it should be learned and taught is reduced. By contrast, weak framing refers to the opposite set of conditions. Bernstein (1971:50-51) writes:

> Where classification is strong, the boundaries between the different contents are sharply drawn. If this is the case then it presupposes strong boundary maintainers. ...strong frame reduces the power of the pupil over what, when and how to receive knowledge and increases the teacher's power in the pedagogical relationship. However, strong classi- fication reduces the power of the teacher over what he transmits as he may not overstep the boundary between contents, and strong classification reduces the power of the teacher vis-a-vis the

boundary maintainers.

It follows, then, that the collection-type
curriculum to which Bernstein refers, having
strong classification and framing, are essentially
similar to what Knowles regards as pedagogy and
what Lawton and Skilbeck call the classical
curriculum, whereas the integrated type of
curriculum, having weak classification and framing,
is essentially the same as the romantic curriculum
or andragogy.

Crucial to Bernstein's analysis is the idea of
boundary maintenance, since here he is reaching
beyond the curricula to the structures of the
organisation in which they are implemented and
ultimately, to the structures of society itself.
Indeed, he (1971:61) claims that 'where knowledge
is regulated through a collection code, the
knowledge is organised and distributed through a
series of well-insulated subject hierarchies.
Such a structure points to oligarchic control of
the institution...'. Elsewhere in the same paper
he (1971:67) maintains that the movement towards
the integrated curriculum which he detected in
the 1960s 'symbolizes that there is a crisis in
society's basic classification and frames, and
therefore a crisis in its structure of power and
principles of control'. While the word 'crisis'
is now seen to be rather too strong, he is
clearly pointing to the fact that the 1960s was a
period of change. Indeed, it was a period of
romanticism when the person as well as the power
structures of society were recognised as important
and it was into this social and philosophical
atmosphere that the concept of andragogy emerged.

The philosophy of progressive education may
be discovered in the history of adult education
before the 1960s. But as was pointed out, the
historical antecedents to Knowles may be traced
back to Dewey and indeed it may be traced back even
further. Yet the significant point about
progressivism is that, with few exceptions, it was
not widely received prior to this time but in the
1960s romanticism appeared to be much more widely
acceptable. The romantic curriculum and ideas
of knowledge for the sake of self-development and
self-expression became the vogue, experience and
project work became commonplace, the integrated day
became a way of life in some schools.

It was into this educational milieu that
andragogy was launched, into a philosophy that was

similar to it, and therefore, quite receptive to
it.   Hence, it is maintained here that andragogy
emerged at a time when the structures of society
were conducive to the philosophy underlying the
theory and that its own structures reflected the
structures of the wider society.   However, the
climate of the 1960s has now disappeared but, as
Martin indicated, many of the innovations of the
period have been incorporated within the mainstream
culture.   This has happened in the case of
andragogy, it has assumed the status of a theory
because it emerged when it did, and yet the debate
about its validity is not yet complete.

Conclusion
The 'two educations' have been examined in this
chapter and it has been shown that 'education from
above' may be depicted in classical curriculum
terms and it has been suggested that it becomes
manifest in societies which have clear and strong
structures whereas 'education of equals' is a more
romantic form of curriculum which appears mainly
at times when the structures of society are less
forceful and the agent may be effective within
society.   Andragogy is a form of 'education of
equals' and fits into this analysis quite easily
but then it contains within it a philosophy of
adulthood which presupposes equality between all
participants in the teaching and learning transaction, whatever their role within it.   However,
it is now necessary to extend this analysis to
various elements of the curriculum and while they
are treated separately here, this is for the
purposes of analyses only since the curriculum
consists of a complex interrelationship between the
traditional four elements, although assessment
rather than evaluation is included here, and the
wider social pressures.

Chapter 5

AIMS, OBJECTIVES AND MEETING NEEDS AND DEMANDS IN
ADULT EDUCATION

Many courses in the education of adults are mounted,
so it is claimed, either as a response to an
expressed demand or need, a claim disputed by
Keddie (1980:54) who, commenting on the findings of
Mee and Wiltshire (1978), suggests 'that adult
education must in part, at least be understood as
operating a provider's model and is less
constrained by the demands of the local community
than is sometimes supposed'. Her analysis was
not really a new criticism of the service ethic
claimed for adult education because Wiltshire (1973)
himself had suggested that the idea of responding
to needs had resulted in a failure of adult
education to think seriously about the theoretical
presuppositions underlying the practice of adult
education. Since that time there have been some
theoretical analyses of these concepts and the
purpose of this chapter is to draw some of them
together and to continue the debate.
    The Open University report on continuing
education (Venables 1976:23-24) suggested that
continuing education had to respond to the following
needs and demands:

        personal - i.e. satisfaction of personal
                   objectives; remedial or
                   compensatory education; the
                   extension of formal education,
                   both immediate and after a
                   lapse of time, for personal
                   development and interest
        economic - i.e. occupational re-orienta-
                   tion; preparation for new
                   jobs, and, after they have
                   been taken up, preparation for
                   new responsibilities and

opportunities in those
jobs; training and
retraining.
vocational- i.e. attainment of professional
and vocational qualifications;
updating courses to offset
obsolence in both knowledge
and experience.
social   - i.e. adaption to changing
circumstances, to changing
social attitudes and habits;
an awareness of personal and
social ethics and values; the
development of social understanding and skills; fulfilment
of particular roles in the
community both voluntary and
professional.

While these four categories are a little artificial
and some of the examples misplaced, it is perhaps
significant that this report should see
continuing education in terms of needs and demands
since both of these ideas are superstructural in
social terms, are responses to infrastructural or
individual imperatives.   They are 'responses'
rather than initiatives and, consequently, they
imply that continuing education is not a
significant agent of change in the social sense.
However, there is a sense in which aims and
objectives are the other side of the same coin, but
in this instance they are more active.   But even
more significantly this demonstrates that no
curriculum in the education of adults may be
divorced from the wider social issues and
imperatives.   Jarvis 1983b:221) has developed a
model of curriculum planning that seeks to
illustrate this point.   Even so, this chapter
commences with a consideration of aims and
objectives and then proceeds to examine the concepts
of need and demand.

Aims and Objectives
Aims, it is generally agreed, are broad philosophical statements of intent while objectives tend to
be more short term and specific.   Yet, occasionally, scholars employ the term 'general objectives'
in a broader manner which is much closer to aims.
However, in order to facilitate this discussion,
this section of the chapter is subdivided.
Aims: Aims, being broadly philosophical, contain

within them ideological implications even though they are explicitly ideological in themselves. The distinction between philosophical aims and ideology is that the former are statements of intent whilst the latter are expressions of belief and value. Nevertheless, it is important to examine briefly some of the statements of aim in order to highlight some of the broader sociological and ideological implications: the selection being employed here is used for no other purpose than to illustrate this discussion.

In vocational continuing education, for instance, the Manpower Services Commission (1983:5) specifies its aims in response to what it perceives to be the national need:

- to raise the productivity and improve the flexibility and motivation of the labour force;
- to enable management and other employees to adjust quickly and effectively to new methods, processes, products, services and technologies;
- to overcome skill shortages which may develop and impede growth or innovation, and to ensure that there is sufficient training in emerging new skills;
- to help those starting up new firms to establish business successfully; and
- to enable individuals to up-date and extend their skills, often on a quite radical basis, and to develop throughout their working lives.

In a similar manner, the Business and Technical Education Council (1983:1) specifies that it:

will develop, approve and validate a range of vocational education courses/units for adults which:

- meet the needs of business, industry and the individual
- is designed to build upon existing knowledge, skills and experience
- is sufficiently flexible to respond to the changing demands of business and industry and the need for continuing training throughout working life
- is designed to develop students' job potential.

Clearly, where the national needs are regarded
as paramount the form of education that is planned
will be an 'education from above'. Its aims will
be to prepare the individual to meet that perceived
need and fit him to play his part in society. No
assessment of the validity of the needs specified
above is undertaken here, suffice it to note that
whatever statement of need that is made it would
reflect the ideological position of those who
make it. If the need is agreed upon by government
then social policy will be implemented and the
educational aims of the courses will be specified,
those aims normally contain an ideological
perspective that assumes that individuals have to
be flexible and change in order to make the social
system function more effectively. In a broad
sense, individuals are regarded as adaptable and
manageable who should accept the role and interpretation of the world that is imposed upon them
by others. Education is seen as mechanism through
which these needs are met and the individual is
moulded.
It is at this point that some radical adult
educators would disagree with a number of issues:
initially the interpretation of the national need
may be disputed, the social policy which is
implemented may not be acceptable and the place of
the individual in the whole process may be spot-
lighted. The place of education within the
governmental process may be called into question.
By contrast, liberal adult education
concentrates on the learner. Paterson (1979:67)
suggests that 'an educational activity is one which
fosters the highest development of individuals or
persons, and that the development of persons
essentially consists in the enlargement of
awareness'. Similarly, it will be recalled,
Hostler (1981:96) claimed that there are three
long-term goals (aims) of liberal adult education:
to foster autonomy, individuality and a relationship of equality between student and teacher.
This last point is perhaps more clearly made by
Freire (1972a:53) when he suggests that the
teacher-student relationship should be regarded as
a mutual one in which the teacher is also a learner
and the student also a teacher in a teacher-student
with the students-teachers interaction. However,
both Paterson and Hostler focus upon the development
of the learner as a person and, in a similar manner,
Kolb (1981:248) claims that experiential learning
is concerned with individual human growth and

development.   Thus it may be seen that the aims of
these forms of education have an underlying
ideology about the individual, that he should be
free to develop through the educational process so
that he may act as an agent in and on the structures
of the world.   Freire (1972a:41) summarises this:

> At all stages in their liberation, the
> oppressed must see themselves as men
> engaged in the ontological and historical
> vocation of becoming more fully human.

It would be unwise, and probably untrue, to claim
that those who expound the aims of education from
above in terms of managing the individual would
deny some of the aims of the education of equals.
Nevertheless, their ideological perspective leads
them to place their emphasis in one direction
while others place theirs in another.   However,
the fact that the structures of society are of a
hierarchical nature does lead to education being
placed within the same framework, so that not only
vocational adult education but much general adult
education is planned and practised in the same
hierarchical manner, indicating the extent to
which hierarchical elements have been internalised
and no other way appears possible.
Objectives: It would be quite possible to analyse
objectives in a similar manner to aims but it is
perhaps easier to highlight the differences by
discussing two types of objectives, behavioural
and expressive.   Davies (1976:28) claims that
behind 'every objective, there are implicit values,
underlying assumptions.   These need to be made
clear and to be brought into the open ...'.   This
is precisely the purpose of this section.
    Behavioural objectives prescribe the outcomes
of the teaching experience; these goals are usually
specified in behavioural terms, as if all learning
necessarily has a behavioural, outcome, which is
one of the weaknesses of many of the traditional
definitions of learning.   Leaving that aside,
the issue behind the explication of behavioural
objectives is that the teacher can pre-specify the
learning outcomes, so that he can write his
objectives.   Thus:

> At the end of the teaching session, the
> learner will be able to ...

Unless such a behavioural objective has been

negotiated between teacher and students in an
egalitarian manner, it is another manifestation of
the idea that the learner can be moulded and
managed in the way that the teacher desires, it is
an expression of education from above. Robinson
and Taylor (1983:368), in a discussion about the
use of behavioural objectives in the training of
adult educators, claim that 'the increasing use of
behavioural objectives in adult education is a
symptom of a threatening economic and political
climate'. Elsewhere they point out that in such
a climate adult educators feel safe in a situation
that they can control. These are by no means the
only reasons why behavioural objectives are
employed in adult education and whether there is an
increasing use of them is debatable. Nevertheless,
the implications of their thesis are similar to
that argued in the previous chapter; that in times
of relative prosperity, such as the 1960s, the
boundary maintenance mechanisms in society are
weakened but in times when resources are scarce the
mechanisms are strengthened and the boundaries are
more clearly demarcated. Hence, adult educators
seek to exert control over their sphere of work
and justify efficiency in behavioural terms.
Behavioural objectives are a symbol of this, even
if they are no guarantee of greater efficiency.
However, the significant point here is that they
imply that the individual can be managed and that
they are a symbol of education from above.
     Yet it may be argued that it is necessary to
have some form of objectives since teaching and
learning need some planning and direction. Few
educators would deny this and some utilise
expressive objectives. Eisner (1969:15-16), writing
about initial education, claimed that

> An expressive objective does not specify
> the behaviour the student is to acquire
> after having engaged in one or more
> learning activities. An expressive
> objective describes an educational encounter.
> It identifies a situation in which children
> are to work, a problem with which they are
> to cope, a task in which they are to engage;
> but it does not specify what from that
> encounter, situation, problem, or task they
> are to learn. An expressive objective
> provides both the teacher and the student
> with an invitation to explore, defer, or
> focus on issues that are of peculiar

interest or import to the inquirer.
An expressive objective is evocative
rather than prescriptive.

Hence, expressive objectives contain the ideological
presupposition that the individual is free to
concentrate upon the task that interests him rather
than having his learning managed or manipulated
so that he learns what he is expected to learn
and he behaves according to the plans.   Expressive
objectives are, therefore, closer to the education
of equals.
     This section has focused upon aims and
objectives and has noted how certain aims and
objectives reflect the ideology of education from
above while others focus upon the individual, his
person and his development.   Having undertaken
the task it is now necessary to examine needs and
demands.

Needs and Demands
In general adult education, Knowles (1980:27) has
suggested that the role and mission of the adult
educator is in 'satisfying three distinct sets of
needs and goals: (1) the needs and goals of
individuals, (2) the needs and goals of institutions,
and (3) the needs and goals of society'.   However,
his (1980:27-36) subsequent analysis concentrates
on the needs and goals of these differing bodies
without ever examining the implications of his
division, so that the two educations do not ever
appear in his analysis nor, therefore, does the
potential conflict between them.   The reason for
this most probably lies in the fact that he devotes
twice as much space to the first as he does to the
other two added together, so that while mention is
made of organization and society, his overall
concern is with the needs of the individual.
Indeed, in liberal adult education the needs of
individuals have always been paramount, so that the
aims of liberal adult education have frequently been
viewed as a response to these needs - a service
ethic.   This latter point will be returned to later
in this chapter but, at present, the discussion will
concentrate upon needs.   How these needs are
discovered remains a problem in adult education, so
that it usually relies on the response to an
advertised programme of courses which are viable,
and this is essentially the operation of a demand
economy (Jarvis 1982:342-348).   This overcomes
the problem of discovering needs since once the

offer is made it is the responsibility of any individual, who feels that he has an educational need, to respond. Certain provisos exist, however: that he is aware of the programme; that he can attend at the time offered; that he can afford it; that the sub-culture of the institution is conducive to his own; that what is actually offered corresponds with what he needs, etc. However, those who actually respond and attend such adult education classes are most frequently from the middle class, so that it does appear that this approach merely enables those individuals who can afford it and have the inclination to study in their leisure time to respond and the educational needs, if they exist, of the remainder of the population are not catered for.

However, the situation may be different in vocational adult education where, as it was suggested earlier, meeting the needs of the society - as interpreted by certain people - was the concern of the educational provision. The implications of that were clearly shown to produce a form of 'education from above' where the individual was prepared to fit into the existing social structures, irrespective of his own needs and interests.

Needs: In everyday speech the term 'need' is employed with a wide variety of meanings, each conveyed through the linguistic structure and the social context within which it is used. Sometimes it is used synonymously with 'wants' but often it relates to the fulfilment of interests. Aditionally, need statements frequently incorporate implications of 'moral ought'. The failure to employ the term with precision in common speech is reflected in the lack to rigour with which it is employed in education. Hirst and Peters (1970:35), for instance, have suggested five types of need: diagnostic, biological, psychological, basic and functional. They claim that 'a major book could be written solely round the problems raised by this emphasis on needs and wants'. Bradshaw (1977), by contrast, considered that needs fall into four categories: normative, felt, expressed and comparative. Halmos (1978) distingui- shed two basic types of need, those which he considered to be primary and those which are secondary. Perhaps, the most significant formula- tion of needs is that specified by Maslow (1954) in which he discussed physiological, safety, social, self-esteem and self-fulfilment needs. There have been a number of criticisms and variations of Maslow's typology, e.g. Jarvis (1983b:14-19), so that it cannot be taken as a basis for this discussion. Such is the profusion of prefixes to the term that it is frequently employed but rarely defined. Hence, it is necessary to examine those analyses that have been made of the term.

Lawson (1975:37), for instance, has suggested that where "a deficiency can be remedied by the help of some educational process an 'educational need' is established". This definition causes a number of problems, as Lawson himself recognised, and he himself was aware of both its normative and, therefore, ideological nature. He (1976:38) points out that:

> Up to a point therefore the educator is inevitably infiltrating his own views about what is educationally relevant and important. He selects those areas of concern among his potential students which he is prepared to make his concern and it is the organiser of programmes who mainly determines what is a valid education need or not.

Hence, Lawson recognised that the adult educator who prepares the programme for an institute is making a selection based on what he thinks is educationally relevant and what his potential students need. But in fact he confuses needs with demands and interests here and perhaps imputes the adult educator with a knowledge of the needs of his potential students that he has not actually discovered. Perhaps Lawson's analysis may be taken to mean that the adult educator's own ideological perspective is the factor that determines the educational programme that is provided and that the use of the concept of need avoids having to analyse the reality of the situation.

At this point, however, it is necessary to consider the concept of need a little more deeply. Dearden (1972:49-53) has argued that there are two criteria for a need to exist: that there is a norm and that it has not been achieved. However, norms and notoriously difficult to discover empirically and the majority of statements of norm tend to be subjective assessments. Unless there is empirical demonstration of norm, then the claim that a need exists can be rejected by refuting the validity of the norm. Even if there is empirical

verification of the norm there is no logical
reason, although there may be an ideological one,
why an individual should achieve that norm.   Hence,
the bases of statements of need are subjective
and ideological, so that it may be as significant
to note who recognises a need as it is to examine
how that need is met.

Management of a company, or a government of a
country, may claim that there are certain company
or national needs that have to be met and that
individuals should be educated in order to meet
them.   In this instance, the expression of need
signifies that the persons to be educated are being
prepared to take their place in a recognised
position within the structure and that their
education is a means to that end.   Consequently, it
is almost inevitably a form of education from
above.   By contrast, the individual desiring to
be educated may claim that he needs education.   In
this instance, what is the difference between a
claim to need and one to want to be educated?
In the one, there is a norm that the learner has
not yet achieved and in the other there is a
condition which he aspires to attain.   Hence, felt
and expressed needs are little different from wants
and interests.   Why then is the term used?   The
term 'need' contains implication of 'moral ought'
that reflects the degree of importance ascribed
to the achievement of a 'want' and the moral
overtones are incorporated in order to endeavour
to influence the social situation towards the
fulfilment of the aspiration.

Another approach to wants, interests and needs
is to recognise·that they are all individualistic
but that wants and interests do stem from a desire
to achieve something within the wider world that
the individual has not yet achieved.   Hence,
Schutz and Luckmann (1974:15) write:

> ... the life world is intersubjective from
> the very beginning.   It presents itself to
> me as a subjective meaning context;   it
> appears meaningful in the explicative acts
> of my conscious.   The life world is
> something to be mastered according to my
> particular interests.   I project my own
> plans into the life world, and it resists
> the realization of my goals, in terms of
> which some things become feasible to me
> and others do not.

The agent is free to pursue his interests so long as the social structures do not prevent him so doing. Realism is recognising the extent to which the agent is free to act in an uninhibited manner in the pursuit of those interests or wants. The use of 'needs' by the agent in such a situation may reflect his desire to influence those who exercise power in order to make it possible for him to pursue those interests.

However, needs may be felt or experienced when an individual has an experience with which his taken-for-granted knowledge cannot cope. Schutz and Luckmann (1974:8) suggests that:

> In the natural attitude, I only become aware of the deficient tone of my stock of knowledge if a novel experience does not fit into what has up until now been taken as the taken-for-granted valid reference schema.

In such situations the individual either seeks to discover new knowledge, his felt need becomes expressed and he seeks answers to his questions. Hence, Aslanian and Brickell (1982) suggest that adults learn in order to cope with life changes. However, if adults do not endeavour to learn as a result of such experiences then there is a tendency to disengage from that element of the life world.

Needs, wants and interests are all related to the individual's position in the social structure and their expression of need or interest is a reflection of their own social experience. Experience is not gained in a neutral world or a neutral culture since, as will be argued elsewhere in this text, both the culture and the selection from it which constitutes formal educational curricula tends to be biased in favour of those socio-economic classes who exercise power and control in society (see Young 1971). That such knowledge and culture is not neutral is a basic fact in Gramsci's concept of hegemony (see Entwistle 1979). However, the individual's perception of the social world and of his place in it is influenced by his exposure to such culture. Therefore, his expressions of need may only reflect his own position in the social structure and be relative to his best interests, rather than reflect those best interests. In other words, his expression of interests or needs may reflect a

'false' expression of his best interest or need.
Hence, it is possible to argue that those who are
more enlightened or whose understanding of the
social processes that have led to this expression of
false interest or need should help them become
more aware of the actual reality of their social
and political situation and, therefore, of their
real needs. Hence it is argued that individuals
should, through an education of equals, be helped
to become aware of the structures of society
that create false consciousness. This is the
perspective adopted by Paulo Freire (1972a, 1972b),
who argues that education should result in
learners discovering 'the reasons behind many of
their attitudes towards cultural reality and
then confront cultural reality in a new way'
(Freire 1972b:35). Elsewhere, he (1972b:81-2)
writes "... since ... men's consciousness is
conditioned by reality,'conscientization' is first
of all the effort to enlighten men about the
obstacles preventing them from a clear perception
of reality". But he is careful always to argue
that the educator should neither prescribe for
the needs of the learners nor specify what the
needs are. Yet when they realize their own needs
and act upon the world, to assist in its
development then they realize their own humanity.

It should be noted that the majority of
adult education provision which it is claimed is a
'needs meeting programme' is actually planned in
response to what are perceived to be the needs of
individuals. Unlike Freire, adult educators tend
to ignore the constraints of social structure and
to assume that the educational process occurs in
relative isolation. (Even if there is a recognition that there are social constraints, the
educational programmes are mounted as if there
were not.) It is therefore based in a liberal
ideological setting and is more likely to attract
those who are relatively free of those constraints.
As Keddie (1980:63-64) claims:

> Adult education responds to the collective
> voice of individualism, but it has to a
> large measure failed to identify or to
> identify with the needs of those who reject
> the premises on which individualism is
> based.

Finally, the idea of responding to needs is at
the heart of the service ethic and the raison d'être

of many adult educators, as it does of many who
claim professional status.   Goode (1973:355)
claims that there are only two central generating
qualities of professionalism, one of these being
the service ethic.   Clearly all professions
endeavour to respond to the needs of individuals
but it may be salutary to recognise that
professionalism has been the subject of severe
structures.   Illich (1977:22-23), for instance,
has suggested that 'Need ... became the fodder
in which the professions were fattened into
dominance' but that needs themselves are created
by advertising.   As adult education operates in
a market economy this may become an increasingly
tempting option for some adult educators.
McKnight (1977:82) summarises the arguments against
the utilisation of the ethic of need in the
following manner:

> ... professionalized services defined need
> as deficiency and at the same time
> individualize and compartmentalize the
> deficient components.   The service systems
> communicate three propositions to the client:
>
> > You are deficient
> > You are the problem
> > You have a collection of problems

To which, he (1977:89) maintains the professional
claim:

> > We are the solution to your problem
> > We know what problem you have
> > You can't understand the problem or
> >   the solution
> > Only we can decide whether the sol-
> >   ution has dealt with your problem

He continues in this vein by arguing that the
preposition can be inverted and expressed in terms
of the professional service system:

> We need to solve your problems
> We need to tell you what they are
> We need to deal with them in our terms
> We need to have you respect our satis-
>   faction with our own work

The altruism of service can be inverted into the
dominance of the professional.   The professional

fits into the social structure and responds to the needs of the individual within the context of the needs of society and the status quo is maintained.
Thus it may be seen that the concept of need in adult and continuing education is both complex and carries with it many implications. The above discussion illustrates that adult education may not actually respond to needs but much more realistically to demands.

Demands: While needs is the ideology of adult education, demand is the practice. Liberal adult education operates in a market economy, sometimes responding to demand. Newman (1979:35) explains precisely how it operates:

> Adult education is designed in the simplest possible way to respond to demand. It is the other side of the numbers game. If classes can be closed on the basis of attendance, then they can also be set up. That is to say, if you have a group of people eager to pursue some activity or if you have evidence of sufficient community interest you can approach your local adult education agency or centre and ask that a course be arranged, a room and basic facilities provided, and a tutor paid.

Sometimes adult educators seem to test the market by offering courses that they are unsure about, Newman (1979:16) calls this the 'Set-'em-up-and-see' approach. Because adult education institutes rarely·have the staff to undertake market research in an systematic manner, the adult educator fills his programme with courses that are untried and hopes that he may get a response. However, part-time staff have to be engaged just in case the chance is successful but if it fails and the class closed, the staff lose their opportunity of employment and carry the financial loss (Hetherington 1980:327). The fact that the part-time staff have few rights of employment means that they can be treated as a reserve army of labour and liberal adult education can be seen to be operating in an economy of supply and demand.
The question must be posed, therefore, as to whether the programme offered is a direct response to the perceived demands of the market or whether it is the adult educator's perception of what will sell in the market. Keddie (1980:54), commenting

on Mee and Wiltshire's (1978) findings suggests
that 'adult education must in part, at least, be
understood as operating a provider's model and is
less constrained by the demands of the local
community than is sometimes supposed'. If she
is correct, then the programme offered is in part
one that is selected by the adult educator for his
clientele, maybe a clientele known both to be
interested in certain popular subjects or are able
to afford the cost of the leisure time pursuit.
However, people seeing the programme but not
coming from the more affluent middle classes may
not be interested in what is offered, so that they
neither enrol nor create a demand for any other
type of provision. The fewer working class
people who enrol, the more middle class aspects
of the enterprise are reinforced. Since schooling
may have already created a negative orientation
to formal education for many from the working
classes the middle class bias of the prospectus
does little to change this perspective. Hence the
supply and demand model of liberal adult education
has the effect of reinforcing the status quo
although it actually has the potentiality to break
away from the class bias.

Much vocational education is also supplied on
demand with the education institution responding
to requests from employing organizations to mount
courses in specific disciplines, areas, etc. for
their employees, and more educational institutions
are creating administrative posts of liaison
officers, etc. whose main occupation is to discover
what demands exist and to organize a course in
response to those demands. For many such
institutions, the continuing education specialist is
this liaison officer and education reduced to the
organization of provision. Clearly this is an
important role but it raises considerable questions
about the nature of the occupation of the
educationalist.

If the educator of adults is one who organizes
courses in response to demand which ironically
enough may actually contain a service ethic, his
occupation is similar in many ways to Goode's
(1961) study of the librarian in which he points
out that since the librarian merely responds to
customer demand his occupation may only be classified as a semi-profession because it does not have
the body of knowledge with which to be prescriptive.
Many of the teachers who teach on the courses that
the continuing education specialist or the adult

71

educator organize may have both the knowledge and
the status of a member of a profession, but this
is not the status of the occupation of the
organizer. Hence, the activity of the educator
of adults either in supplying education or in
responding to the demand for education precludes
its being a profession. Since further reference
to the professionalization of adult education will
be made in a subsequent chapter, further discussion
on the topic will be deferred.

Conclusion
This chapter began with a consideration of the aims
and objectives of the educator, and in this
instance these are part of the curriculum in the
traditional sense. It was shown that education
from above and education of equals operate within
this situation. However, it was recognised that
the aims and objectives of the educator must be
seen within a wider context of needs, wants,
interest and supply and demand, so that these
concepts have been explored in some detail. Need
was shown to be a very complex concept which, when
operationalized, led to prescription by the
professional, and ultimately had within it overtones
of an education from above. If the adult
educator were to respond to demand, however, which
might have implications for education of equals
his occupation would be seen as no more than a
semi-profession. If he operated an entrepreneurial
supply model, however, he could be accused of
managerial exploitation of part-time staff and
seeking to impose his perception of what adults
need for their education and this would result in
the take-up of popular low-status subjects or
reinforcement of the middle class image of adult
education.

Chapter Six

THE CONTENT OF THE CURRICULUM

Few studies in the education of adults have
concerned themselves specifically with curriculum
content although the topic has arisen in a variety
of published material, so that while no attempt
is made here to examine every reference to it, it
is essential to explore much of it in order to
highlight some of the sociological issues involved.
Much recent debate in the sociology of education,
however, has focused upon the sociology of
knowledge and this was stimulated by the symposium
edited by Young (1971). Indeed, Flew (1976:20)
has accused him of trying to place the sociology
of knowledge in the centre of the sociology of
education. While there is little or no evidence
to support Flew's accusation, it is an important
area of the current debate and one upon which this
chapter concentrates. Consequently, it commences
with a sociological discussion on the nature of
knowledge, thereafter it examines how curriculum
knowledge is selected from culture and, finally,
it raises issues about the extent to which
education is from above or between equals.

A Sociological Understanding of the Nature of
Knowledge
Sociological understanding of knowledge claims
that the 'principal thesis of the sociology of
knowledge is that there are modes of thought which
cannot be adequately understood as long as their
social origins are obscured' (Mannheim 1936:2).
However, two philosophers of adult education have
concentrated upon knowledge, Paterson (1979) as
an exponent of liberal adult education and Lawson
(1982) in an attempt to refute what he understood
to be the radical position in regard to knowledge.
It is, therefore, important to understand the

position that they espouse in order to contrast
it to a more rigorous sociological analysis.
    Paterson (1979:67-102) suggests that knowledge
is a united phenomenon although not quite 'a
seamless robe' (op cit:86) and that as knowledge
it is necessarily directed towards some object,
or objects, of which it is the knowledge (op cit:
83).   Hence he regards it as always reflecting an
objective reality.   He claims that knowledge can
be classified by subject matter or by the
procedures used in constructing that knowledge
(op cit:75) although he concentrates on the former:

> In distinguishing one kind of knowledge
> from another, then, it is to the nature
> of the subject-matter under study, not to
> the nature of the procedures by means of
> which it is brought under study, that we
> must above all give our attention.
> (op cit:83)

Thus it may be seen that Paterson claims that
knowledge always reflects objective reality.
However, sociologists are not really so concerned
about the nature of objective reality, or even if
there is one, but they are concerned about how
individuals construct their reality, or realities,
since the former is a philosophical question and
the latter a sociological one.   Hence Paterson's
concern with the subject matter of knowledge is
perfectly understandable from a philosophical
perspective but it does not provide many clues about
a sociological understanding of knowledge.
    By contrast, Lawson (1982) regards his work as
a deliberate attempt to refute what he perceives
to be the relativism of the radical sociological
analysis of adult education contained in Thompson
(1980).   While he disputes the fact that he is
trying to attack sociological understanding from a
philosophical perspective, this is actually what
he appears to be doing.   Unfortunately, he does not
produce an analysis of his own understanding of the
nature of knowledge in his polemic on sociological
relativism, so that it has to be extracted from the
argument that he produces.   He claims that
relativity in knowledge has no guideline and that
there are universal guidelines that can be employed
to judge the validity of knowledge, stating that:

> Relatively few people would claim that the
> anti-Jewish policy of the Nazis were good

> because the Nazis saw it as good within
> their own frame of reference. There are
> values that are so universal that they can
> be used to judge on issues of this kind,
> and they are used by members of many groups.
> (Lawson 1982:15)

However, Lawson recognises that from their own frame
of reference the Nazis might have regarded their
policies as good, and that from another frame of
reference other groups judge it to be evil.
Therefore, there is no universal self-evident
principle even though it may be one that the
majority accept, so that at the point where he
claims to refute relativism he employs a relativist
perspective. This is not to claim that there is
no objective good, only that the argument that he
employs does not demonstrate it.
    Having briefly examined the work of two
philosophers of adult education and having seen that
Lawson's position is inconsistent, it is now
necessary to return to the element that Paterson
omitted from his deliberations, the procedures
of constructing a body of knowledge about reality.
This philosopher Scheffler (1965) suggested that
there are three types of knowledge: rationalistic,
empiricistic and pragmatic. However, it will be
recalled that earlier in this text it was suggested
that rationality may itself be conceived as being
ideological, so that Scheffler's first form of
knowledge will be referred to here as logical
knowledge. Perhaps one of the best examples
of this form of knowledge is mathematics. Through
the exercise of reason knowledge may be deduced
that links it back to self-evident truth. The
significance of this form of knowledge is that it
is not dependent upon experience, socio-economic
class or national group. It is the one form of
knowledge that is in no way relative and as such
it is the only form of knowledge that Lawson could
have legitimately employed in this attempted
refutation of relativism. Even then, he would
still have had to have pursued another major issue:
there is no logical reason why logical knowledge
must necessarily be included in any curriculum, and
that raises an issue that will be discussed in the
next section of this chapter.
    Empirical knowledge has as its exemplar natural
science, although there are other forms of social
science knowledge that may have an empirical base.
Natural phenomena are revealed through sense

experience and are then interpreted. The experience may in itself be indisputable but the interpretation is much more open to the subjective perspectives of the interpreter. Hence the more interpretation is necessary in order to give the empirical facts meaning the more the knowledge may be regarded as a personal or a social construction. Thus the historian E.H. Carr (1964: 30) in seeking to answer the question 'What is History?' writes:

> The historian without his facts is rootless and futile; the facts without the historian are dead and meaningless. My first answer therefore to the question 'What is History?' is that it is a continuous process of interaction between the historian and his facts, an unending dialogue between the present and the past.

The empirical facts of any discipline are meaningless without interpretation and that interpretation must be a personal or a social construction and, in the former case, that relates to the previous knowledge, experience, perceptions and values of the interpreter. Hence, empirical facts may be interpreted in totally different ways by different people, despite Lawson's (1982:13) fear that it is apparently inconsistent for different people to view liberal adult education as good and bad simultaneously.

Pragmatic knowledge involves the utilisation of logical and/or empirical knowledge in order to learn something significant about the world, and this involves experimentation. However, experimentation in social living will not bring the same results for different people. For instance, men and women experimenting with the same ideas in similar social situations may discover that different things work for them as a result of their gender differences; children and older adults doing the same may also discover different things work on their behalf because of their age differences. The same claim could be made about people from different ethnic groups and even social classes. Different persons in a variety of social situations will experience the constraints of the social structure in different ways, so that pragmatic knowledge has a basis within the social structure. The process of learning from experience is an active one for the pragmatist, but the outcome of that experience may well be affected by the social structures within which the learner is located. This is not to deny the fact that individuals may transcend the limitations and constraints of their social situation and this will be discussed in the next chapter.

In addition to these three types of knowledge individuals hold perceptions of reality, universes of meanings and world views that find no verification through these processes, although some forms of religious belief or superstitution may find some justification in pragmatism (e.g. Jarvis 1980). However, many of these beliefs tend to be objectified, as if they were actually founded upon one of the above processes, classified as if they were actually knowledge and then taught as if they have such verification (see, for example, Berger 1969, Jarvis 1976). Yet even these beliefs and meaning systems are frequently related to an individual's place within the social structure. Mannheim (1936:3) exemplifies this claim:

> Men living in groups do not merely coexist physically as discrete individuals. They do not confront the objects of the world from the abstract levels of a contempla- ting mind as such, nor do they do so as solitary beings. On the contrary they act with and against one another in diversely organised groups, and while doing so they think with and against one another. These persons, bound together in groups, strive in accordance with the character and position of the groups to which they belong to change the surrounding world of nature and society or attempt to maintain it in a given condition. It is the direction of this will to change or to maintain, of this collective activity, which produces the guiding thread for the emergence of their problems, their concepts, and their forms of thought.

Hence, it is maintained here that with certain specific exceptions much knowledge has its basis in people in society. Yet some who maintain this sociological view of knowledge expound it crudely (e.g. Blum 1971) and are rightly attacked for it (e.g. Flew 1976). Yet those who do attack the relativist position, such as Flew (1976) and Lawson (1982), do so from an epistomologically

weak basis.   Paterson (1979), by contrast, omits
to consider the way in which a body of knowledge
is constructed, so that his analysis does not
focus upon quite the same issues.   Even so, there
is another point that is as significant in the
consideration of curriculum knowledge and that is
how it is selected for inclusion within a
curriculum and this entails consideration of both
dominant and relevant knowledge.

Curriculum Content as a Selection from Culture
In sociological terms culture means the some total-
ity of knowledge, beliefs, values, etc. of a
society and Lawton (1973:23) regarded curriculum
as a selection from culture.   The term 'curriculum'
has been discussed more fully elsewhere (Jarvis
1983b:211-250) so that it is unnecessary to
elaborate upon it here since the focus of this
section is actually the curriculum content rather
than the curriculum per se.   The idea that
Lawton raises here is quite significant, especially
when it is realized that one of the functions
of adult education is cultural reproduction, but he
is perhaps misleading in as much as he employed
the singular form 'culture' rather than the
plural.   Yet there are a variety of sub-cultural
forms based upon ethnicity, socio-economic class,
region, etc.   However, it is suggested here that
there is a single dominant culture and a number of
major sub-cultural variations.   Hence, it might
be argued that either the curriculum is a selection
from the dominant culture or a selection from the
sub-cultures of a multi-cultural society.   Perhaps
the former is more realistic.   The dominant
culture clearly relates to those who exercise power
in society.   Marx and Engels, for instance,
claimed in 'The German Ideology' that:

> The ideas of the ruling class are, in
> every age, the ruling ideas: i.e. the
> class which is the dominant material force
> in society is at the same time its domi-
> nant intellectual force.   The class which
> has the means of material production at
> its disposal, has control at the same time
> over the means of mental production, so
> that in consequence the ideas of those who
> lack the means of mental production are,
> in general, subject to it.   The dominant
> ideas are nothing more than the ideal
> expression of the dominant material

> relationships, the dominant material
> relationships grasped as ideas, and thus
> of the relationships which make one class
> the ruling one; they are consequently
> the ideas of its dominance.   The
> individuals composing the ruling class
> possess, among other things, consciousness,
> and therefore think.   In so far, therefore,
> as they rule as a class and determine the
> whole extent of an epoch, it is self-evident
> that they do this in their whole range and
> thus, among other things, rule also as
> thinkers, as producers of ideas, and
> regulate the production and distribution
> of the ideas of their age.
> (cited from Bottomore and Rubel, 1963:93)

Thus Marx and Engels claim that not only do the
ideas of the ruling elite dominate the culture of
a society, it is they who actually create new
ideas.   Perhaps this claim is rather excessive
since it has long been recognised within the
sociology of religion that sectarian religion is
often a lower class counter culture to the religion
of the elite and it frequently generates new
religious ideas, and Mannheim (1936:36) also
stresses how oppressed groups devise utopian ideals
that are distinctly different from the dominant
ideas.   However, the significant point about
this discussion is that these ideas are not incorporated easily, if ever, into the dominant culture .
As Musgrove (1979:60) claims: 'Hegemony is the
power to shape our consciousness.   In the field of
education it is the power to define what is
valid knowledge'.   Hence, the dominant culture is
itself not neutral, even though it may appear to
be rational.   Indeed, the dominant culture is
often presented by intellectuals as if it were
rational and objective and Mannheim (1936:78)
points out:

> Thus we are faced with the curiously
> appalling trend of modern thought, in
> which the absolute which was once a means
> of entering communion with the divine,
> has now become an instrument used by
> those who profit from it, to distort,
> pervert,and conceal the meaning of the
> present.

However, it might be claimed that this position is

rather more extreme than that presented in the last
section, since not all knowledge is necessarily a
social construct. This is true, but it must be
recognised that not all logical or empirical
knowledge necessarily gets embedded into the
dominant culture, but much knowledge and belief that
is not capable of verification by these methods
does so occur and is sometimes presented as if it
were logical or empirical knowledge. Therefore,
it is necessary to recognise that the dominant
culture from which the curriculum is selected may
itself be of a biased nature.

Thus far culture has been recognised as being
heterogeneous but it has been treated as if it
were static, yet the culture of a society also
relates to its structural elements. Earlier in
this study it was claimed that the division of
labour has been a major constituent factor in the
evolution of societies, so that it is not surprising
that the division of labour has caused changes
in the structure of knowledge in society. Without
emphasizing the division of labour, Scheler (1980:
76), writing in the 1920s, was one of the first
to recognise that different types of knowledge
changed at different rates. He suggested a
sevenfold division of knowledge: myth and legend,
knowledge implicit in everyday natural language,
religious knowledge, mystical knowledge,
philosophic-metaphysical knowledge, positive
knowledge of mathematics, natural sciences and
humanities, and technological knowledge. Scheler
regards those forms of knowledge that reflect a
relative natural world-view are changing slowly
whereas those forms that relate to a learned
world-view change rapidly and are artificial.
Merton (1968:525) is rightly a little critical of
Scheler because he does not provide the principles
of his classification, does not even define
artificiality, nor does he consider the consequences
of his categorization. Despite these criticisms,
Scheler's classification highlights the fact that
certain forms of knowledge do change more rapidly
than others and that the change is actually a
consequence of the division of labour. This
latter point is made most clearly by Berger and
Luckmann (1967:95):

> Given the historical accumulation of
> knowledge in a society we can assume that,
> because of the division of labour, role
> specific knowledge will grow at a faster

rate than generally relevant and accessible knowledge. The multiplication of specific tasks brought about by the division of labour requires standardized solutions that can be readily learned and transmitted. These in turn require specialized knowledge of certain situations, and of the means/ends relationships in terms of which the situations are socially defined. In other words, specialists will arise, each of whom will have to know whatever is seemed necessary for the fulfilment of his particular task.

Hence the division of labour is responsible for the growth in the body of knowledge, especially that which relates to occupational specialisms. Yet the division of labour is not merely a horizontal division, there is also a hierarchical one. This is not a phenomenon peculiar to modern industrial capitalist society, for Visalberghi (1979:33) argues "that the class divisions associated with the social division of labour are as old as 'civilization' itself". Hence, the knowledge that relates to the upper stratum of society will be accorded high status while that which is specifically relevant to the lower echelons of society is given low status. Freire (1973:50-1) epitomises this position in respect to the Third World:

> It is not by co-incidence that the colonizers refer to their own cultural practices as an art, but refer to the cultural production of the colonized as folk-lore. Similarly, the colonizers speak of their language, but speak of the language of the colonized as dialect.

This process occurs only in the Third World, but as Young (1971) endeavours to demonstrate, it also occurs in the industrial societies of the world. Hence, the question remains as to whom should select knowledge for the curriculum. Clearly this is a matter of power and control, it is also a matter of education from above or the education of equals. In the former certain knowledge is defined as curriculum knowledge and given high status, or as Marx (in Hoare 1975:112) neatly summarizes it in his 'Critique of Hegel's

Doctrine of the State', that inclusion in the
examination syllabus is 'the official recognition
of the trans-substantiation of profane knowledge
into sacred knowledge'. The latter then receives
no recognition and remains low status or 'profane'
knowledge.

Education from Above
Before embarking upon an analysis of the content
of the curriculum in education from above it is
necessary to recapitulate the argument thus far.
Initially it was maintained that some knowledge,
i.e. logical knowledge, was totally free of social
or personal construction but that all other forms
of knowledge were open to a greater or lesser
degree of influence from the wider society. By
contrast, knowledge may be viewed as an entity
which continues to sub-divide as the division of
labour is perpetuated in contemporary industrial
society. At the same time knowledge is not only
sub-divided horizontally, but its division
reflects the hierarchical division of labour in
society, so that some knowledge is accorded higher
status than other. It was recognised that there
is a degree of relativity in social and personal
knowledge and those who attacked the so-called
radical adult educators on this score did so from
an epistemologically weak position. Nevertheless,
a crucial question remains and this is, who
selects the content of the curriculum from the
wider cultural knowledge, and this section focuses
upon those forms of education in which the
selection is made without consultation with the
learner. Three types of education are discussed
briefly here; vocational, adult liberal education
and distance education, the first two being two of
the major forms of education for adults and the
third because it is a mode of delivery of
educational material that has become increasingly
popular since the foundation of the Open University
in the United Kingdom. It is recognized that
further and higher education could also have been
discussed here but as adults are increasingly able
to continue their education in both of these
spheres and vocational and adult liberal education
incorporate many of the same issues, they are
only referred to in the course of this discussion.

Vocational Education: Thus far knowledge has been
related to the division of labour, so that it
would be surprising if this argument were not

pursued further here.   This section will
concentrate first upon this in respect to work
in general and, thereafter, to the professions in
particular.   However, it must be noted immediately
that professional knowledge is, in the same way,
a consequence of the social division of labour, in
as much as the professions have been traditionally
regarded as a part of the elite and only more
recently have they been regarded as occupationally
based.   Overall, vocational education reflects
the division of labour and the social acclaim that
accompanies it.   Gelpi (1972:Vol 2:7), citing the
work of Gintis in America, indicates how education
supports the division of labour.

> The division of labour is sustained by the
> dualistic system of education, where there
> are two educational channels, one for the
> masses and one for the elite.   But in many
> countries this system is to some extent in
> a crisis ... because there are contradictions
> between the logic of these institutions and
> that of production.   In an analysis of the
> situation in the U.S.A., Gintis has pointed
> out the conflicts between a higher education
> which confers elite status and the
> exigencies of an increasing bureaucratiza-
> tion and stratification of labour, which
> imposes different objectives on
> education ...
>   This contradiction, in post-high
> school education (and increasingly even in
> high schools), takes the form of admini-
> strators and teachers consciously having
> to sully the principles of free enquiry
> to the reality of repressive organization
> and economic need.

Educational methods constitute the focus of the
next chapter, so that no comment will be made about
that here, but it is obvious that the content of
higher education is also being adversely affected,
in the minds of Gelpi and Gintis.   They see the
aims of higher education changing from producing
critically aware individuals to producing ones who
will acquire the necessary knowledge to assume a
place within the structures of society, structures
which are themselves partially a result of the
division of labour.   However, it is clear that
because of the increasingly rapid rate of
technological change the education of adults, as

a sub-section of education per se, has expanded
rapidly. Again Gelpi (1979:Vol 2:3) points out
that this is of necessity an education from above:

> The important expansion of educational
> activities for the adult population has its
> origins in industrialised countries, and
> more specifically in the continuing need
> of enterprises to bring the training of
> their managers and workers up to date.
> The educational requirements of workers
> do not always correspond to the vocational
> needs of enterprises, even when their
> demands do not have a purely cultural
> character. The workers are interested in
> an educational development which would help
> to diminish the gap between managers and
> workers, and which would not lead to new
> forms of domination in modern society. A
> strictly vocational training programme
> does not respond to these educational
> requirements, except perhaps in terms of
> the individual advancement of workers
> which, in fact, estranges them from the
> group to which they belong.

Thus it may be seen that the content of vocational
education is basically a form of education from
above and that it has expanded in order to respond
to the demands of the division of labour in a
rapidly changing technological society. However,
it is perhaps significant to investigate whether
the rapidly changing technology now has a life of
its own so that it simply continues to produce new
technological knowledge, or whether there is
another social impetus behind this social situation.
Innovation rarely occurs in a mindless manner and
it could be argued that it is a specific response
to a social situation. Hence, Gorz (1980:387)
argues that 'the main purposes of research and
innovations is to create new opportunities for
profitable capital investment'. If he is correct,
then it might be argued that new knowledge is
itself often the result of capital investment in
research, so that even the production of new
knowledge is not totally free. Gorz (1980:394)
follows the argument documented by Marglin that
'technology has been shaped by capitalism so as
to secure maximum control over and exploitation of
labour, not to secure the maximum production of
goods'. Hence, he (ibid) continues that this

'implies that capitalism uses the most efficient
production technology only so far as the latter is
compatible with maximum control and exploitation'.
This radical thesis requires careful examination
since it implies that the content of vocational
pre-service and in-service education does not
merely serve to equip the individual to fill his
place within the social structure but that it
ultimately helps to ensure that he remains within
it since the level of knowledge in the curriculum
is determined by the needs of that technology and
its ensuing division of labour.

Control is also the theme of Elliott's
(1972:11) understanding of the professions:

> The professional group controls a body
> of knowledge which is applied to specialist
> tasks.   This poses special problems of
> social control.   Such problems can be
> seen in the relationship between the
> professional and the unskilled client or,
> more generally, the tension between values
> developed within the profession and the
> values of the wider society.   Social
> control in the professional group takes two
> forms.   The professional institutions
> oversee all the functions of the profession.
> They lay down standards controlling entry
> to the group.   Through the training
> necessary to achieve these qualifications,
> and through association with professional
> peers, the individual acquires the norms and
> values of the group.

Elliott notes how the professions have changed from
status professions which demanded a traditional
liberal education for entry to occupations which
are more role based and require more role specific
knowledge.   Hence, the new professions especially
require a body of knowledge to be transmitted to
the new recruit, a body of knowledge deemed
necessary to be learned prior to entry into
professional practice and which is, consequently,
included in the curriculum of professional training.
As this knowledge has become more technical and
role specific the notion of professional education
being based on a traditional liberal education
has receded: some professions now require
candidates for the professions to hold a degree
prior to entry for professional preparation while
some writers consider that the humanities, etc.

should be regarded as leisure time interests only,
e.g. Kerr et al (1973:47). However, industrialization has meant that not only do recruits to
the new professions have a great deal of new
technological knowledge but that this technological
knowledge 'increases so rapidly that what a student
learns early in the pre-service curriculum may be
out of date or wrong by the time of graduation'
(Houle 1980:85).   Hence, the Advisory Council
Report claimed that:

> In recent years the obsolescence of
> knowledge has been most marked in the
> professions.   Many professional bodies
> now encourage, and sometimes require, their
> members to undertake regular courses in
> continuing education and professional
> development.   This need for regular
> updating will broaden across much more
> of the working population.   There is
> also going to be an increasing demand
> for retraining as structural shifts in
> the economy make some jobs redundant and
> create new ones.

Implicit in this clear statement of education from
above in order to assist individuals to cope with
structural changes is the notion of control:
professions require their members to be educated in
order to keep up with the technical innovation,
rather than to evaluate the knowledge and its
place in contemporary society.   Thus it may be
seen that the control of the curriculum in
vocational education is related to the social
processes in the society in which it occurs.

Liberal Adult Education: It has already been
should how both Lawson (1982) and Paterson (1980)
regard liberal adult education as initiating those
who wish into the body of knowledge of the
discipline that they are studying.   However, as
a leisure time pursuit adult education is very
much the preserve of the middle classes, as will
be shown later in this text, a concern that has
been expressed by some adult educators (e.g.
Thompson 1980).   Lawson (1982:16-17), commenting
on this concern for the working classes' education,
states:

> The fact that many members of the working
> class do not recognize the above criteria

(reasons for including specific aspects
of knowledge in the curriculum) does not
mean that they cannot come to recognise
them.   The possibility of ignorance,
inappropriate experience and similar
contingent factors have to be allowed for
and there is no logical reason why, for
example, traditional liberal adult
education should not be seen as relevant,
or indeed, be relevant.
     The argument, therefore, turns on the
issue of whether or not an imperative
exists which says that members of the
working class ought not to be encouraged
to accept the traditional form of education.

The issues of relativism have already been
discussed in this chapter and so there is no need
to pursue them here.   However, it may be seen
that the tenor of Lawson's argument is that working
class people should be encouraged to accept the
traditional form of education because it might be
relevant to them.   Since revelance is itself a
matter of subjectivity, individualism and
relativity it does appear that Lawson's own
criteria are as equally open to criticism as are
those which he seeks to oppose.   Nevertheless,
it may well be that the working classes (and other
classes in the population) are actually being
presented with a liberal adult education which
encourages them to accept a traditional middle
class adult education.   Mee and Wiltshire (1978:41)
conclude that there is a consistency of provision
despite the different types of institutions that
offer adult education classes:

     Together these (data) seem to constitute
     a core curriculum which is common to most
     institutions.   That this is so should be
     surprising when one considers that adult
     education institutions are free of any
     constraints of externally imposed
     syllabuses and examinations, that they
     differ widely in structure and philosophy
     and that their programmes are planned by
     adult educators many of whom have a
     considerable degree of autonomy.   They
     can in theory teach what they like, yet
     three-quarters of their work is in fact
     basically similar.   There seems to be
     some sort of natural consensus that these

are the kinds of things that institutions
of adult education ought to be offering
the public and that there is something
wrong if those subjects are not given
something like their due place in the
programme.

Mee and Wiltshire appear a little perplexed about
the manner in which this 'national consensus'
operates, since they labour under the impression
that these institutions are responding to either
the expressed 'need' or 'demand'. Yet few, if
any, adult education institutions had conducted
rigorous market research in their catchment areas
in order to discover if what was offered
constituted either a need or a demand. However,
they were offering programmes which they thought
would attract sufficient response to justify
mounting the class, irrespective of whom the
clientele happened to be. That the student body
was primarily of middle class background, as will
be discussed later, was not the concern of many
adult educators. Moreover, that the programmes
that they prepared were their own and that many of
them may have got inspiration for new topics from
reading the prospectus of another institution
(- as was revealed in a piece of research in which
the author was involved) did not really enter into
the consideration of Mee and Wiltshire. However,
the national consensus may well have been the
consensus of the adult educators, 'a providers'
model of adult education' (Keddie 1980:54), rather
than a model that responded to the free pressures
of the market. Yet there is a sense in which
the providers' model is a market model. Since
the providers decide what they are going to offer
on the market and, thereafter, advertise it.
That which they sell successfully constitutes the
viable programme for the ensuing academic year.
Hence, liberal adult education may be viewed as
'education from above' both in what is included
in the programme and what topics are included
in the actual syllabus of any specific topic,
although it should be pointed out that in some
institutions of adult education tutors are
encouraged to negotiate the syllabi with their
students, a point that will be discussed below.

Distance Education: A recent innovation in adult
education is the Open University in which the
teaching method employed tends to be didactic

(Jarvis 1981).   Hence, the content of any course
has to be specified in the published learning
materials and while there are occasional variations
in teaching method, in the main students are
expected to learn pre-selected knowledge and to
reproduce it in a traditional examination format.
Students are expected to learn and pass a specific
number of course contents in order to gain their
degree.   Hence, the curriculum of the Open
University may be regarded as a collection-type
curriculum, even though there has been some attempt
to integrate knowledge in some of the courses.
However, it is merely that the new parameters of
knowledge-to-be-learned has been defined by a
course team in a slightly different manner.
Bernstein (1970:63) has argued that:

> Where knowledge is regulated by collection
> codes, social order arises out of the
> hierarchical nature of the authority
> relationships, out of the systematic
> ordering of the differentiated knowledge
> in time and space, out of an explicit,
> usually predictable examining procedure.

While there are different teaching methods that
may be used in distance education, as will be
discussed in the next chapter, it is maintained
here that the Open University, in common with
other institutions of liberal adult education,
offers an education that may best be described as
an 'education from above'.
    Throughout this discussion it has been
recognised that there is a more radical stream of
education that is critical of education from
above.   Giroux (1981:64) suggests that the
cornerstone of the position of the radicals who
criticise this position 'lies in (the) stress in
the relationship between the economic and
political structures of capitalism and the
ideological superstructures'.   Hence, the content
of education offered to the learners is such that
it helps to legitimize the structures of society
as they are.   That this goes unrecognised by
many is at the heart of the hegemonic principle,
which suggests that the knowledge and values which
favour the elite are regarded as rational,
commonsense and even self-evidently true.   It is,
nevertheless, a selection from culture.   Thus
the processes by which the dominant culture's
traditions are selected and transmitted is a

significant one.   Is this to imply that adult
educators are deliberately misleading their
students?   By no means so.   Indeed, it can be
argued that the criteria for selection include
objectivity (Paterson 1984), worthwhileness
(Peters 1966), balance (Mee and Wiltshire 1978)
and the demands of professional practice (Jarvis
1983a).   It has been argued that Lawson and
Paterson argue from an epistemologically
questionable position (Mannheim 1936:70).
However, it is in the nature of the hegemonic
principle that ultimately that which is selected
acts as a means whereby the dominant culture and
ideology are reproduced in a conservative manner.

Education of Equals
In contrast to education from above, some educationalists have discussed approaches whereby the
learner rather than the teacher selects what
content is to be learned.   Two approaches are
discussed briefly in this section: contract
learning and self-directed learning.

Contract Learning: One of the foremost exponents
of this approach to teaching and learning is
Knowles (1980:382 ff), whose approach to adult
teaching has already been mentioned in this
theory of andragogy.   Here Knowles views the
teacher as a resource person whose task is to
assist the learner with his learning activities.
Consequently, the learner is encouraged to:
diagnose his own learning needs; specify his own
learning objectives; specify the learning
resources and strategies; specify the target
dates; specify the evidence of his accomplishment;
specify how the evidence will be evaluated;
review his contract with consultants; carry out
the contract; evaluate his own learning.   This
approach is as much a method as it is a theory
of curriculum content, so that it will also be
mentioned in the following chapter.   Nevertheless,
it is a method that allows the individual to
focus upon his own learning needs and this is
something that Jarvis (1983a) also argued for
within the context of professional education, since
the professional is aware of any deficiencies he
may have in terms of the knowledge necessary for
him to practice to the best of his ability.
Nevertheless, it has to be recognised that these
approaches are individualistic and that the learning
outcome may be that the individual is more competent

to fill his place in the social structure, so that it may merely be a more efficient method of achieving a conservative outcome since the knowledge may actually be in existence for the learner to acquire. However, this need not always be the case since the method allows for the rejection of that which exists if it is not suitable for the demands of professional practice. However, methods constitute the focus of the next chapter so that subsequent discussion on this will be deferred.

Self-Directed Learning: Tough (1979) has focused upon this aspect of adult learning and his contribution to adult education theory must be seen from the interest he has provoked in this field. He (1979:17) discovered a 98 per cent participation rate from his small sample of sixty-six individuals in learning projects of at least seven hours duration over a six-month period. Not only was Tough's sample extremely small but there are other inconsistencies with his method that throw some doubt on the high participation rate he originally discovered. For instance, he (1979:8) regarded his work as investigating deliberate learning episodes but he (1979:14) notes how his interviewers help interviewees to understand that they themselves have actually been undertaking learning episodes. Despite his methodological weaknesses, Tough's (1979:191ff) work has been replicated sufficiently to indicate that self-directed learning is a very common phenomenon among adults. In this form of education, the learner selects whatever knowledge he wishes to study, for whatever purpose, in order to pursue his own concerns. Hence, the curriculum content is totally selected from the wider culture by the learner for whatever reasons and, as such, it is the education of equals. Nevertheless, it should be recognised that interests, etc. are themselves socially constructed so that even in this form of education it is possible to argue that if consideration is given only to the content of learning, then it is easy to see how radicals can argue that false consciousness are produced.

Conclusion

If the content of the curriculum is a selection of culture, a selection from the dominant culture, however that selection is made and if the learner merely internalizes it, he may do no more than to

internalize that knowledge and values which are
favoured by the elite.   As such the education
process merely locates individuals in their social
position, reinforces the social structures and
helps produce a sense of false consciousness in
the learner.   However, in the education of equals
the learner is more free to select from minority
cultures and learn knowledge that is not
necessarily regarded as being of value.   Nevertheless, such selection of knowledge is more rare
than the selection from the dominant culture and
will depend upon the membership and reference
groups of the individual concerned.   Such knowledge
is accorded lower status, even if it is given the
status of knowledge at all.   However, not all of
the educational process should be regarded as a
transmission of culture to be learned and reproduced
for, as Giroux (1981:65) points out, there are not
only content-based radicals but there are also
strategy-based radicals, so that it is now
necessary to examine teaching and learning.

Chapter Seven

TEACHING METHODS AND LEARNING

> The strategy-based position springs from
> a long tradition of thought including such
> diverse notables as Rousseau, Wilhelm
> Reich, A. S. Neil, Carl Rogers and Erich
> Fromm. Shaped in what can be generally
> termed a radical humanism, this group
> acknowledges the oppressive power and
> control exercised by schools, but they
> differ from the content-focused radicals
> in their assessment of the nature of such
> control. For the strategy-based radicals
> the essence of schooling lies in its
> reproduction of traditional, hierarchical,
> social relationships. In general these
> relationships replicate top-to-down models
> of authority and sanction social conformity
> rather than student initiative and
> imagination. The strategy-based radicals
> believe that the process of schooling
> inculcates in students a form of domination
> that is deeply felt, lived and experienced
> as part of one's own history and self-
> formation.
> (Giroux 1981:65)

By virtue of the nature of adulthood, many adult
educators would regard their approach to teaching
within the framework of what Giroux calls
strategy-based radicalism, even though they may
not see themselves as radicals - this is a point to
which further reference will be made later in
this chapter. However, adult educators who adopt
this position might well argue that since students
are adults, there is a degree of equality
between teacher and taught. It will be recalled
that one of Hostler's (1981:56) aims of adult

education was 'to achieve the student's equality
in his relationship with the tutor'.   Nevertheless,
Giroux does spotlight why such equality is
espoused - the ideology of radical humanism.
Such humanism is explicit in many adult educators'
writings, such as Rogers (1969), Knowles (1978,
1980), Jarvis (1983a, 1983b).   One of the most
significant of all adult educators to adopt this
position and to pursue it to its logical
conclusion is Paulo Freire (1972a, 1972b) and his
work will be discussed separately in the final
section of this chapter.   However, before this
can be done it is necessary to explore both
teaching methods in general and the particular
elements of the strategy-based position.
      One of the main aims of adult educators who
have adopted a humanistic position is the development of the self of the learner (Bergevin 1967:30)
and at the heart of Knowles' (1980:45-49) theory
of andragogy lies the idea of the self of the
learner.   It is, in part, this emphasis that led
to andragogy being classified as an expression of
romantic curriculum earlier in this section of the
text.   However, no analysis of the self has thus
far been undertaken, so that the second section of
this chapter will concentrate upon this.   This
will lead to a discussion of the learning cycle in
which learning is viewed as a process of reflection
upon experience rather than memorization of data.
Thereafter some of the criticisms of the strategy-
based radicalism that were implied in this chapter
will be analysed in order to assess their relevance.
Finally, the work of Paulo Freire will provide the
focus for the concluding section of the chapter.

Methods of Teaching

Education is often regarded, in some way, as the
transmission of knowledge (Peters 1966).   But
implicit in this type of definition is an
extremely limited teaching methodology.   This
methodology is reflected in the idea that teaching
is a one-way communication process and that
education is merely the communication of knowledge
that should be acquired and reproduced.   However,
there are a variety of other approaches to teaching
which Jarvis (1938b:120-129) outlined.   These
methods are classified within a framework of three
broad types: didactic, socratic and facilitative.
Each of these is now briefly discussed.

Didactic Methods: Didactic approaches to teaching

generally assume a one-way communication approach
and that a selection of culture (body of knowledge)
should, for a variety of reasons, be transmitted to
the students to learn.   This knowledge is usually
taught by the lecture, or some other similar mode
of instruction.   Indeed, there is a sense in
which the education-versus-training debate can be
placed within this context.   Training, it is
assumed, emphasizes the learner's dependence and
education is viewed as creating a much more
autonomous individual.   Mannheim and Stewart
(1962:13) suggest that 'training is probably
linked with vocational preparation, and education
is linked with liberal preparation'.   Such a
distinction may have been valid in the past when
entry into the professions was often related to
having received a liberal education while entry
into other occupations was related to role specific
knowledge.   However, with the increasing
industrialization of society, such a distinction
now appears rather simplistic, although it is
possible to understand why occupations have changed
the title of their preparation from 'training'
to 'education' as they have professionalized.
Apart from this, the debate about education and
training appears to be a rather futile one in
the light of the fact that both may employ similar
one-way communication processes and that a more
important debate may be between the different
modes of communication that may occur in the
teaching and learning process.
    Didacticism signifies a form of education from
above in which the learner is regarded as an empty
receptacle that needs to be filled with the
knowledge and wisdom that emanates from the teacher.
This approach does imply a concept of man that is
to be moulded by external forces, so that it is
not surprising that Bourdieu and Passeron (1977:5)
claim that 'all pedagogic action is objectively
symbolic violence insofar as it is the imposition
of a cultural arbitrary by an arbitrary power'.
Hence, in the process of teaching the social
relationships of the wider society are reproduced
and the knowledge to be learned is presented to
the learner.   Bourdieu and Passeron are also as
clearly concerned about the curriculum content as
about the method whereby the content is presented
but they are mentioned here simply because their
approach emphasizes the method.   However, they
proceed to point out that such pedagogic action
presupposes an authority to impose such symbolic

violence upon individuals, authority which reinforces the arbitrary power which establishes it and which it conceals.

It might be claimed that this form of analysis is valid for initial education but it is not true for the education of adults because the learners are voluntarily present and that outside of the context of the classroom some of the learners may be in higher positions in the social hierarchy than the teacher so that education is not reproducing the social situation. However, this argument does not hold good, since in the context of the teaching and learning, didacticism does reproduce a hierarchical relationship and the fact that some of the learners may forego their status within such a relationship merely serves to reinforce the validity of such a hierarchical structure. That the learner is not always compelled to attend adult and continuing education classes hardly alters the fact that the learner may be prepared to have his self moulded by agencies other than himself in a manner that some might view as symbolic violence.

Didacticism is, therefore, a technique of control insofar as the method by which the content presented is authoritative and often authoritarian. Frequently, the learner is expected to reproduce it but rarely is he given the opportunity to debate it. In some liberal adult education classes, debate often follows a didactic presentation, and in these instances it is clear that Bourdieu's and Passeron's claim would be less valid, but then it might also be that ultimately this teaching method may not be totally didactic! Overall, didacticism that allows for no debate and expects the memorization and reproduction of knowledge presented in a form of education from above and, as such, seeks to mould the individual to fit into the structures of the wider society.

Socratic Approaches: Unlike the previous technique in which learners are required only to memorize what is presented to them from above, this approach encourages the human process of learning. Socratic teaching methods are sometimes employed in adult and continuing education: in this approach the teacher either takes the students through a prepared, logical sequence of questions or the teacher responds to the students' response with further questions, so that the onus is always

on the learners to formulate their reply to the
teacher.   One outcome of this process may be
that the students reach a new position in logical
knowledge from that which they had reached
previously.   Alternatively the teacher may have so
controlled the process that the outcome of the
teaching and learning process is that the students
are left with the culturally accepted knowledge and
that since it appeared to be arrived at in a
democratic manner it may be accepted and acted
upon more readily by the group as a whole, since
Lewin and his associates (cited in Krech et
al 1962:228-229) discovered that where the
participants had helped to set group goals they
would more likely to be committed to the outcome.
In this instance, therefore, while an impression
of democracy is given, the outcome may merely be a
more effective method of control than didactic
teaching and, as such, it remains a form of
education from above.
     However, the fact that in this instance
students are given the opportunity to reach their
own conclusions actually does create a situation
in which a more explicit reflective learning
process is encouraged.   In this instance, the
agent is less constrained by social pressures than
he is when he is merely required to memorize and
to reproduce that which he has been presented.
Hence, the possibility of the learners reaching
conclusions other than those held by the teacher
must exist and, provided that there are no other
methods of control such as examinations, therefore,
the teacher may be seen to be embarking upon an
educational process of equals.

Facilitative Methods: In this approach the
educator of adults creates a situation in which
learning may occur.   He may, for instance, seek
to create an awareness of a special learning need
in the student;   endeavour to confront a student,
or students, with a problem requiring a solution;
provide the student(s) with an experience and
encourage reflection upon it.   In all of these
instances an outcome of the activity should be that
learning has occurred, but the teacher's role has
not been to control the learning outcome but to
facilitate the learning process.   Hence, the
potentiality exists in such a situation for the
learning outcomes to be totally different from
those which the teacher had perhaps anticipated.
This reflects the earlier discussion on

behavioural and expressive objectives, for in
facilitative teaching the only possible form of
objectives that the teacher may legitimately have
is expressive, for the learning outcome should in
no way be controlled by the teacher.   Thus, the
education of equals appears when this teaching
method is employed.   Even so, it might be
objected that the teacher is in a position to mani-
pulate the environment, so that the learning
outcomes are still under the teacher's control.
Such a possibility must always exist but strategy-
based radicals would claim that this is an abuse of
the teacher's office.   As Dewey (1938:71-72),
writing about the eudcation of children, claims:

> It is possible of course to abuse the
> office, and to force the activity of the
> young into channels which express the
> teacher's purpose rather than that of the
> pupils.   But the way to avoid this danger
> is not for the adult to withdraw entirely.
> The way is, first, for the teacher to be
> intelligently aware of the capacities,
> needs, and past experience of those under
> instruction, and, secondly, to allow the
> suggestion made to develop into a plan
> and project by means of the further
> suggestions contributed and organized
> into a whole by the members of the group.
> The plan, in other words, is a coopera-
> tive enterprise, not a dictation.   ...

While Dewey's terminology may not be that which an
educator of adults might use, this sentiments are
those of which strategy-based radicals might
approve.

Three broad categories of teaching method have been
examined: didactic, socratic and facilitative.
It has been seen that didactic approaches tend to
be a form of education from above since it seeks
to transmit accepted content within a teacher-
controlled situation while facilitative is more
likely to be an expression of the education of
equals since the teacher does not seek to control
the learning outcomes.   Socratic teaching may
be both education from above or the education of
equals, depending upon how the method is employed.
    It was claimed in the previous chapter that
distance learning need not always be a form of
education from above although much of it appears

to be so since it is both content based and
examined according to the traditional methods.
Nevertheless, distance learning can be a form
of the education of equals, using both socratic
and facilitative techniques. For instance, content
may be provided and critical and probing exercises
may be set on it using a socratic format, or it is
quite possible for distance learning to utilise
facilitative techniques in which the learner is
enabled to choose the topic to be studied or
the project to be undertaken and the learning
outcome is left to the responsibility of the
student. An example of this latter approach is
the project-type approach used in some more
recent Open University courses.

Methods of teaching are, therefore, not immune
from sociological analysis since they are always
techniques of control, even though some of them
allow for freedom. Hence, the teacher's role
must also be analysed within this context. The
more control that a profession, for instance,
seeks to exercise over the body of professional
knowledge the more likely the teacher's role will
be a didactic exercise of control over the learners
but the more that the learning process is important
in itself irrespective of what is learned the less
the teacher's role may be seen to be one of
control. In this latter instance, the teacher of
adults may be viewed as a strategy-based radical
whose concern is for the humanity of the learner
rather than the body of knowledge, even though it
must be acknowledged that this dichotomy is over-
simplistic in many instances.

The Self

The strategy-based radicals are in various ways
concerned with the humanity of the learner.
Rogers (1969), for instance, focuses upon both the
self of the learner and the achievement of freedom.
Yet Rogers, like others of this school, spends
little time considering the constraints of the
social structure on the self, this is a point to
which further reference will be made below.
Knowles (1980:45), it will be recalled, locates
his first major difference between andragogy and
pedagogy in the concept of the learner, claiming
that:

> ... something dramatic happens to their self
> concepts when people define themselves as
> adults. They begin to see their normal role

in life no longer as being full-time learners.   They see themselves increasingly as
producers or doers.   Their chief sources
of self-fulfilment are now their perform-
ances as workers, spouses, parents, and
citizens.

The development of the person is clearly central to
this perspective but the above quotation raises a
number of questions that require further examination.
      Knowles focuses upon the self concept of the
learner but produces no evidence to substantiate
his claim that adults see themselves as self-
directed, even though he acknowledges that
children may also be self-directed and he accuses
society of preventing this occurring. Nevertheless, he makes no reference to the thorough
discussion of the self that various social
interactionists and phenomenologists have undertaken.   For instance, Mead (1934) argues that the
self is the product of interaction between the
individual and, initially, significant others.
In this early socialization process a body of
knowledge, meaning and experience acquired by
individuals becomes detached from the immediate
experience of the individual and assumes an
independence.   This detachment leads to an
individuation of consciousness which permits the
construction of schemes of meaning which allow
for the individual to interact with himself as
an objective reality in an I-Me dialogue.   Hence,
he argues that both reason and self-consciousness
emerge in an individual as a result of interaction
with others.
      Two questions immediately demand discussion
here: is not the conception that the self is a
creation of social interaction a confirmation that
man is created by society and, therefore, evidence
that there is only one sociology and, secondly, is
Knowles correct when he claims that something
dramatic happens to the self concept when people
define themselves as adults?
      Mead was aware of the issue of the social
self and he discussed, but rightly rejected, the
possibility that the self is an independent entity.
However, is the assertion that the self is social
evidence that man is merely the product of the
social group into which he is born? This is a view
that was prevalent in sociology during a stage in
its development but it is not one that now finds

favour with sociologists. Wrong (1961), drawing
on the work of Freud, sought to show that this
resulted in an over-socialized conception of man
and one that is false to experience. Hence, the
problem is to explain how an independent self
can emerge in an individual since it is the product
of society in any case. In a pluralist society
the individual will be exposed to several different
interpretations of any reality, especially over a
period of time, so that in order to understand that
reality the individual has to decide upon which of
the interpretations, if any, to accept and espouse.
The more that the individual is enabled to
reflect and decide from alternatives the more likely
he is to emerge as a self-directed person. Not
all people achieve the same degree of independence
and self-direction and initial education, with its
traditional didactic methods, with the exception of
primary education, may not encourage the process.
Riesman (1950) showed that while some adults are
'inner directed', others are 'tradition directed'
and even 'other directed'. Hence, it is
suggested that since the self is a social construct,
some individuals do not acquire as high a degree of
self-direction as others during their socialization
and initial education. Such self-direction does
not, therefore, emerge with adulthood: for some
it occurs early in their lives and for others it
may not appear until much later, if at all.
Indeed, other directed individuals may have what
Lifton has called a 'protean self'. Sennett
(1980:101) describes this:

> as a belief that one's personality is always
> undergoing fundamental changes, or is
> capable of doing so. There is no core of
> 'innate' human nature or fixed social
> condition that defines it. It is a self
> so immanent in the world that it is a
> creature of immediate appearances and
> sensations. This selfhood puts an immense
> premium on 'direct' experiences with other
> people; it detests reserves or masks behind
> which other people are felt to lurk, because
> in being distant they seem to be inauthentic,
> not taking the immediate moment of human
> contact as an absolute.

There is a sense in which some forms of adult
education, especially in its affective form, seek
to remove the barriers that prevent self-disclosure

and endeavour to facilitate a community feeling in
which the participants reveal themselves to each
other. Sennett (1980:92) regards self 'disclosure
of one's feelings to others' in an attempt to
create Gemeinschaft as something destructive to the
participants since advanced industrial societies
demand individuals who do not necessarily seek to
share their feelings and certainly do not need to
do so. This inner-direction or self-direction may
be a condition of social maturity in such a society,
but this is not necessarily to be equated with
adulthood in the manner that Knowles implies.
Whenever self-direction begins it does not,
however, imply the strategy-based humanistic aim of
seeking to ensure the development of the self in
the teaching and learning transaction, it merely
points to the fact that adults are at different
levels of self-development and independence when
they embark upon a learning project and that
adult educators may need to diagnose the degree
of individual development if they are to employ
facilitative methods of teaching and learning.
    The third point in the quotation from Knowles
that requires examination is his assumption that
the chief source of adults' fulfilment is their
performance as workers, spouses, etc.   The
assumption here is that adulthood will result in a
social conformity and that in performing socially
prescribed roles the individual discovers self-
fulfilment.   The implications of this position
are implicitly conservative and that the social
structures exercise no constraint upon the
individual.   No consideration is given to the
fact that for many able persons the constraints of
the social structure do inhibit their self-fulfilment.   Indeed, it is very difficult for those lower
in the social hierarchy to be socially mobile
upwards and to obtain the type of employment that
is intrinsically satisfying, so that individuals
are not all totally free agents in the way that
liberal adult education assumes.   While a person
may be free to think he may be constrained from
acting by the structures of society and this is a
phenomenon that is examined in greater detail in
the following section.

The Learning Cycle
Thus far in this study the dichotomy between
education from above and the education of equals has
been maintained since it reflects both the two
sociologies and the problems of structure and

agency. However, there is one process in which this dichotomy should find some resolution, that of human learning. It must be emphasized that it is learning, and not memorization, that may enable the individual to become an agent and to act upon the societal structures in order to help fashion them anew. Since it is learning rather than teaching, it may be seen that any method of teaching employed may result in changes in the student, even though they may not be those intended by the didactic teacher! However, facilitative methods are more likely to produce learning as opposed to memorization. However, this learning may only really occur if the human being has the opportunity to reflect upon his learning experience and providing other factors of social control do not operate.

Learning in the sense being used here is similar to Mezirow's (1981:6) concept of perspective transformation, which he defines as:

> the emancipatory process of becoming critically aware of how and why the structure of psycho-cultural assumptions has come to constrain the way we see ourselves and our relationships, reconstituting this structure to permit a more inclusive and discriminating integration of experience and acting upon these new understandings.

While Mezirow's argument is extremely important it must be pointed out that this definition contains one of the same weaknesses that was referred to earlier about liberal adult education, it assumes that the learner is free to act upon any new understanding he may gain. This is clearly not the case and the lower in the social hierarchy learners may be the more inhibiting they may find the social structures, if they seek to be socially mobile. Kolb and Fry (1975:33-37), for instance, recognised that one element in human learning must be testing the implications of any learning and they depicted the learning process as a cycle.

Jarvis (1983b) has discussed the above learning process very thoroughly and so there is little need to trace the learning cycle through its psychological stages but it is necessary to examine it from a sociological perspective. However, it is necessary to recognise that the phases that Kolb and Fry distinguish may not be totally discrete and that reflection and conceptualization and generalization may actually merge together in one phase.   Even so, each of the four stages are discussed here separately.

Figure 7.1:   The Learning Cycle - following Kolb and Fry

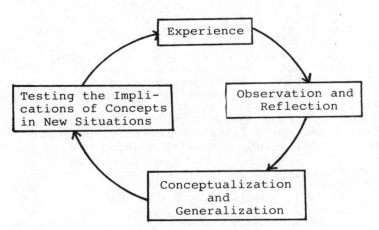

Experience: Every learning situation whether it is listening to a lecture or participating in a workshop may be viewed as a human experience.   This point must be emphasized because this terminology is usually only applied to affective, experiential learning in adult and continuing education rather than to all human learning.   Such a restriction is regarded here as detrimental to a complete understanding of human learning.

The experience, through whatever senses the learner receives it, is not one to be treated in total isolation since the learner brings to the situation himself, and he may be regarded as more than the sum total of all of his previous experiences, knowledge, interpretation of reality and systems of meaning.   He is the human physical organism with all of its drives, etc. and the complex self in an interacting whole.   Hence, the longer a person has lived the greater the accumulation of all of the experiences etc. that constitutes the person so that the adult is more likely, but not necessarily, going to bring a greater richness and diversity of knowledge, etc.

to the learning situation than is a child.   Hence,
a significant element in adult learning is that
the sum of all those previous experiences provides
a springboard for any new learning.   Obviously,
the closer a new experience is to the orientation
of the self, or the more that it relates to a
self-perceived deficiency, the easier it is to
learn.   But if there has been a false consciousness
in the individual (Mannheim 1936:84-87) then the
learning experience may be of a more traumatic
nature, as it may if the experience is considerably
removed from the self-orientation of the learner.

Reflection: Reflection is at the heart of Mead's
I-Me dialogue.   The individual is able to reflect
upon any learning experience in the light of
other experiences that are stored in the memory.
In the same way Mezirow (1981:6) suggests that
'meaning perspectives refers to the structures of
psycho-cultural assumptions within which new
experience is assimilated and transformed by
one's past experiences'.   However, this formulation is incomplete since Mezirow's thinking stops
with the present.   But reflection also places
the learning experience within the whole conception
of time (Jarvis 1983c) so that the omission of the
future leaves the analysis incomplete.   The
individual is not able to predict only to anticipate
and imagine the future but this may be a significant
element in the process of reflection.   Hence,
the process of time is an important element, first
in building up the store of memories but also in
allowing anticipation of future events, in any
consideration of human learning.   However, it is
this ability to draw together the interpretations
of the past and anticipation of the future in a
confrontation with the present that releases the
individual from the bonds of past experience.
Human learning occurs at the point in the process
at which the individual is free to be an agent
within himself.
      However, it might be argued that this still
does not demonstrate that the individual is free
because his mind is merely like a complex computer
that has been programmed by previous experiences,
so that the person is the sum total of his
experiences, and that if his biography were fully
known then his learning response to any new
learning experience would be predictable.   This
argument would be quite strong were it not for
the fact that the only way that a computer can

take the future into consideration as if it were
programmed to do so by a human mind. However,
it cannot do so unless the human first programmes
it so that it is maintained here that the
consideration of both the past and the future is a
significant factor in recognising that at the
point of reflection the individual is able to be
free from the psycho-cultural structures of his
biography. This does not mean necessarily that
the individual will exercise the freedom of the
agent, only that potentiality for the individual
as agent exists at this point.

Mezirow (1981:11-14) suggests that there are
seven levels of reflectivity:
- reflectivity, awareness of specific
  perceptions
- affective reflectivity, awareness of how
  the perceiver feels about the perceptions
- discriminant reflectivity, assessment of the
  efficacy of perception
- judgmental reflectivity, making and becoming
  aware of value judgments in perceptions
- conceptual reflectivity, evaluating the
  bases of making judgments
- psychic reflectivity, recognising the habit
  of making precipiant judgments on the
  basis of limited information
- theoretical reflectivity, being aware of the
  reasons why precipiant judgments are made
  is a set of taken-for-granted cultural
  or psychological assumptions which explain
  personal experience less satisfactorily
  than another perspective.

Mezirow argues that theoretical reflectivity is the
process central to perspective transformation and
that the latter three forms of reflectivity are all
forms of critical consciousness. This analysis
highlights the fact that individuals reflect at
different levels, although it assumes that critical
reflectivity results in change rather than, in
some instances, in reinforcing the present
perception of reality. This implies a limited
conceptualization of the notion of 'critical' but
this does not detract from the significance of
his analysis.

Hence it may be seen that the structure-and-
agency debate may in part be resolved by the
incorporation of time into the discussion.
Clearly the self is partially a product of the
forces operating in the social system but through
the process of time it initially achieves

individuation and, thereafter, the potential to become an agent able to confront those forces operating in the social world and to modify them.

Conceptualization and Generalization: Reflection does not finish when it has worked through the immediate implications of a learning experience because the learner may seek to generalize from the experience or to develop abstract concepts from it. Hence, the learning experience may not only be projected into the future but it may be extended to the wider parameters of social living. Hence Kolb and Fry employ a third stage in their learning cycle but it may be an unnecessary complication or merely an extension of the process of reflection.

Some adult educators advocate that the processes of reflection and conceptualization should occur in small groups of learners, so they use the small group discussion method to facilitate reflection. Small group discussion may facilitate the presentation of alternative solutions, different interpretations of experiences and additions to a body of knowledge but since the group is a dynamic entity exercising pressures upon its members it is quite unsound to treat a group as an agglomeration of individuals. Asch (cited Krech et al 1962:507-508) has demonstrated how 123 subjects were tested on twelve critical judgements in groups and none of the subjects reported that they disregarded the pressure of the group and 37% of their judgements were in error in conformity with a false group perspective, while virtually none of the control subjects made error of judgements when assessing alone. Similar experiments by Crutchfield (cited Krech et al 1962:508-509) also demonstrate precisely the same conclusion, that group pressure leads to conformity. Hence, reflection may occur only when the individual is free to reflect for himself, alone and away from the pressures of the social groups. Having reached conclusions, it is necessary for the learner to test out their implications.

Testing the Implications: Since everybody, almost without exception, has to live in the wider society it is necessary for the learner to test the implications of the conclusions reached in the process of reflection in the wider society. Sometimes the conclusions reached may be in accord with the direction of the prevailing social

forces and in such instances the individual would
have no difficulty in playing his role in the wider
society and in conforming to its pressures.   But
it is possible that the conclusions reached may
be contrary to those social forces, whether they
are spatial forces that lead to segregation or
political pressures that demand conformity.   The
actor then has alternative strategies: either
to conform to the social pressures even though
such a course of action would be contrary to the
conclusions that have been reached, or to resist
the prevailing social forces which may ultimately
result in a conflict situation.   Hence, it is
essential in any resolution of the structure/
agency discussion to recognise that both the
temporal and the power dimensions have to be
included.   Additionally, it must be recognised
that learning, as opposed to memorization, does not
automatically result in conformity.   Hence, not
all education from above results in individuals
being moulded in precisely the manner that
educators or the elite in the social groups may
desire.   However, it may be useful at this stage
to reconstruct the learning cycle.

Figure 7.2:   A Re-Constructed Learning Cycle

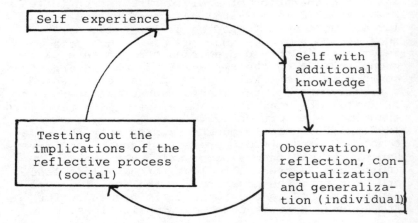

Learning can result in conformity or conflict
but the significant factor in this discussion is
that agency can be created through the process of
human learning and teaching strategies that
encourage this process are more likely to produce
agents able to play their part in changing the
structures of society.

It is perhaps significant to note here that
Mannheim (1936:10) considered that the intelligentsia would be free to act as agents in the wider
world. However, this freedom only exists so long
as the universities are allowed to operate in some
way independently of the wider society. Once
universities have to seek funding by research
contracts from government and commercial organizations then the production of knowledge is itself
controlled to some extent by those who control and
funding, so that the freedom of the intelligentsia
is itself perhaps a utopian ideal.
   Having thus examined the strategy-based
position and examined its possibilities in assisting to produce agents within the wider society,
it is now necessary to assess some of the
criticisms of the position mentioned by Giroux.

Criticisms of the Strategy-Based Position
Giroux (1981:65-67) perhaps levels the most forceful criticisms at the strategy-based radical
position. However, it has to be recalled that
much of his criticism is more applicable to
initial education than it is to adult and
continuing education because, as the students are
adults, there may be more of a tendency to teach
them as adults. Hence, within the ideology of
adult education there actually are elements of
egalitarianism between teacher and taught, which
may be regarded by some as radical, but by other
practitioners it may not even by regarded as
radical. Overall, however, the tenor of Giroux's
position is that strategy-based radicalism is
utopian because it depoliticizes the function of
methodology so that the social relations of the
classroom are not explored by establishing their
meaning within the context of corresponding socio-
political forces in the larger society. Hence,
he claims that this produces a 'happy but no less
mystifying false consciousness'.
   However, strategy-based adult educators might
well wish to dispute these criticisms initially
by denying that the social relations of the
classroom are not explored within a wider
political context with adult students. It would
have to be acknowledged, however, that in some
instances the accusation may be valid since,
some adult educators practice egalitarian teaching
methods for no other reason than their effectiveness in producing learning in the students rather
than memorization. But more significantly, they

may wish to claim that in treating people as equals
they are demonstrating an alternative strategy,
one that is indicative of a better way of social
living and, whilst it may be utopian, it is
practical since it has been shown that adults
learn effectively in these surroundings. Similarly,
they may wish to claim that where management has
introduced more egalitarian methods of production,
especially where workers are encouraged to use
their own initiative, productivity may actually
increase and the turnover among the workforce fall.
Finally, strategy-based radicalism does not
prevent examination of any political position or
ideology, but it is being true to itself in not
seeking to indoctrinate any learner into accepting
any interpretation of reality, whether it is
radical, reformist, liberal or conservative,
without first considering it as fully as possible.

It is perhaps important to note here that
indoctrination may occur when the teacher intends
the learner to acquire specific knowledge, so that
it is presented in such a manner as to appear
to be true and by such a method as to inhibit the
learner from exploring alternatives. Hence, it
may be seen that indoctrination requires a
combination of aims and objectives, content and
methods in order to occur. However, it may
actually happen without all three being apparent
in the teaching and learning process. Nevertheless, it may be a fairly common occurrence in
education, especially in initial education. For
instance, Wilson (1964:44) writes:

> Naturally I do not at all want to say that
> all teaching in all societies today is
> indoctrination. But I incline to think
> that most of it is either indoctrinatory
> or irrelevant to that territory in the
> human personality which we wish to conquer
> and which is now occupied by indoctrination.

While Wilson's claim is not based on empirical
evidence, it is the conclusion of his own
philosophical examination of teaching and learning.
However, it is only applicable to school children
and it may be less true of a great deal of the
education of adults. Even so, it will be argued
that one of the functions of adult and continuing
education is cultural reproduction, so that if this
occurs then it would be valid to assume that some
indoctrination does occur in the education of

adults and it is evident from the above discussions
that it is more likely to occur in education from
above than it is in the education of equals.

The Teaching Strategy of Paulo Freire

Any examination of the works of Freire would reveal
that at the heart of his approach is a strategy-
based radicalism based upon a humanism that stems
from his concern for the human being.   Indeed, it
is his ideological background in a radical
Christian-Marxism that makes his theory and practice
so unique and important to any understanding of
the education of adults.   As it will be seen in
this brief section, his theoretical perspectives
fit clearly into the ideas of reflectivity,
structure and agency and human learning that have
been discussed in this chapter.

However, in examining Freire's approach it has
to be borne in mind that his ideas emerged from the
Third World, where the dominant elite exercise
power in a much more overt manner than they do in
some other parts of the world.   This cultural
difference is enough to lead Giroux (1981:139) to
claim and it 'would be misleading as well as
dangerous to extend without qualification Freire's
theory and methods to the industrialized and
urbanized societies of the West'.   However, he
does acknowledge that some of the themes would
enrich pedagogy but Giroux's strictures are really
only applicable to the process of schooling and
it must be remembered that Freire was really
concerned with the education of adults.   Hence,
in adult education, especially in community
education, his approach may have validity and,
perhaps, in literacy education there may be more
place for it than there appears in the literature
of adult basic education.   However, it has to be
recognised that the exercise of power in the
industrialised countries of the world is more
covert and it is Gramsci's considerable contribution to sociological analysis to make explicit
the principle of hegemony.   Williams (1976:205)
describes hegemony as:

> ... a whole body of practices and
> expectations, our assignments of energy, our
> ordinary understanding of the nature of man
> and of his world.   It is a set of meanings
> and values which as they are experienced as
> practices appear as reciprocally confirming.
> It thus constitutes a sense of reality for

> most people in society, a sense of absolute
> because experienced reality beyond which
> it is very difficult for most members of
> society to move, in most areas of their
> lives.

Thus while Gramsci recognized the significance of
the dominant culture in the industrialized
societies of the world, Freire highlights a similar
principle in the colonized countries of the Third
World. The masses of such countries are
conditioned into accepting the interpretation of
the world provided by the dominant culture so that
they have a false consciousness and there exists,
therefore, a culture of silence. They are,
consequently, oppressed and the 'pedagogy of the
oppressed ... (is) a humanist and libertarian
pedagogy' (Freire 1972a:31). Its aim is to assist
the oppressed unveil this world of oppression and
to commit themselves to its transformation. When
this ideal society has been achieved its techniques
should belong to all people ensuring the permanent
process of liberation. Herein lies a major
weakness in Freire's thinking since it assumes an
egalitarian society will be achieved, an assumption
that, thereafter, will require permanent liberating
forces to prevent the structures of society being
reformed with another dominating elite. Such a
process was tried in the latter years of Mao
Tse-tung in China without a great deal of success,
since the process of time cannot be stopped. Yet
such an ideal, with similar problems of accounting
for the process of time without change in the
social structures, may be discovered in many
revolutionary thinkers from Christ to Marx. Nevertheless, the fact that the ideal may be impractical,
within the context of current development, does
not actually invalidate the ideal and, in part,
Freire overcomes the objection when he (1976:225)
claims that only 'those who are continually
denouncing and announcing committed and engaged in
the transformation of the world, are utopian and
create hope' as if the process of world-building is
never completed.
    Freire recognises that there may be cultural
differences between the educators and the learners
so that his method begins by 'participant
observation of educators "tuning in" to the
vernacular universe of the people' (Goulet in
Freire 1974:viii). The educator, therefore, goes
to the people but he does so not initially as a

teacher but as a learner so that he can understand
the language and the thought patterns of the
people.   This educator-student relationship is
one that is a problem that has to be overcome:
education from above reproduces the power relationships of which Freire disapproves so that from
the outset the education of equals is the only
strategy that should be employed.   Since educators
also learn from the people, they are the people's
students but the students also learn in dialogue
from the teachers, so that education of equals is
also practised.
    From the outset of his literacy programme,
Freire's aims were clear: they were to help people
learn rather than memorize using the medium of
literacy to create a critical consciousness.   He
(1972b:29) explains it thus:

> If learning to read and write is to
> constitute an act of knowing, the learners
> must assume from the beginning the role
> of creative subjects.   It is not a matter
> of memorizing and repeating given syllables,
> words and phrases, but rather of reflecting
> critically on the project of reading and
> writing itself, and on the profound
> significance of language.

In his writings he describes fully the types of
learning strategies to which the students were
exposed, including: working from their own level
of experience, active projects and group discussion.
The educator is a member of the group rather than
its leader and his task may be that of problem
setter rather than problem solver!   Hence, the
learners are encouraged to generate their own
meanings and to realize that there is a difference
between appearance and meaning so that they are
encouraged to analyse the influence of the dominant
culture upon the social reality that they experience.   Liberation begins when they realize that
apparently objective knowledge is ideological.
This process of reflection is, according to Freire
(1976:224) one of the characteristics of man
himself and problem solving is an element in the
development of the humanity of the learner.

> Problem-posing education affirms men as
> being in the process of becoming - as
> unfinished, uncompleted beings in and with
> a likewise unfinished reality.   Indeed, in

> contrast to other animals who are
> unfinished but not historical, men know
> themselves to be unfinished; they are
> aware of their incompleteness. In this
> incompleteness and this awareness lie the
> very roots of education as an exclusively
> human manifestation. The unfinished
> character of men and the transformational
> character of reality necessitate that
> education be an on-going reality.
> (Freire 1972a:56-57)

It is through problem solving that individuals
become conscious of the world in which they live
and by which they can be freed from the process of
conditioning. In the act of learning individuals
become potential agents, freed to act upon the
world. Through the process of learning man becomes
conscious of reality and the process of conscientization is at the heart of Freire's thinking, it
is defined as 'the process in which men, not as
recipients, but as knowing subjects, achieve a
deepening awareness both of the socio-cultural
reality which shapes their lives and of their
capacity to transform that reality' (Freire 1972b:
51 footnote). The process of transforming the
world is for him a process of humanizing it, so
that the end product of the process of reflection
and action is one in helping to create a world
where individuals may be more truly human. It is
a utopian ideal but he himself claims that unless
education is utopian either the future has lost
its meaning for men or men are afraid to risk living
in the future as creative human beings. Hence,
man is involved in a struggle against the
oppressive and dehumanizing structures of the world
in a 'precarious adventure of transforming and
recreating the world' (Freire 1972b:72).
        Among the strengths of Freire's position are
that: it combines theory with practice; it
contains a theory of human learning that is in
accord with theorists that do not necessarily
espouse his ideological position; it locates
education within the wider socio-political process;
it places the individual within the context of
a sociological framework within which contemporary
sociological theorizing is seen to be relevant; it
combines Christianity, humanism and Marxism in a
radical, humanist, ideological position that is
quite unique within educational theory; it is
utopian.

One of the weaknesses of Freire's position was
pointed out earlier. In addition, he appears to
assume that those of the masses who have been
educated will become revolutionary and this could
open him to the criticism that he is actually
using education to produce revolutionaries. This
would be a contradiction in his position in as
much as it would be an imposition of the utopian
ideology that he espouses upon those who learn.
Consequently he may need to be more explicit about
those who do not accept the revolutionary
position once they have learned about the social
processes that have produced the results that they
have. Nevertheless, it will be seen that he
espouses the radical humanist position about which
this chapter began and since there has been a
considerable volume of literature about him it is
unnecessary to pursue his ideas further in this
context.

Conclusion

This chapter has examined the processes of teaching
and learning. Initially, it was shown that
didactic teaching tends to be education from above
while facilitative teaching epitomises the
education of equals. However, it was recognised
that since the process of learning involves
reflection, wherever learning occurs where exists
the possibility that the learner could be freed
from the social pressures that have constrained
him in order to act as an agent. However,
few leading theorists, especially in the education
of adults, have located learning within the socio-
political context in the manner that Freire does.
Hence, he makes explicit the potentially
revolutionary nature of human learning whereas
others deal with learning in an individualistic
manner unrelated to the wider society in which
learning occurs. Yet one other technique of
control exists, that of assessment and that
constitutes the final chapter of the second section
of this study.

Chapter Eight

EXAMINATIONS AND ASSESSMENT

In the traditional curriculum model the fourth
element is usually evaluation and it is generally
agreed that this is actually part of the
curriculum process.   However, in the teaching and
learning model that is under discussion here the
examination and assessment of students constitutes
the fourth element.   Assessment is used throughout this chapter to refer to any form of
evaluation of students in their educational work,
grading to indicate a symbolic representation of
the assessment and examination to the process,
usually formal, of setting exercises that are
completed, assessed, graded and the results
published so that usually the students obtain some
form of certificate or diploma.   It will be
recalled from Table 4.3 that education from above
assumes that examinations and assessment involves
public examinations, competition, teacher-set
tasks and an emphasis on standards.   By contrast,
the education of equals emphasizes assessment by
peers and by self and what has been learned
rather than what is known.   It is clear that these
two forms are closely related to the teaching
methods that were discussed in the previous chapter:
in fact, it is emphasized here just how distinct
these two forms are.   Nevertheless, there has
been an occasional overlap between the types of
education in the aforegoing discussion and one
other will occur in the following analysis.
     It is perhaps significant that different types
of assessment may be more well known than, for
instance, different types of teaching method.
However, for the purposes of focusing the discussion
it is noted that among the different types of
assessment that occur in education from above are:
national and public examinations, e.g. General

Certificate examinations;locally set examinations
with national validity, e.g. university degree
examinations; local examinations with assessment
but with no widely recognised validity, e.g.
college diplomas and attendance certificates. By
contrast, there are less formal examinations and
peer and self assessment, which are more   likely
to occur in the education of equals.

While it is perhaps still generally assumed
that most educational examinations occur in
initial education, it is becoming a much more common
phenomenon for adults to sit both the school type
General Certificate of Education examinations
(e.g. Butler 1981), and for them to take vocational
examinations throughout a considerable proportion
of their early occupational career. Since the
advent of the Open University many adults are also
sitting university degree examinations within the
context of liberal adult education, while much
liberal adult education is still conducted without
a formal examination although teacher-set exercises
do often occur. However, there is an increasing
emphasis on self and peer assessment, so that it
will be necessary to explore these elements within
this chapter.

It is important to note from the outset of
this analysis that there will be some slight overlap with some of the discussion in sociological
literature about the functions of education within
the social context. Such an overlap is unavoida-
ble since less emphasis has actually be placed
upon this topic in that literature than has been
placed upon education as a whole. However, it is
considered here that the topic is significant
enough to merit a separate chapter and that it is
especially important as continuing education is
institutionalising and more adults are actually
sitting examinations and being assessed educationally for various purposes. It is suggested here
that assessment and examinations: help to define
a social reality and then legitimate it; reproduce
the hierarchical relations in society; reproduce
some of the social mechanisms through which
society operates; reduce education to a commodity;
provide status and identity for the candidate;
reflect the individual's subsequent performance
in the educational system. Each of these issues
are now discussed and that is followed with a
brief analysis of self assessment and a conclusion.

Definition and Legitimation of Social Reality

It will be recalled that in the analysis of the concept of 'need' it was discovered how difficult it is to determine a national norm empirically. Since examinations are often about standards, frequently claimed to be national standards, which are norms, the same problem about determining these exist. But in this sense examinations define the standard but even this is problematic. There is ample evidence to show that work assessed by one academic will be graded differently by another, even when a comprehensive marking scheme is employed. There is evidence to show that markers vary in the grades that they award according to many variables, including the time of the day that the assessment is undertaken, the handwriting of the candidate, etc. (Jarvis 1978). Hence, grading provides a spurious objectivity to both assessment of assignments and to examinations. This does not deny that there are standards, it only questions whether such apparent objectivity as a percentage actually means very much. The grade may reflect the standards of the assessor at the time that the work is being marked, but even this necessarily includes factors that are contingent upon the process rather than only the essence of the work being assessed. All of this is well known to educators and many attempts have been made to eradicate some of the factors that causes such subjectivity and unreliability in examinations but, as yet, the problem has not been successfully solved. But that is almost certainly an impossible undertaking, since whether there is an absolute standard behind the apparent standard is a nice philosophical question. Even though this debate is well known among educationalists it is necessary to enquire why examinations and assessments are perpetuated in education as if there were no problem about them.

It would be possible to argue that since assessment is an essential part of the learning process in the form of diagnosis of what is known and what needs to be learned, it is fundamental to education. Additionally, it might be claimed that in the education of equals certain forms of assessment need to occur if one colleague is able to share his strengths with another in order to achieve the highest possible standards. None of this would be denied, but in none of these instances would it be claimed that there are absolute and objective standards and, in addition, assessment in

the process of teaching and learning is a rather
different process to that which occurs in either
national or local examinations.   These have a
more significant place in society.

If there is no real possibility in determining
a national norm, or standard, then national
examinations do not reflect one but rather they
create the illusion of there being one.   Yet, as
Rowntree (1977:54) points out, 'the standard of
an examination adjusts itself to the standard of
those taking it'.   But even this an over-simplifi-
cation of reality since he, himself, suggests
that the standard is actually adjusted by those who
control the examination for a variety of reasons,
including the necessity to have failures.
However, it is not actually the standard of the
performance reflected by the grades awarded to
whose who are sitting the examination at that time
that is adjusted.   This may appear a trifle
pedantic but the fact remains that over a period
of time the pass grade may have remained the same
but the grades of a variety of markers adjusted
each time the examination is taken.   Hence, the
pass grade reflects a spurious objectivity of
examination success or failure and it is this that
defines a social reality of those who 'more able'
or 'less able' members of society.

Hence, it is these who are labelled 'more
able' and awarded the educational certificate as an
insignia of merit who are then permitted to
proceed to more responsible positions in society.
Since they are 'the more able' is appears self-
evident that they should assume such responsibility
and does it really matter if the examination has
been subjective, since those who pass may have
been the more able in their cohort?   Even allowing
for this, it does not allow for comparison between
cohorts, but the question remains has the
examination actually measured who are the more able
or has it merely defined some as more able than
others?   This is a much more significant question
and it may be necessary to look at other measures
of ability to answer this question.   Berg (1973:
110) concludes that:

> A search of the considerable body of
> literature on productivity, absenteeism
> and turnover has yielded little concrete
> evidence of a positive relationship
> between workers' educational achieve-
> ments and their performance records in

the private sector (of work).

The whole tenor of Berg's argument is to suggest that the level of educational assessment and work performance may not be correlated in America. A similar conclusion was reached by Bowles and Gintis (1976:123) who suggest that:

> the basis for assessing merit - competitive academic performances - is only weakly associated with the personal attributes indicative of individual success in economic life. Thus the legitimation process in education assumes a largely symbolic form.

Since both the examination achievement and the work performance may both be regarded as indications of ability, then it must not be assumed automatically that the former actually suceeds in measuring it but it does define ability since the examination grade is regarded as a symbol of the ability required to enter many responsible occupations and professions. Therefore, adults sit the same examinations as school children, so that they can acquire the certificate of ability necessary to enter, or to change, an occupation. Hence, it must be argued that the examination defines who are the more able and, thereafter, it legitimates the individual's right to hold a position in the social system even if his work performance does not justify it. Irrespective of how able the practitioner is in the performance of his occupation, he is able to display his degree certificate, diploma of professional qualification, etc. to demonstrate his right to practise. As mandatory continuing education appears in various professions, additional qualifications and certificates are awarded and those too are displayed for clients to see, which perpetuates the process of legitimation.

Examinations Reproduce the Hierarchical Relations in Society

From the earlier discussion it might have been included that educational success is a mechanism whereby individuals might be socially upwardly mobile. Indeed, this may be a motive behind many people when they study for and sit examinations yet it is undoubtedly true that many courses are instituted with the highest of professional motives

but the result of new courses and examinations may
not quite be in line with the intention.   Many
years ago, Max Weber commented on this phenomenon:

> When we hear from all sides the demand for
> the introduction of regular curricula and
> special examinations, the reason behind it
> is, of course, not a suddenly awakened
> 'thirst for education' but the desire for
> restricting the supply for these positions
> and their monopolization by the owners of
> educational certificates.   Today the
> 'examination' is the universal means of
> this monopolization, and therefore
> examinations irresistibly advance.   As
> the education prerequisite to the
> acquisition of the educational
> certificate requires considerable expense
> and a period of waiting for full remune-
> ration, the striving means a setback for
> talent (charisma) in favor of property.
> (Gerth and Mills 1948:241-242)

Two points arise from this that requires some
consideration at this juncture.   Firstly, it may
be seen that every new educational course and
certificate creates both those who are able to
acquire the certificate and those who, for
whatever reason, are unable to do so.   Hence,
every educational innovation creates a new rich
and a new poor.   The more the financial reward
is withheld until the successful acquisition of
the educational certificate, the more it favours
whose who have sufficient wealth not to require
that additional remuneration.   Of course financial
grants and bursaries are available in some
instances but these are not awarded to all adults
as of right and neither do they necessarily
provide sufficient income and to allow the adult
to meet all his domestic commitments and to pursue
that course of learning and some might argue
that if such awards were available the perpetual
student would appear.   Hence recurrent educationalists have argued that everybody should, of right,
be entitled to a fixed number of years of
educational study after the completion of compulsory education.   Clearly this is a policy decision
that would enable some of the less wealthy to
pursue such activities but few societies in the

world have implemented it.   Of course, those who
are very highly motivated, but who have not
sufficient wealth, may still acquire such
accreditation by dint of hard work and sacrifice,
but this is often exacerbated by the fact that
there is considerable resistance in the
universities and the professions to the introduction
of part-time degree level study.
     The second point that must be raised is the
extent to which Weber's claim is correct.   Has,
for instance, the introduction of part-time further
education (as opposed to higher education) provided
an alternative route to educational success?
Halsey et al (1980:193) conclude from their study
of education and mobility that the expansion of
education in the United Kingdom was sufficient to
provide more opportunity for individuals from all
socio-economic classes but that 'the largest
absolute gains' went to the service, or white-
collar, class.   The curtailment of the post-
compulsory education service will, therefore,
restrict the opportunities of all groups but it
will probably affect the poorer more than the more
wealthy.   Hence, it may be concluded that those
with wealth, social position, etc. took greater
advantage of the expansion of education which is
circumstantial evidence in support of Weber.   In
addition, there is considerable evidence in the
sociology of initial education that demonstrates
that the attrition rate in schools is related to
class, with there being an inverse relationship
between class and attrition.   Therefore, it is
suggested here that while Weber's hypothesis has
not absolutely conclusive proof, there is
considerable evidence to suggest that he is
substantially correct.

Examinations and the Reproduction of Society's Mode of Operation

Much of the ethos of adult education is about
cooperation between learners, so that all can share
in the learning experiences, resources etc. of the
group.   Methods of teaching are employed that
assume this form of co-operative enterprise.
Adult education is, therefore, often a form of
education of equals.   However, examinations are
individualistic, any form of sharing of knowledge
is regarded as cheating;   they are competitive in
as much as the perceived standard is adjusted so
that some candidates will pass and others fail
thereby demanding competition between the entrants.

Vandome and his colleagues consider that one of
the side effects of competitive assessment at
college level is:

> Students feel that they will gain through
> the poor performance of others and suffer
> by imparting their knowledge to fellow
> students. In this way a potentially rich
> source of knowledge - communication of
> ideas among students - tends to be stifled.
> To the extent it does take place, any
> exchange is biased by the way in which a
> student's 'self-image' and his image of
> his fellows is affected by their grades.
> A 50% student for instance will think
> twice before putting forward one of his
> ideas for discussion with a group of 60%
> students. This is relevant not only to
> informal interchange between students but
> also to tutorial discussion. Competitive
> rather than co-operative behaviour may be
> manifest in other ways such as the 'illegal
> borrowing' of library books.
> (cited from Rowntree 1977:56)

Thus it may be seen that assessment and examinations produce an individualistic and competitive
situation but, in addition, in the above quotation
they produce a social hierarchy in which students
locate themselves and behave accordingly. Hence,
it may be seen that this reflects the ideology of
the type of society in which the fittest individuals, industrial or commercial concerns, flourish
in the battle for survival.
    To some extent peer assessment overcomes this
problem in as much as it places the emphasis upon
the groups of equals seeking to help each other
achieve better standards but, in other ways, peer
assessment also makes colleagues aware of each
others strengths and weaknesses, so that it may
produce a situation in which the less able feel
inhibited from contributing to the learning
situation. Hence, it becomes apparent why some
types of education, such as liberal adult education,
emphasize cooperation but eschew examinations
and assessment. Obviously it thereby opens itself
to the charge that it is utopian but that accusation
has been answered elsewhere in this text.

Education as a Commodity
Liberal adult education and the education of equals

place considerable emphasis on learning for learning's sake. Paterson (1979:17-18) claims that education, as a concept, connotes something that is intrinsically valuable, rather than a process undertaken for instrumental ends. However, once educational qualifications are required for entry to the professions or even to further or higher education, then education becomes a means to an end rather than an end in itself. Hence, students seek good grades not for the sake of being perceived to have completed an excellent piece of work but because they may affect the overall standard of the degree, etc. Learning, therefore, is not undertaken for its own sake, not undertaken to satisfy a desire to know or to respond to a question in the human mind, but it is only undertaken to meet the requirement of achieving a certain grade. Hence, the learning may not be satisfying in itself, it may be an alien activity, undertaken as a means to achieve another end. Such an argument is remarkably familiar to sociology, for it was Marx (1975:326) who asked in 'Economic and Philosophical Manu-scripts':

> What constitutes the alienation of labour? Firstly, the fact that the labour is external to the worker, i.e. does not belong to his essential being; that he therefore does not confirm himself in his work, but denies himself, feels miserable and not happy, does not develop free mental and physical energy, but mortifies his flesh and ruins his mind. Hence the worker feels himself only when he is not working; when he is working he does not feel him-self ... His labour ... is therefore not the satisfaction of a need but a mere means to satisfy needs outside of himself.

It would be quite easy to rephrase the above quotation to relate to the learner seeking only to satisfy the demands of educational certification in order to proceed to still more learning! Marx (1975:328) continues to elaborate upon the conditions of alienated labour concluding that the logical outcome is that life 'itself appears only as a means to life'. Once education is reduced to a commodity in this way, learning is reduced to memorization so that the essence of learning is no longer to respond to human curiosity and it is,

therefore, no longer intrinsically satisfying nor
is it directly essential to the process of living.
Yet individuals subject themselves to the system
for ends other than the acquisition of knowledge
and education becomes a commodity to be bought and
sold in the market place in which the educational
certificate may be equated to the receipt of
purchase and which permits the holder to live and
work in specific social situations. Thus there is
the antithesis of liberal adult education in which
learning is seen as a direct response to human
need, interest, curiosity, etc.

An Identity Ritual
Alienation is an estrangement from self, yet it is
clear from many writers on adult education that the
self-concept is important for adult learners.
Brundage and Mackeracher (1980:26) claim that:

> Adults with positive self-concept and high
> esteem are more responsive to learning and
> less threatened by learning environments.
> Adults with negative self-concept and low
> self-esteem are less likely to enter
> learning activities willingly and are often
> threatened by such environments.

Hence, it is clear that if learning is not related
to the self it can result in alienation but if it
is related to the self, then it is central to
adult activity and will be related to the self-
concept. But it is also a fact that each
individual sees himself to some extent in the way
that he is seen by others. As Mead argued 'The
origins and foundations of the self, like those of
thinking, are social' (cited from Thompson and
Tunstall 1971:155). Self-identity is, therefore
created and sustained to a considerable extent
by interaction with other people. Individuals
whose academic work is assessed by tutors or peers
as successful, will begin to see themselves as
successful and will, consequently, be more
responsive to learning. By contrast, those who
are adjudged to be weak will see themselves in
this light and be less willing, therefore, to
enter subsequent learning activities willingly.
Learners will develop an identity that corresponds
to the way that other people view them, although
obviously this is neither automatic nor absolute.
However, it must be borne in mind that since there
are no absolutes nor objective standards, there is

a sense in which society not only 'creates' its own successes and failures but 'creates', therefore, the positive and negative self-concepts that affect learning thereafter.   This is a point to which further reference will be made in the next section.

   This argument assumes even greater cogency when it is recalled that there are no absolute nor objective standards in examinations either.   Those standards are determined by the members of society who exercise responsibility or control over the relevant examination system.   But the candidate who is successful in the examination is regarded as a success, even though the success has been 'created' by society, but the failure is labelled a failure through the same process.   The self-image of the candidate is affected by the way that he is labelled success or failure.   Society has in effect 'created' its own successes and failures and those so labelled may actually come to see themselves in this light.   The formal organization of the examination and the subsequent publication of the results may be regarded as a ritual process through which individuals are expected to pass by society and in it society confers an identity upon the candidate.   Thereafter, the labelled individual is likely to associate with other people who confirm that identity of success or failure either because they have also been through the process or because they are aware of the identity conferred upon the person concerned.   Berger (1966:119) suggests that 'every identity requires specific social affiliations for its survival. Birds of a feather flock together not as a luxury but as a necessity'.

   When Knowles (1980:45-49) discussed the self-concept of the learner he concentrated upon the self-identity with respect to adulthood but omitted discussion of the process described above. Yet it might be fair to assume that the type of learning climate that he seeks to engender in the teaching and learning transaction is one in which a person whose self-identity is that of academic failure might well discover opportunity to change.   Many adult educators are aware of the need to help adult learners to see themselves in a different light.   Belbin and Belbin (1972:167-168) note that the instructor with the most successful training record with London Transport declared that he always acted as if learners were going to pass their test but another with one of the poorest records claimed that he could see 'who

isn't going to make it' (Belbin and Belbin
1972:187). Hence, society 'creates' its successes
and its failures in a number of different ways but
the examination system merely ritualises the
process. The examination, publication of results
and any subsequent award ceremony are merely a
ritual process in which that status and identity
are formally conferred. It may be seen as a
similar process to Garfinkel's (1956) 'status
degradation ceremonies' or Goffman's (1968:27-30)
'admission procedures' to a total institution.
Hence society both 'creates' and then confirms the
identity of the individual self.

It is perhaps significant to note here that
peer assessment acts in precisely the same manner,
the self is nearly always affected by social
interaction. It may not elaborate nor ritualise
the process in quite the same way as do the more
formal examination systems, but the more the self
is exposed to peers and their assessment the more
it will be the recipient of those social pressures.
Hence, in this instance the education from above
and this form of education of equals act in
precisely the same manner.

An Aftermath of Examinations?
Individuals who have been through this process
bring to subsequent learning experiences the
products of the past, they also bring with them
the self-identity that they have acquired. As
was pointed out earlier, many adult educators
are aware that they have to try to create a learning
climate in which adults may achieve a self-identity
that is orientated towards a successful outcome of
a learning experience. Some adults may bring to
a learning situation a successful work identity but
a less successful educational one. Belbin and
Belbin (1972:168) describe such an example:

> An example might ... be quoted of one of
> 'the most intelligent personnel' who was
> offered day release from a chemical firm
> in preparation for a City and Guilds
> examination. This man passed his first
> year examination and towards the end of
> his second year left - not the classes but
> the firm. His explanation was '... I was
> scared of not passing the second year
> examination or of falling behind the others.
> You see I've been a leading hand and I've
> a reputation to keep up. I might fail to

do so'.

Society, then, 'creates' its failures - perhaps even those who have a self-identity of success in other situations in which ability is measured.

Self-Assessment

Unlike all the other forms of assessment, self-assessment does not require external standards, external assessors nor certification. Self-assessment encourages the learner to concentrate upon the extent to which he has achieved his own aims in the learning situation and whether he has learned what he has wished to learn. This is a significant form of assessment in adult education. In some situations educators prepare instruments of assessment that the learner can employ to assist him to assess his own learning but in others the students are merely encouraged to assess for themselves. This is a manifestation of the education of equals in which there need be no interaction and, therefore, no outside influence either upon the assessment of upon the self. However, self-defined success is not the same as socially defined success; self-defined standards are not the same as socially defined standards. Hence, there is no recognised authority to define the social situation and to pronounce upon the fact that the learning has occurred. In the same way as illness requires a medical certificate to make the illness socially acceptable, so learning achievement requires an educational one to do the same. Self-assessment which may be a very valid method of learner self-diagnosis has little or no currency in the market place of social living. Hence, organizations are appearing that will award the symbols of success, such as degrees and certificates, upon a statement about what has been learned in the experience of living. Obviously, these organizations are not genuine institutions of learning but living is genuine so that they award false certificates for real experience! Their presence demonstrates the need for some form of social definition of success and failure in the present social system unless, of course, the learning is undertaken for its own sake!

Conclusion

Much of the above discussion has not concentrated specifically upon assessment and examination in adult and continuing education but upon the process in general. Nevertheless, many of the conclusions drawn from this analysis are relevant to the education of adults, especially as continuing education becomes institutionalised and more examinations occur. Yet every new course and every new examination, claimed Weber, is a barrier to inhibit social mobility upwards and to protect those in privileged positions. At the same time every new course and every new examination presents opportunities to the most tenacious of the less privileged to aspire to greater heights within the social structure, although many may aspire but few may achieve. Even so, this makes education a commodity and a means to an end rather than an end in itself. Philosophers may debate whether it is, therefore, truly education, for it would be true to claim that what is socially defined as education is frequently a means to a social end. But liberal adult education without examinations is frequently accorded low status and this is precisely because there is no social definition of its standards or of its utility.

This second section has concentrated upon some of the elements in the teaching and learning curriculum and they have been examined from a variety of sociological perspectives. However, having undertaken this exercise in which the process has been analysed, it is now necessary to locate adult and continuing education within the wider social context.

PART III

ADULT AND CONTINUING EDUCATION IN THE CONTEXT
OF SOCIETY

Chapter Nine

THE FUNCTIONS OF ADULT AND CONTINUING EDUCATION

The term 'function' has been traditionally
associated with the structural functionalism in
sociology, some of the weaknesses of which have
already been illustrated. However, in education,
there has been a tendency to confuse it with
'aims' and so it is necessary at the outset to
clarify the concept and to demonstrate how it
differs from aims. Additionally, it is essential
to rescue the term from its conservative connotations, so that this introduction will concentrate
upon these tasks. Thereafter the chapter will
highlight six opposing sets of interpretations of
the function of the education of adults.
      Within the structural functionalism of Talcott
Parsons the term 'function' meant very broadly the
contribution that the existence of a phenomenon
makes to the coherence of the social system. It
may be seen immediately that this has ideological
conservative undertones because it assumes that
the existence of every phenomenon contributes to
the coherence of the social system. However,
another sociological definition overcomes some of
these problems so that a phenomenon's functions may
be seen to be the consequence of its existence.
It will be noted that there is no ideological bias
here, although it does assume that every phenomenon's existence has social consequences. This is
an assumption that is not debated here, although
the potentiality that this might not be so is
acknowledged.
      By contrast to aim, a function is an event or
consequence that occurs after the phenomenon has
begun to exist whereas an aim is an intention in
the mind of the designer or provider. Hence,
the term 'function' may be used about social
phenomena that may, or may not, have a designer;

discussions of this nature are metaphysical rather
than sociological. However, Durkheim (1956:62),
following Kant, almost confuses the two concepts
by suggesting that 'the end of education is to
develop in each individual all the perfection of
which he is capable', whereas Bergevin (1967:30-31)
is more specific when he claims that among the
major goals of adult education are helping the
adult achieve happiness, meaning in life, fulfil
his talents, etc.   Now neither Durkheim nor
Bergevin claim that education actually achieves
these aims but a function is something that does
occur.   It may be the fulfilment of an aim but it
may be an unintended and even unrecognised
occurrence.   Hence, Merton (1968:105) distinguishes
between manifest functions, both intended and
recognised consequences, and latent functions,
which were neither intended nor recognised.
However, the problem with this very useful distinction is that it does not exhaust the possible
combinations of intention and recognition, so that
it can only be employed if the intention, or the
aim, is omitted entirely.   This is precisely how
the terms are used here.

Another factor that requires recognition is
that the aims of education tend to relate to
specific learners whereas any discussion of function
is social, so that the individual process may not
be as significant sociologically as it is
educationally since the former discipline is more
concerned with the social and the patterns that
occur as a result of repeated educational processes
of a similar nature.   Thus it may be that many of
the functions of education, especially the education
of adults, may be latent rather than manifest.
Another reason why this may be true is because
adult educators have traditionally been more
concerned with meeting individual needs that with
recognising the social significance of the process
in which they have been involved.

This chapter is more concerned with the social
than with the personal but, as it was pointed out
earlier in this book, in order to give meaning to
any social phenomenon it is necessary to bring to
it theoretical, ideological and value
orientations.   Since functional analysis is
actually a process of ascribing social meaning to
the educational process it is possible to bring to
it diametrically opposed ideologies and, thereby,
provide it with different social meanings.   This
is not disadvantageous since it is possible for

both interpretations to be compatible with the
phenomenon, even though they are incompatible with
each other. Hence, the task to be undertaken here
is to present both sides of the argument simultaneously, both the conservative and the radical.
This must necessarily be a tentative undertaking
since there is insufficient evidence in adult and
continuing education to allow claims of a substantive nature. Six sets of functions are discussed
in the following pages and while in each case the
more conservative interpretation is discussed
first, the only reason for this is because it is
more likely to be the manifest function and relate
to the original intention than is the latter.
These six sets of functions are: maintenance of the
social system and reproduction of the existing
social relations; transmission of knowledge, and
the reproduction of the cultural system; individual
advancement and selection; second chance and
legitimation; leisure time pursuit and institutional expansion to fill non-work time; development
and liberation.

Maintenance of the Social System and Reproduction of Existing Social Relations

Talcott Parsons (1951, 1971) argued that there
are certain functional pre-requisites for the
maintenance of the social system: integration,
pattern maintenance, goal attainment and
adaptation.   These functional pre-requisites are
discussed in the following sections but both
integration and adaptation are important here.
However, a significant point about Parson's analysis
is that provided society has the mechanisms to
co-ordinate its constituent units, maintain its
cultural system, allow its members to achieve their
goals and help them to adapt to differing
experiences it will retain its identity.   He was
concerned to demonstrate how the social system
remained an integrated entity which he (1951:36n)
recognised as having two elements: compatibility of
components and maintenance of the distinctiveness
of the system within specified boundaries.   He
recognised that initial education has a part to
play in this since it acts as a major socializing
agency through which individuals learn how to play
the roles that they do in society and the
institutionalization of roles is significant in
integration.   This is clearly even more significant
in initial vocational education because in this
process some major social roles of adulthood are

prescribed and taught.   Hence, initial vocational
education has an integrating function within the
wider society, it helps to maintain the social
system.
     Yet the social system is not static but
dynamic: it was argued earlier that society is
continually evolving and changing, so that the
social system seeks always to re-establish dynamic
equilibrium.   This means that when one part of
the system changes, others must change also, so that
when the technological institution changes all
other institutions need to change as well.   Hence,
Kerr et al (1973:47-48) described education as
the 'hand-maiden of industrialization' since
education is continually changing in response to
technological pressures.   Education itself adapts
to social change and emerging social needs, so
that it continues to fulfil its function of
socializing individuals into the social system.
Since the system is changing, the new forms of
education assist individuals to perform new roles
within it, so that continuing education is helping
individuals to play these roles.   In short, it is
assisting in their process of adaptation to
changing conditions.   It is acting in an integra-
tive capacity in the system, which is merely
extending the function that initial education
originally performed.   But such a process does
no more than reproduce the existing social relations
of production and the social structures remain
unaltered.   Indeed, the social relations of
continuing education reflect the social relations
of initial education in this respect.   Continuing
education is itself institutionalizing and
becoming the third educational system (Ontario
Ministry of Education) and in the process there is
centralization and control occurring.   Janne
(1976:170-172) notes the dangers in this happening
but recognises that 'there is ... a need for
central co-ordination' in lifelong education, so
that it will become hierarchical and bureaucratic
at both the institutional and the organizational
levels.   In addition, stratification occurs in
continuing education since the middle classes
receive their in-service education at universities,
polytechnics and in plush hotels in courses run
by private providers while the working classes
receive theirs in colleges of further education or
in-house.   Hence, the structure of continuing
education provision confirms Gelpi's (1979 vol 2:7)
claim that the 'division of labour is sustained by

the dualistic system of education, where there
are two educational channels, one for the masses
and oné for the elite'. Not only does continuing
education reflect the division of labour but it
reproduces it in its provision . Bryant (1983:
57) points out that managers and other professionals are more likely to have paid educational leave
entitlement 'built into their conditions of service
and/or to be more liberally treated in determining
for themselves the educational content of any
discretionary leave'. Finally, once awards occur
in continuing education, such as the Physician
Recognition Awards in America (Houle 1980:239),
then the system of external incentives for undertaking continuing education will be similar to those
which occur in the world of occupational work and
the reason for taking the course may become the
award rather than the learning. Bowles and Gintis
(1976:48) claim that the 'educational system
serves - though the correspondence of its social
relations with those of economic life - to
reproduce economic inequality and to distort
personal development'. In as much as a function
of the education of adults is to mould individuals
to fit into the demands of the social system their
claim is a criticism of education from above.
However, this raises significant questions about
the concept of personal development and this will
be referred to in a later section of this chapter.
    Thus continuing education may be seen as a
mechanism that assists the maintenance of the social
system and reproduces the social relations of
production.

Transmission of Knowledge and the Reproduction of Culture

It appears to be stating the obvious to assert that
one function of the education of adults is the
transmission of knowledge since: examinations
record the specific knowledge that has been
memorized; students return to adult and continuing
education course because they have learned new
knowledge in their previous courses; employers
grant in-service leave (paid, assisted or unpaid)
to their employees, always at cost to themselves,
and however altruistic they may be it would not
occur with such frequency unless it were of some
benefit to their organization. Here, then, is a
combination of a manifest function in the
transmission of knowledge and a latent one in as
far as the acquisition of new knowledge and skill

is positively related to economic development.
Indeed, Kerr et al (1973:47) argue that industrialization 'requires an educational system function-
ally related to the skills and professions
imperative to its technology'. They proceed to
argue that this will result in a technologically
orientated curriculum and that the 'increased
leisure time of industrialism, can afford a
broader public appreciation of humanities and
the arts' (ibid). The leisure time function of
adult education is discussed later in this chapter
so that there will be no further discussion on
that at this point, but it is clear from the claims
of Kerr et al that curriculum knowledge is not
neutral. Hence, the transmission of knowledge
does not really specify precisely what is the
function being performed by the education of adults.
    But this has long been recognised by philoso-
phers who have suggested that education is about
'worthwhile knowledge' (Peters 1960:45). Indeed,
Paterson (1979:85) claims that 'in constructing a
curriculum for adult education designed to enlarge
the student's awareness and put him in more
meaningful touch with reality by building up in
him rich and coherent bodies of worthwhile knowledge
...' But what is 'worthwhile' and who determines
its worthwhileness? Mill (cited in Lester-Smith
1966:9) regarded education as a deliberate attempt
by one generation to pass on to the succeeding
generation the culture which it values. While
Mill isolated the factor of control in education,
he never suggested whose culture or knowledge was
being transmitted. Neither Paterson nor Peters do
this either. Yet Marx claimed that the ruling
ideas in every generation are those of the class
which controls the means of production. Neither
the knowledge nor the wider culture that is
transmitted is neutral, a point that was thoroughly
discussed in the second section of this study.
Nevertheless, that which is transmitted often
appears objective and neutral and this is how
hegemony operates.
    However, education does not merely serve to
reproduce the cultural system by transmitting the
dominant culture. Bourdieu (1973:71-112) has
argued that those most likely to be the recipients
of the dominant culture are those who, as a result
of birth and upbringing, have already acquired
the cultural capital to receive it. By this, he
means that those who have already been socialized
into a culture that is sympathetic to the dominant

culture, or into the dominant culture itself, are more likely to acquire the fruits of education than those who have not. Indeed, he (1973:73) demonstrates quite clearly that:

> The statistics of theatre, concert, and, above all, museum attendance ... are sufficient reminder that the inheritance of cultural wealth which has been accumulated and bequeathed by previous generations only really belongs ... to those endowed with the means of appropriating it for themselves.

This argument may, in itself, be sufficient to explain why liberal adult education tends to be a middle class pursuit. Hence, Westwood (1980:43) can claim that:

> Adult education with its middle class bias, its uniformity within a common core of the curriculum ... has a reinforcing role. But in relation to the concept of hegemony it can be seen to have a much clearer role in maintaining the status quo, engendering a state of consensus and contributing positively to the mechanisms whereby hegemony is maintained.

Hence, the education of adults transmits the dominant culture and in the process it reproduces the cultural system which, in itself, is a force for the retention of the status quo rather than social change.

Individual Advancement and Selection

It has frequently been claimed that education is a vehicle of upwards social mobility but this usually refers to initial education only. However, it may be seen from the work of Goldthorpe (1980) that adult vocational education has facilitated the social advancement of those with the motivation during their work life. He (1980:232) records a number of life histories in which the respondents record how they have been socially mobile as a result of day release and evening studies. Such mobility suggests that there is an openness in the structures of society that allows individuals to penetrate the class barriers with a degree of ease if they have the necessary motivation. Such a conclusion would, however, be quite misleading for a number of reasons, but the appearance of openness may itself be an element in the legitimation of the status quo, a function that is discussed in the next section of this chapter. Among the reasons why the conclusion would be wrong is the fact that the economic expansion of the post-war period resulted in considerable structural changes in the occupational profile of many countries, especially Britain. These changes have led Goldthorpe to draw the following conclusion:

> The rate of expansion of the service class in Britain, outstripping that of the institutions of higher education until the later 1960s, has meant that indirect routes into service class position have 'necessarily' remained of very considerable importance up to the time of our enquiry. But the influence of bureaucratic selection procedures is, we would argue, already apparent in the growing relative importance of direct routes ...
> (Goldthorpe 1980:257)

Thus he suggests that the relative importance of adult and continuing education in individual social advancement after having commenced their work life is declining as the children of the new middle class begin to follow in their parents' footsteps and occupy middle class positions in the social structure. Hence , adult education may not perform this function to the same degree in the future. Another feature of this social mobility that needs to be noted here is that those who are socially mobile upwards may experience a degree of isolation within their new position in the social structure because they have not necessarily acquired the culture of the class that they have entered. Education may be the vehicle of the mobility but unless the mobile are able to experience other aspects of the culture, e.g. the extra-curricular activities, they will not feel integrated into their new position. Hence, adult vocational education may be an individuating experience for some of the mobile. That they are not always readily or easily accepted within their new class position in the social structure may reflect Goldthorpe's (1980:275) assertion that the class structures actually sustain inequality and resist social change.
    While some who have been socially mobile

upwards may feel that they have actively exploited
the educational system to their own advantage, it
must be recognised that the system itself is a part
of the selection mechanism. Indeed, this is a
traditional function of initial education and
Turner (1971) has suggested that there are two
normative patterns of mobility: sponsored and
contest. Contest mobility, according to Turner
(1971:74) 'is like a sporting event in which many
compete but few are recognised' whereas sponsored
mobility favours a controlled selection process
whereby:

> The elite or their agents, deemed to be
> the best qualified to judge merit choose
> individuals for elite status who have
> appropriate qualifications. Individuals
> do not win or seize elite status; mobility
> is rather a process of sponsored induction
> into the elite.
> (Turner 1971:74)

While post-school education may appear to be like
contest mobility, a great deal of continuing
education may actually be much closer to sponsored
mobility in which individuals are selected and
prepared for promotion. Hence, Killeen and Bird
(1981:61) point out that:

> Men receive more paid educational leave
> because they engage in occupations where
> it is more frequently given for vocational
> purposes - so far as extended first training
> for work is concerned ... and later in life
> as managers and professional workers.
> The young receive it more frequently ...
> because forms of training associated with
> promotion tend to be given in 'early
> middle' career.

Killeen and Bird discuss the distribution of paid
educational leave and note that it is not given in
relation to the scale of occupational difficulty.
Hence, it may well be that some forms of
continuing education are an element in the
selection mechanism of sponsored mobility. In
this way individual advancement may be viewed in
some instances as a form of co-optation.

Second Chance and Legitimation
When the Open University was established in the

United Kingdom it was widely regarded as 'the university of the second chance'. For many students it has indeed performed this function: but, second chance for what? For some, merely a second chance to study at a level of higher education since they had either been denied or declined the opportunity during their initial education. For others, a second chance to improve their academic qualifications, so that they might change their occupation and become socially mobile. Indeed, in recent years the element of vocational counselling has played an increasingly significant part in the work of the Open University counselling service, and full-time vocational counsellors are now in its employment. Yet, for others, the Open University is a university of the first chance since, for those able to pay its fees which are becoming increasingly high - although there is a student hardship fund, it provides the first opportunity that they have had to study at higher education level.

However, adult education has provided second chance opportunities to many different people in a variety of ways. In higher education, there has been the opportunity to study for an external degree of the University of London and a number of colleges organised courses that prepared students to sit these examinations. In addition, Birkbeck College has provided opportunities for part-time higher education for adults but, as Tight (1982) shows, the majority of higher education part-time provision has been located in the southeast of Britain and it has been in very limited supply.

There has, however, been a much wider provision of second chance through part-time courses in the General Certificate of Education, at both ordinary and advanced levels, offered by Colleges of Further Education. These have enabled adults, especially women, to acquire the minimum qualifications necessary for entry into occupations, such as nursing, demanding such academic certification. The fact that most of these examination syllabi had been prepared for children in initial education and that the General Certificate of Education Boards have not been enabled to produce syllabi for adult students indicates another of the barriers that adults face when they wish to pursue education for a second chance.

More recently, there have been courses especially designed for adults who wish to avail themselves to a second chance, some of these are primarily for women (Hutchinson E & E 1978) who have been discriminated against in their initial education. Fresh Horizon courses, and others of a similar kind, provided opportunity for women to redirect their careers but, even courses of this type are of a limited nature and Thompson (1983: 104) records the comments of one person who did not complete the programme: 'older working class women have been given little opportunity to learn about mathematics, physics and other subjects'. Clearly women are discriminated against in society generally but education is providing something of a second chance for some.

In addition to the above, there are other second chance projects (Yarnit 1980) and some of the residential adult education colleges, i.e. Fircroft, Hillcroft, Ruskin, all provide opportunity for adults to return to education and to have a second chance.

Another significant area of second chance that adult education provides is Adult Basic Education Schemes (ACACE 1979b) where many disadvantaged adults are provided with the opportunity to gain skills in literacy and numeracy later in life. For a variety of reasons, including the fact that the government has been prepared to fund this work, adult educationalists have been very active in undertaking this work and a variety of research projects have been undertaken in this area, i.e. Blamire and Dawkins, (n.d.)

Adult and continuing education has, therefore, provided a second chance to many adults in different parts of the social system. Hence, it may rightly be claimed that one of the consequences of the existence of this service is that it provides individuals with the opportunity to play a different role in society than that for which their initial education prepared them. Even so, it will be recognised that this is still a function that re-inforces the status quo, in as much as the structures of the social system remain unquestioned. Indeed, the existence of second chance education actually produces an appearance of greater equality of opportunity and, hence, reinforces the existing social structures since it provides additional support for the right of those in powerful positions in society to hold them because of their success in the educational system - even though it was in their initial education. Lynch (1982:10) has argued that:

> ... as the supply of material rewards and promotions, from which members of society have learned to glean a meaningful identity, is reduced, the consciousness of inequalities among members of society is accentuated and the awareness of the contradictions inherent in the basic ideology of Western democracy grows apace.

Hence, the appearance of equality of opportunity serves as a legitimation of the structure of the social system.

Legitimation is the social process that occurs through which individuals learn to accept that the state has the right to govern and that the resulting structures of the social system are made to appear acceptable to its members. This is the process of hegemony which Joll (1977:99) describes thus:

> The hegemony of a political class meant for Gramsci that that class had succeeded in persuading the other classes of society to accept its own moral, political and cultural values. If the ruling class is successful, then this will involve the minimum use of force, as was the case with the successful liberal regimes of the nineteenth century.

The manner through which the elite achieve this is, according to Althusser (1972), through the operation of various social institutions which he calls ideological state apparatuses. Amongst these he (1972:258) regards education as the most dominant in contemporary industrial society. He concentrates his discussion on initial education and demonstrates how it functions in society to reproduce the social relations of production even though the school itself is presented as a neutral environment. However, his argument is applicable to adult and continuing education since the opportunity of second chance merely reinforces the idea that those who occupy positions of power and responsibility in society do so on their merit and those who occupy other positions do so because of their mobility, despite the fact that society actually gives them another chance if they did not accept the first opportunity if offered. Thus, second chance education legitimates the status quo in society with all its manifest inequalities of opportunity.

Leisure Time Pursuit and Institutional Expansion

Leisure is a subject that has come to the fore in recent years because it has been claimed that advanced technology is producing a world in which mankind will not have to work for as much of his lifetime. By leisure, it is meant here, time away from paid employment rather than the opposite to the expenditure of energy. Yet many people have a lifestyle that is orientated to employment from which they gain not only financial rewards but also personal and social identity. Hence, leisure time is not something that all welcome. Traditionally, also, a great deal of education has had a vocational orientation and general education has been rather the poor relation and to which a lower status has been attributed. Yet education does play an important part in leisure and Parker (1976) distinguishes between education for leisure and education as leisure. It is the latter that is the main concern here.

Education as a leisure time pursuit may be understood quite simply as an activity that is voluntarily undertaken in non-employment time in order to enrich the life of the participant. Carlson (cited Parker 1976:92) claims that:

> the goals of recreation and education are not poles apart, since both are working toward enrichment of life for individuals. Learning is more rapid and lasting if it is pleasurable and satisfying in itself and the finest educational experiences take a recreational nature.

However, it is clear that education as a leisure time pursuit is only followed by those who have the cultural capital (Bourdieu 1978:73) to enjoy it. By contrast, Johnstone (cited Parker 1976: 100) asserts that

> The typical lower class person does not think of education in terms of personal growth or self-realisation, and as a consequence is even less ready to turn to adult education for recreational purposes than he is for vocational purposes.

Hence, it would appear that education reproduces the social relations of production even in leisure time. However, Bergsten (1977:128) did not find 'any large differences between white collar and blue collar workers with respect to interest in participation in adult education' in Sweden. But what he did find was that blue collar workers with little experience in education had greater difficulties in turning their interest into participation than did white collar workers with little previous educational experience. This may reflect the content of the curriculum offered by an educational institution or a difficulty in joining organizations as well as the explanation that Bergsten gives that white collar employees have more opportunity to interact with others who have a positive orientation to education. Bergsten (1977:134-136) did discover that:

> The interest in adult education for the present job and in non-competence giving adult education can be seen as part of a leisure style consisting of 'cultural' activities and active membership in organizations.

This clearly supports Bourdieu's cultural capital thesis and it does also suggest, as Bergsten notes, that increased leisure does not necessarily mean that large groups of people would automatically commence adult education. Nevertheless, it is possible to argue that the educational system has expanded to fill the gap left by the declining demands of work upon individual's time. Kumar (1978:255) writes:

> Keeping young people off the labour market then appears to be one latent function and dynamic of the educational system. Keeping them off the streets, and attached to their allotted tasks, seems to be another, perhaps in the end more important.

Not only does the education system absorb surplus manpower but it provides something for the unemployed to do. Hence, in the United Kingdom the Manpower Services Commission has funded many such educational activities and these have been organised by institutes of adult education and colleges of further education.
Education is also expanding into the area of old age and educational gerontology is becoming a significant area of study now that there are more

146

elderly people alive who wish to undertake learning activities. Wherever the demands of work do not exist, education is expanding to fill the gap.

Hence, education may be both a leisure time pursuit and a forced leisure time pursuit but, nevertheless, it is clear that while its manifest function in this case is a leisure time activity its latent function is the retention of stability in the social system at a time when many people do not have work to occupy their time and their minds.

Development and Liberation

It is almost commonplace among philosophers, especially those who work in the field of liberal adult education, to regard one of the aims of education to be the development of the person. Paterson (1979:17) suggests that 'education is the development of persons as independent centres of value whose development is seen to be an intrinsically worthwhile undertaking'. While it is possible to question the idea that education is about the development of persons as independent centres of value since they may have value as persons per se, it is clear that Paterson would concur that education is about the development of the person. Similarly, Knowles (1980:29) regards 'maturity' as a goal of education and he proceeds to outline fifteen continua along which that maturity may develop. Once again it would be possible to question some of these since they obviously reflect his own values and this is clearly one of the major problems concerned with the concept of development. Indeed, there is no agreement about this normative concept and, consequently, it is difficult to assess it. Unlike the previous two authors, Dewey (1916:51) made less expansive claims for education:

> Since life means growth, a living creature
> lives as truly and positively at one stage
> as at another, with the same intrinsic
> fullness and the same absolute claims.
> Hence education means the enterprise of
> supplying the conditions which ensure
> growth, or adequacy of life, irrespective
> of age.

Since it is obvious that development is a difficult concept to define and its precise place relative to education is itself debatable, it is much more

147

difficult to claim that development is a function
of education than to assert that it is an aim of
education. However, many learners and teachers
would claim that as a result of some learning
experiences they have grown and developed, so that
it would be perhaps a little pedantic to dispute
the claim that development is a function of
education. Hence, it will not be disputed here
although it may be that development is more
significantly a function of learning rather than
education. Nevertheless, what is much more
significant sociologically is the type of
development that occurs.

This is not the place to debate the nature of
the concept of staff development, although the
following discussion will highlight one of the
significant aspects of the debate. It is almost
self-evident that certain forms of development
can, like education from above, be designed to
assist the individual to fit more easily into the
niche prepared for him in the structures of the
social system in which he is employed. By
contrast, it is possible to consider a form of
development that results in the individual being
critical of the constraints that the structures of
the system impose and trying to alter them.
Taylor (1980:327-339) has argued quite convincingly
that continuing education for school teachers
should result in a form of professional development
that is also personal growth. This may be a valid
argument for professionals who practise relatively
independently, albeit within the bureaucratic
framework of the school or college, but his
argument is less valid for those whose main work
orientation is within a much more rigid bureaucracy.
Taylor actually claims that professional development
may be identified with personal growth but this is
open to serious questioning in the context of
bureaucratic employment. In addition, it is
possible to consider situations in which individuals
claim to have experienced personal growth but
which may not be regarded as professional
development.

Indeed, it is possible to consider certain
forms of learning that result in individuals
becoming critically aware thinkers. Freire's
(1972a, 1972b, 1974) idea of conscientization
refers to the deepening awareness that learners
cn achieve of the socio-cultural reality that shapes
their lives and also that they have the capacity
to change that reality. It will be recalled that

148

in the discussion on the learning cycle it was
recognised that through the process of reflection,
individuals' learning can result in their becoming
agents, freed of the constraints of the social
structure and enabled to act back upon those
structures in order to change them.   This
recognition led Freire to the position in which
he regards education as 'the practice of freedom'
(Freire 1974).   For him, education is a liberating
process.   Within the socio-political context in
which he writes, recognition of the liberating
function of education led Freire into a position
that is clearly radical and revolutionary.   Indeed,
some of those who learned with him and through his
approach, realized the inequality of their social
situation and recognised that they were able to
transform and recreate their world.   For Freire,
this was both revolutionary and utopian but for the
elite of his society it was perceived as revolutionary and dangerous.
      Whenever education liberates, it can result in
agents who might, but also need not, seek structural
reform.   This may occur in the socio-political
context about which Freire writes or even in
vocational or community education.   Hence, the more
vocational education encourages the recruits to
the professions to think in a critical manner, the
more the potentiality of producing agents for
change is increased.   Wherever agents who seek
structural reform, or other changes, are produced,
it might be claimed that, in structural functional
terms, education is dysfunctional to the social
system.   Hence, it is hardly surprising that some
elites neither encourage the existence nor the
growth of education that can result in 'the
practice of freedom'.

Conclusion
This chapter has attempted to demonstrate how the
functions of adult and continuing education can
be interpreted from both a conservative and a
radical perspective.   Both sets of interpretations
may be valid from whatever ideological stance
the interpreter adopts and yet they may be
incompatible with each other.   This is precisely
how underdetermination operates, since analyses of
adult and continuing education cannot demonstrate
conclusively which theoretical perspective is
correct.
      Having analysed the function of adult and
continuing education in contemporary society, it is

now important to analyse some of the alternative
forms of education for adults that have appeared in
contemporary society.

Chapter Ten

ALTERNATIVE APPROACHES TO THE EDUCATION OF ADULTS

There is a general agreement among sociologists that
the changes in the patterns of social living since
the outset of industrialization have been quite
considerable. Toennies (1957) regarded it as a
change from community (Gemeinschaft) to one of
association (Gesellschaft) and Durkheim (1964)
from mechanical to organic solidarity. From
the Industrial Revolution there has been an
increasing division of labour that has had an
individuating effect on social living. However,
this division of labour has not occurred in
isolation, since it was argued earlier that the
technological innovation was itself the result of
enterpreneurial capitalism. Coupled with these
is the growth in bureaucracy, so that contemporary
industrial society may be typified by the fact that
it has resulted in individuals being in a hierarchical relationship which is characterised by
impersonality and anonymity. The growth of
bureaucracy and technological production led Berger,
Berger and Kellner (1974) to describe modern
consciousness as 'the homeless mind'. Their
approach reflects Simmel's (1971) early analysis
in 1903 of the effect of the metropolis upon mental
life in which he suggested that the modern mind
is more calculating, rational and intellectual.
He (1971:84) claimed that 'Money economy and the
dominance of the intellect are intrinsically
connected.'
    From these two brief references it is clear
that the loss of Gemeinschaft has not necessarily
been regarded by sociologists as a totally
beneficial social change. Indeed, the loss of
community was regarded quite widely as a 'bad'
thing during the 1960s the early 1970s and anything
that pointed to the rediscovery of community was

widely regarded with approbation.
It is this peculiar manifestation of social
living that forms the basis of this chapter since
education has not remained totally unaffected by
either the loss of, nor the attempt to rediscover,
community. Three distinct types of adult
education are analysed within this context:
education of the affect or the attempt to rediscover community; community education, or the
attempt to recreate community; distance education,
which is a denial of community.

Education of the Affect

Studies of Gemeinschaft-type societies reveal the
way in which the whole community was involved in
the socialization and welfare of children in the
tribe. Children learned to play together, compete
together and live together. Turnbull (1984:39)
points out that by being allowed the freedom to
explore the camp in which they lived, the Mbuti
children became 'increasingly sensitive (to the)
emotional relationships within the camp'.
Because the children live in community, they
acquire an education of the affect during their
primary socialization. However, Gemeinschaft has
almost disappeared and contemporary society is
hierarchical, individual, impersonal and anonymous
and children are reared in nuclear, or even one-
parent families. Here they are denied the
opportunity to learn widely about education of
their emotions and even, occasionally, denied the
opportunity to express them. Heron (1982:4)
claims that 'childrearing and (the) educational
system has no adequate working theory of affect'.
Indeed, education has been so controlled by the
Greek emphasis on the intellect, which has
traditionally been regarded as the controller of
the emotions. Heron (1982:5) claims that
contemporary culture 'offers only one guiding norm
and about feelings: control'. However, education
of the emotions has become an increasingly
significant aspect of vocational continuing
education as may be seen from the fact that Heron,
himself, is employed by the British Post Graduate
Medical Federation and many other adult educators
who specialize in this area work with a variety
of different occupations and professions. That
there is such an interest from management and
from the professions for this type of education
indicates that there is a weakness in the
conception of bureaucracy that is totally impersonal

and also that the modern emphasis on impersonal
anonymity is not an adequate reflection of man.
Indeed, it has been clear from other sections of
this book that man is regarded here as more than
the product of his previous experiences.

This type of education frequently occurs in
Encounter Groups or Therapy Groups, one of the
major exponents being Rogers. In these groups
he seeks to facilitate a situation in which all
the members are open to each other, discussing
their personal feelings, concerns, values and
aspirations. The group becomes an affective
entity in which all the members are encouraged to
open themselves to each other, to relate to each
other and to be sensitive to each others' needs.
Rogers (1969:73) writes about his own involvement:

> In an encounter group I love to give, both
> to the participants and to myself, the
> maximum freedom of expression. This
> attitude usually gets across fairly
> quickly because it is real. I do trust
> the group, and find it often wiser than I
> in its reactions to particular situations.

Thus it may be seen that encounter groups seek to
achieve a situation in which there is mutual self-
giving in which all its members learn to achieve
an emotive relationship of love and trust with each
other. Neither this relationship, nor the actual
experience, can be long lasting because of the
transient nature of the group but, even so, it is
one that at that time creates a temporary community
and a memorable experience for many of the
participants. However, this temporary community
is not actually about social living, which is an
aspect quite fundamental to the concept of
community from a sociological perspective, but it
is a phenomenon familiar to sociologists and
anthropologists. Turner calls it communitas.
Communitas is an experience that occurs within the
liminal period of ritual. He (1969:82) writes:

> It is as though there are two major 'models'
> for human interrelatedness, juxtaposed and
> alternating. The first is of society as a
> structured, differentiated, and often hier-
> archical system of politico-legal-economic
> positions with many types of evaluation,
> separating men in terms of 'more' or 'less'.
> The second,which emerges recognizably in

> the liminal period, is of society as an
> unstructured or rudimentarily structured
> and relatively undifferentiated comitatus,
> community, or even communion of equal in-
> dividuals who submit together to the
> general authority of the ritual elders.

In the case of encounter groups, the ritual elders
are the facilitators. Turner suggests that life
for many people contains alternating exposure to
structure and communitas. In his eloquent ex-
position of the concept, Turner (1969:115)
highlights the fact that many religious groups have
sought the experience of communitas and that
frequently its manifestation is a sacred event.

> Communitas breaks in through the interestices
> of structure in liminality; at the edges of
> structure and marginality; and from
> beneath structure, in inferiority. It
> is almost everywhere held to be sacred or
> 'holy', possibly because it transgresses
> or dissolves the norms that govern
> structured and institutionalized relation-
> ships and is accompanied by experience of
> unprecedented potency.

Like religious fellowship, the encounter group
creates a situation in which human relationships
are experienced unhampered by the social structures
and in so doing experience something that are
regarded as compelling and significant; indeed, as
life changing experiences in some instances. It
is perhaps significant to recall that Durkheim
(1915:47) defined a church as a moral community
and that he regarded God as the projection of its
unity. Hence, it is maintained here that the
encounter group recreates the type of experience
that is at the heart of religion and at this point
education and religion overlap, although there are
other points at which the two may also be seen
together (Jarvis 1983 d).
Heron (1982:10) recognises that there is a
relationship between education of the affect and
religion but Rogers does not dwell on this.
However, he (1969:79-83) records some of the
positive reactions to his students to their
experience of communitas. One such recorded reaction was: 'The weekend workshops were terrific.
I wish there was some way to make them a
continuous part of the doctoral program'. Here

the desire to recapture the 'magic moment' of the
communitas experience is evident.   However, Rogers
(1969:83) also records one negative reaction to
the groups and it is significantly from someone who
considered that the personal problems that were
exposed and explored in the group were problems
that should have been solved by belief in God,
which itself confirms something of the religious
nature of the experience.
     Not all analysts are unsceptical about the
process as it occurs in contemporary industrial
society.   Sennett (1980:107), for instance,
claims that:

> It operates on the principle that selfhood
> can be generated through mutual confession
> and revelation, and under the illusion
> that experiences of power, inequality and
> domination all have a meaning subsumed and
> psychological categories.   The destructive
> quality of this gemeinschaft when tested
> by external or internal conflicts is that
> questions of unity of impulse become   more
> important than discussion or defense of
> common interests.

Hence, Sennett argues that the encounter group is
an agglomeration of individuals each seeking self-
fulfilment rather than the creation of a genuine
community.   He regards the two as distinctly
different entities and that in some instances the
encounter group may be destructive.   Yet this
insightful analysis perhaps provides a reason why
education of the affect has assumed such a
significant place in some areas of continuing
education.   This is not because it generates a
feeling of community but because it erases the
necessity of the world of impersonal reality.
Reality has now become a matter of feeling,
impression and sensation and a form of social
interrelatedness is perceived beyond the power
structures of society in which people commune with
each other in a personal and affective manner.
Consequently, individuals are enabled to cope with
the impersonal bureaucratic and hierarchical world
in which they actually live.   Like some forms of
religion, affective education is fundamentally
conservative, offering a mechanism that enables
people to cope and, thereby, re-inforcing the social
structures.

Community Education

Affective education, so it was claimed in the previous section, is a response to the decline in Gemeinschaft in which it performs similar functions to those performed by the members of the community in the normal course of social living. Its exponents regard it as a form of adult and continuing education in which the life of the individual is enriched. Similarly, exponents of community education claim that its concern is with the quality of life, but in this instance it is the quality of life in a community rather than that of an individual. Hence, in Boucouvalas' (1979:35) tautological definition of community education, she claims that:

> the ultimate goal of community education
> is the development of self-guiding, self
> directing communities which are able to
> identify and satisfy the needs of all
> their community members through the co-
> ordination, co-operation, and collaboration
> of all community resources.
> (cited from Brookfield 1983:67)

As Brookfield notes, this is extremely idealistic but it does combine the ideas of people's quality of life within a specific geographical location. These are the basic elements in a sociological definition of community: people in relationship and a specific geographical location. However, Boucouvalas and many other writers on community education also include implicitly in their writings a concept of social change, but theories of social change do not often appear to be the concern of the adult educator. It is for this reason, among others, that there appears to considerable confusion about the phenomenon of community education. Jarvis (1983b:44-51) endeavoured to clarify this concept by suggesting that there are three broad categories of community education: education for action and for development; education in the community; extra-mural education. It was argued that only the first of these should be regarded as community education and, it will be noted, that this is the only one that requires a theory of social change. However, no such undertaking was attempted in that instance.

Nevertheless, in order to devise a theory of change, it is necessary to relate it to an understanding of the social structure and to

156

ideology.   Indeed, community education has suffe-
red theoretically by not having an adequate analysis
of any of these concepts.   However, it will be
recalled that in the first chapter of this book,
structural and ideological perspectives were
discussed and it is now necessary to examine their
implications for community education.

Of the four types of ideology discussed,
conservatism is the only one that requires or allows
for no theory of social change.   It may occur in
a variety of social structures and political forms,
it may be prevalent in a capitalist or a communist
society, and wherever it is manifest it is an
ideology to retain the status quo.   Each of the
other three either allow for a theory of change
to be elaborated within them or demand such, so that
they are now discussed in greater detail.

Liberalism assumes that individual needs are
the paramount concern.   The state or local
government should interfere but minimally in all
private activities since the individual knows
best what he needs.   As the individual is aware of
his needs or interests and is free to act upon
them in an independent and rational manner, it is
the individual's own decision to decide to act.
Like the state and local government, education
should not intervene in the private affairs of
individuals but if any person's interest can be
furthered by enrolment on a course of education,
then it is his responsibility to act.   If, having
learned more about his interest, he wishes to
pursue it in a social or a community matter, that
is his concern but not that of the educator.
Hence, the former student may start an interest or
a pressure group in order to prosecute his interest
and the role of the state, or local government,
is to be neutral and respond to the pressure of
interest groups in a balanced manner.   This
approach may be detected in Lawson's (1977:6-13)
critical analysis of community education: it is
an approach that is entirely consistent with the
ideology of liberal adult education which he
espouses.

However, it is possible to assume a more
reformist perspective, in which it is argued that
the individual is only partially free because he is
also constrained by the social structures.
Supporters of this view maintain that some of the
real interests of the individual may be hidden
from him because of the dominant interests of the
more powerful.   Indeed, individuals may not

Alternative Approaches to the Education of Adults

even consider that their interests can be realized
because of the manner in which the more powerful
pursue their own concerns.   Therefore, the state
and local government should be supportive of the
individual and seek to provide for his interests
and needs.   Community education may be viewed as
one of the ways in which the state provides for
the welfare of people, as it offers support to them
in deprived areas.   Two aspects emerge from this:
firstly, education is received as welfare and an
object of social welfare policy and, secondly,
that the community schools, colleges and community
education officers, etc. are a result of this
policy.   Indeed, there is in this ideological
approach a number of similarities to that
definition of Boucouvalas which was mentioned above.
Social change, it is noted, comes from above in
this instance since it is the state or local
government which, recognising the needs of the
community, responds to them.   Thus some of the
forms of education in the community, discussed by
Jarvis (1983b:47-48) may be classified within this
category.
     Finally, the writings of Freire (1972a, 1972b,
etc.), Lovett (1975, 1983) and other community
adult educators, espouse a radicalism.   Much
radicalism is contemporary society adopts a marxist
perspective although, as was pointed out earlier,
marxism is only one form of radicalism, albeit one
which has the most consistently elaborated
theoretical perspective.   This claims that individuals are moulded by the social forces and social
structures, so that their real needs might be
totally unrecognised.   Since power resides in the
hands of those who control the infrastructure of
society, there will be little change in society
until the elite have been changed.   Hence,
community education then assumes a political
perspective and, since the elite will not lay down
its power voluntarily, a theory of change that
involves conflict.   Consequently, the adult
educator needs to be committed to the ideals of
the people with whom he is working, believing that
only within the framework of a different social
structures will be the individual be free to pursue
his own needs and interests unconstrained by the
structure of society.   It might be claimed that
this form of community education is implicitly a
form of indoctrination since the community educator
is claiming to have recognised the real needs of
the people and he is then teaching them how to

become activists in order to change the social
structure.   Obviously, all forms of education run
the risk of being regarded as indoctrination but
it may be regarded as a form of education of
equals when educators and students problem-solve
about social living together, and Freire's approach
to teaching is but one form of this education of
equals.
     One issue that needs to be discussed although
it cannot be resolved here is the difference
between these latter approaches: the first is much
more a policy of development and the second one is
action;   the first has a theory of change that is
evolutionary and the second a theory that involves
conflict between different groups in society.
Are these perspectives irresolvable?   Basically,
it was argued in the first part of this text that
interpretation of social phenomena is a complex
process and that it would not be detrimental to
understanding them if there were different, even
incompatible, interpretations.   Since this is the
case with community education it has to be noted
that the interpretations and the ideologies and
strategies are different and that is not detrimental to an understanding of community education.
But in both cases the community educator is
committed to helping the residents in a specific
geographical location improve of quality of their
lives through different forms of education.
     Unlike the previous two approaches to
education, the third one to be discussed in this
chapter makes no reference to community but, even
so, it could not have occurred at all had the
decline in community not happened, for distance
education is a product of the impersonal,
technological society of the industrial period;
indeed it is very much a sign of the twentieth
century with its individuated man.

Distance Education
The decline of Gemeinschaft-type society was almost
a prerequisite for the emergence of distance
education.   It may be recalled that in Durkheim's
formulation of mechanical and organic solidarity
he recognised that the division of labour was a
casual factor in the decline of mechanical
solidarity.   However, Durkheim was still convinced
that society is more than the aggregate of its
members since there are bonds that hold them
together, which is what he sought to demonstrate
with his idea of organic solidarity.   In organic

solidarity there is a functional interdependence in the division of labour and this is perhaps demonstrated best in distance education by the definition proposed by Otto Peters (cited Wedemeyer 1981:49) which is:

> a rationalized means for transmitting knowledge, skills and attitudes based upon divisions of labour, which involves the use of comprehensive technical means and the appropriate application of organization techniques through which the possibility of the reproduction of optimal learning materials takes place for a great number of learners without consideration of the place of domicile or prior education of the participants.

While there are a number of points in the above definition which are disputable educationally, i.e. the idea of transmission suggests only teaching method, a point which has been criticised elsewhere (Jarvis 1981), there is much here that reflects the present argument that distance education is a 'functional fit' to societies having organic solidarity. This form of solidarity emphasizes individual differences rather than similarities, with Giddens (1971:73) suggesting that:

> Organic solidarity ... presupposes not identity but difference between individuals in their beliefs and actions. The growth of organic solidarity and the expansion of the division of labour are hence associated with increasing individualism.

It is the fact that learners can be themselves, individual and different, and yet still follow the course of study without fear of peer pressure and by integrating their 'learning into the ideosyncratic patterns of their occupational and domestic lives as and when appropriate (ACACE 1983:4). Attendance at a traditional institution of education is often prevented by one or other of these factors.
   Analysis of contemporary society reveals a number of structural features that indicate that distance learning is functional, including geographical mobility, rationalization (see Simmel 1971) and technological expertise. In addition,

the greater the division of labour within a society,
the more occupational specialisms that emerge and
the greater the likelihood that individuals will
be employed and will reside a great distance from
the source of expertise in their occupation.
Hence, with continuing education becoming more
important as technical knowledge changes and
develops, the more significant will distance
education become.   Thus it is argued here that
distance education is a 'functional fit' to
contemporary, technological society and that the
decline in the Gemeinschaft-type society was a
necessary prerequisite for its emergence.
Having appeared, however, its benefits may be
utilised on an ever wider geographical basis and
developing societies may actually use this method.
Indeed, at the University of Surrey in the United
Kingdom there is one distance education course,
in higher education, that has been developed
especially for the Third World (ACACE 1983:26).
This enables students to continue to work in their
own countries whilst they take a university
qualification in another.

However, distance education in Third World
societies may actually serve another purpose.
Students are often militant and university campuses
are frequently places where unrest occurs, simply
because students are enabled to come together in
the university.   This is a function that Marx and
Engels (1967:89) recognized that the introduction
of the factory system did for the workers:

> But with the development of industry the
> proletariat not only increases in number;
> it becomes concentrated in greater masses,
> its strength grows, and it feels that
> strength more.

By contrast, distance education prevents students
coming together in one place at one time, so that
separated the students are not aware of any common
interest or concern.   Hence, with the development
of distance teaching universities, the political
implications of control need to be recognised.
Another feature of the above definition by
Peters that requires discussion is that not only is
there a division of labour but he regards it as
'rationalized means' of the production and
transmission of knowledge.   However, it must be
borne in mind that Weber's (1947:329-341) conception of bureaucracy was of an organization of

people in a rational manner in order to operate efficiently. Hence, the actual shape and organization of the educational provider is a significant feature in sociological study and it will be discussed in the final section of this book. But the shape of the organization is also related to the structure of knowledge that is produced and transmitted. This was clearly recognised by Bernstein (1971:61-63) in his analysis of the two types of curricula, which was discussed in the fourth chapter. He (1971:62) claimed that the production of integrated curricula 'require teachers of different subjects to enter into social relationships with each other which will arise not simply out of non-task areas but out of a shared, co-operative, educational task'. This is a necessary horizontal organizational arrangement that enables academics to work together in the production of a course and which will require an organizational ethos that facilitates such co-operation. Obviously this occurs in the Open University in the United Kingdom, where courses are created by course teams, but it is clear that for some the course team is an inefficient system (Stringer 1980). However, it must be recognised that the Open University was established in the late 1960s, at a time when the boundaries of the social system were quite weak and which actually allowed for an expressive revolution. But the production of integrated curricula through the use of course teams is a relatively expensive process and one which more recently established distance education institutions have not considered to be cost-effective. Hence at Athabasca (Stringer 1980) and at the Open Learning Institute in British Columbia (Ellis and Mugridge 1983) courses are produced with smaller teams. Indeed, in the Open Learning Institute each course is produced by a single course writer, in co-operation with a course designer who works on a number of courses simultaneously, and with the approval of a course consultant. Hence, the courses are in single disciplines and a student's overall course of study is more like a collection of small single discipline modules. But the organization of the Open Learning Institute in vertical, with course writers working at a distance and with no co-operation with each other. Without horizontal relationships integrated themes are less likely to occur. However, it has to be recognised that the Open Learning Institute was established in the

late 1970s, when the boundaries of society were
much stronger so that the lack of integration is
hardly surprising.

Terms like Open University and Open Learning
Institute suggest that they are open to anybody
and, indeed, Peters' definition, which was cited
earlier, also gave that impression. However, it
was argued earlier, following Bourdieu (1973), that
only those who had sufficient cultural capital are
likely to enrol in any form of learning and this is
also true for distance education. Woolfe (1977:79)
showed the validity of Bourdieu's thesis when he
recorded that only 9 per cent of all Open University
students could be described as working class and
fewer, 8.5 per cent in 1974, had no previous educational qualifications. By contrast, and as would be
expected, 69.9 per cent had at least one advanced
level pass in the General Certificate of Education
and about 60 per cent of the 1971 intake had
attended grammar school. Hence, Westwood (1980:38)
argues that:

> The Open University may be analysed in
> relation to the social relations of
> production under capitalism. Briefly,
> the centre controls the knowledge and its
> production and consequently the nature of
> the teaching that takes place. In addition,
> the pace of work and form in which knowledge
> is presented is all carefully controlled
> from the centre. Courses are pre-packaged
> and they come through the door like
> commodities. To re-inforce the production
> and transmission of knowledge there exists
> a large bureaucratic structure.

Yet that structure actually determines the way that
the knowledge is presented, so that it is both the
force that shapes and the one which produces and
transmits the knowledge. But the organization of
distance education does not occur in isolation nor
is it unaffected by the wider social forces within
the society in which it operates. Hence, the
structures of knowledge reflect the structures of
the system that produce that knowledge which, in
turn, reflect the structures of the social system.
This analysis does not deny any benefits that may
be gained by learners through distance
learning but it does indicate that it functions in
the same manner as do other forms of education.
Hence, it may be asked, does this mean that it can
also liberate the learners from the structures of

the social system?   Obviously, there are fewer
opportunities for learners to meet with each other
and to enjoy the stimulus of dialogue and discuss
a pluralism of interpretations of social phenomena.
Nevertheless, this does not deny that if learning
is to occur then there must be an opportunity to
reflect and, whenever reflection occurs, as it was
argued in the seventh chapter, the possibility
of the production of agents must exist. Hence, it may
be functional in an unstable state to introduce
distance education because, at least, the agents
are kept apart.

Conclusion

This chapter has examined three alternative
strategies of the education of adults, all of which
relate to the overall structure of society and to
the decline of Gemeinschaft.   Education always
relates to those wider structures and this is a
feature in the traditional models of the curriculum
that is frequently absent.   Yet in some models
of the curriculum (Jarvis 1983b:221), all education
is affected by social policy, and this constitutes
the subject of the following chapter.

Chapter Eleven

ADULT AND CONTINUING EDUCATION AND SOCIAL POLICY

One of the features of any sociological analysis
of a phenomenon is that it locates it within its
wider social context and the social implications of
its existence are analysed.   Yet it is relatively
rare in sociological studies of initial education
to find social policy analysis.   Indeed, it is
often maintained by sociologists (Meighan 1981:370)
that issues in social policy are not really their
concern since they regard it as a matter of
prescription but marxist sociologists do assume
that sociological analysis is related to policy
formation.   However, policy is also a social
phenomenon and as such it is open to the same type
of analysis as is any other social phenomenon.
But it is extremely rare to see social policy in
education treated this way, the studies by Silver
(1980) and Finch (1984) being exceptions.   As
Silver (1980:19) actually notes, it is usually left
to historians to evaluate the motives of the policy
makers, although there is no legitimate reason
why sociologists should not also be involved in
this enterprise.   since initial education has not
been subjected to a great deal of analysis of
policy theorists, it is hardly surprising that
adult and continuing education has received even
less, although Griffin (1983a:217-244; 1983b:92-
117) in the United Kingdom and Wharples and
Rivera (1982) in the United States have begun the
process.
      The intention of this chapter is to continue
this process, using some of the theoretical models
that Finch employs in initial education and
applying them to adult and continuing education.
At the same time it will become apparent that
the theoretical perspectives already adopted in
this book do relate closely to the models used.

The chapter commences with a discussion of the
concept of social policy, it then utilises three
basic theoretical perspectives employed by Finch
and applies them to adult and continuing education
and the chapter concludes with a brief discussion
in which some of the implications of the aforegoing
are examined.

Social Policy and Legislation

There is a distinct difference between legislation
and social policy that should be recognised from
the outset.   Nevertheless, the fact that there
has been an increasing amount of legislation about
adult and continuing education in recent years
indicates that it has become a more significant
object of social policy (Titmus and Pardoen 1981:
129-161).   Indeed, they make the point that
legislation only becomes necessary when the state
acts as a provider or a facilitator of adult and
continuing education but in Britain there were
mechanics institutes and Sunday Schools long
before the state formulated any regulations for
adult education and it was only when the state
wished to control the direction that the movement
took that it offered financial assistance to
science courses 'because it was believed
necessary to encourage the training of more highly
skilled craftsmen in order to meet foreign
industrial competition' (Titmus and Pardoen 1981:
135).   Herein lies one of the elements about how
social policy uses education for a social end, but
it must be recognised that in some instances
education may be an end in itself for social policy.
It is perhaps significant to note how Silver
(1980:19) perceives the relationship between
education and social policy:

> Education in all its forms ... has always
> been a social instrument and historians
> have constantly to evaluate the motives
> of the makers and users of the instrument.
> Its most recent declared purposes have
> included the protection of democracy and
> social values, the improvement of national
> efficiency and the protection of the nation.
> It has also been seen both as a means of
> selecting and protecting elites, and as
> a means of social justice and undermining
> elites.   It is discussed in terms of class
> domination and social control, but also
> of social liberation and progress.

Perhaps this list appears as familiar to adult educators as it does to those who are involved in initial education, since adult and continuing education has clearly been an instrument of social policy in the same way as has been initial education. silver's list also reflects some of the functions of adult and continuing education that have already been discussed in this part of the book. Even so, this list suggests that Townsend's (1967:2) definition of social policy as 'policy concerned with the public administration of welfare' is a little restrictive, which he himself recognises, although this is not to deny that education may be analysed from a welfare policy perspective. Hence, it is necessary to broaden this approach. Indeed, Finch (1984:4) maintains that there are a variety of approaches to social policy, and while the following is not a conceptual definition, it is illumunative. Social policy, she suggests, may be seen as:

> ... action designed by government to
> engineer social change; as a mechanism
> for identifying human needs and devising
> the means of meeting them; as a mechanism
> for solving social problems; as redistri-
> butive justice; as the means of regulating
> subordinate groups.

This approach is akin to Silver's (1980:17) recognition of how education has been used throughout its history:

> Whatever the functions of the increasingly
> large and complex system of education, its
> history can be written in terms of social
> policy - the attempt to use education to
> solve social problems, to influence social
> structures, to improve one or more aspects
> of the social condition, to anticipate
> crisis.

Hence, social policy about the educational system, irrespective of the educational aims and objectives of the educators, is about how government, both national and local, can use education within the wider social system. Social policy is, therefore, both ideological and normative. Hence, it is a far broader concept than legislation, although the latter forms one element within it. Clearly then, the history of adult education could be written

from a social policy perspective, illustrating:
how government has directed the choice of its
subjects; used it to promote hopes of a new
society in a period of social reconstruction after
the 1914-18 War and how government inactivity
thereafter was also a manifestation of social
policy; used it as an instrument of social
welfare e.g. the Russell Report (1973); used it
fend off crisis in unemployment etc.

Hence, social policy may be seen in terms
of the social aims of government which respect of
education, so that in order to analyse adult and
continuing education from this perspective it is
now necessary to examine some of the theoretical
models of social policy.

Models of Social Policy
Finch (1984) suggests three approaches to examining
social policy in education: welfare, beneficiary
and social engineering. Each of these three are
now examined briefly and then applied to adult and
continuing education in the next section.

The Welfare Model: It is perhaps significant that
the 1944 Education Act, which placed a duty upon
Local Education Authorities to 'secure the provision for their area of adequate facilities for
further education' (cited from Stock 1982:12), was
a precursor to the establishment of the Welfare
State. Indeed, in that Act the welfare of children
is considered from a perspective far wider than
just their education, so that it not surprising
that social policy models of welfare are applicable
to adult and continuing education. Welfare
analysis have contributed a great deal to social
policy analysis and Griffin (1983a; 198b)
records two theoretical models, one by Titmuss
(1974) and the other by Pinker (1971). Titmuss
(1974:30-32) produces a model in which he suggests
there are three normative approaches to social
policy:

> The Residual Welfare Model - social welfare
> institutions perform temporary functions on
> behalf of the private market and the family
> in order to meet individual needs but it is
> only a temporary provision and people
> should learn to meet their own needs with-
> out help.

The Industrial Achievement Performance
Model - social welfare institutions are
additions to the economy and treat people's
needs on the basis of merit, work-perform-
ance, productivity. etc.

The Institutional Redistribution Model -
social welfare responds to need universally
and pursues social equality through
redistribution of resources.

In many ways, Pinker's (1971:97-104) model is
similar to Titmuss' although it has only two
facets:

The Residual Model - social welfare should
focus selectively on residual and declining
minority of needy groups, but as the wealth
of the nation increases so these will
require less assistance.

The Institutional Model - since the market
is totally unable to insure that there is
a just allocation of resources throughout
society there will always be a need for
the social services.

Naturally, Titmuss' model is later than Pinker's
and to some extent it is an elaboration of it but
both sets of models reflect some of the same
ideological perspectives that have been discussed
earlier in this book. The first two models of
Titmuss and Pinker's residual model both have
liberal conservative implications in which the
individual is treated as free, rational and able
to act independently and the state is neutral,
passive and its interventions are much more
limited and usually to balance the demands of
pressure groups etc. It will be borne in mind,
however, that this is a philosophy of 'the survival
of the fittest' when not all start equal, so that
effectively it gives free rein to the interests of
the powerful. By contrast, Titmuss' institutional
redistribution model and the latter of Pinker's
models contain a reformist ideology, which
recognises that the real needs of individuals may
be hidden from them or that they may not be free
to pursue them, so that the state should
intervene and support those who are less able to
support themselves. Since this two-way division
fits into the previous analysis it will be used

in the next section in order to illustrate how it
may be utilised in the analysis of adult and
continuing education.

The Beneficiary Model: Underlying this approach
is the idea that education is a valuable commodity,
too valuable to be offered on the market (Jarvis
1982), so that it should be offered to all for
their benefit. Finch (1984:85) suggests that
'some examples can be found of educational policy
presented primarily in these terms and where there
does seem a prima facie case for evaluating the
provision of the action of a benevolent state,
mindful of the "good" of its citizens'. She
notes that the provision may be analysed in terms
of education as a right and as a response to
individual need and social problems. However, is
the state actually that benevolent? Policy is
frequently introduced in 'the national interest',
so that the needs of the nation have to be met
and may even be assumed to be paramount even though
a policy is introduced as a response to the needs
of the people. National interest is itself a
problematic concept since there is an unequal
distribution of rewards in society and frequently
the main beneficiaries of national interest
policies are the more powerful and wealthy members
of society. If education, for instance, is to be
in the national interest it would necessarily have
to be in a controlled form and, therefore,
'education from above', whereas if it were to be
for individual benefit it might assume an 'education
of equals' perspective. Hence, it will be seen
that while this approach is self-evident it may
raise significant issues when applied to adult and
continuing education.

Social Engineering: By and large the beneficiary
approach is individualistic, whereas the social
engineering perspective is more concerned with the
social institutions and social structures.
Finch (1984:114-115) suggests that it has three
conceptually different strands to it:

> Change in education, designed to change
> educational outcomes: Changes in the
> structure of education, such as the
> abolition of selection at eleven years
> of age, designed to bring about major
> changes in the system thereafter. The
> result of this approach does tend to

allow successful individuals to change
their position in the social structures
rather than actually altering the social
and economic structures themselves.

Change in other areas of social policy,
designed to change educational outcomes:
Finch suggests that urban renewal might be
encouraged in order to produce better
living conditions, thus enabling children
to perform better at school.   The result
of this is that groups of people , rather
than individuals, benefit by the change.

Change in education, designed to produce
social change outside of education: This
approach is to use education as an
instrument of social change, so that as
the result of educational reform,
innovation, etc. the social structures are
changed.   This is the most ambitious
and difficult.

Each of the above approaches are applicable to
adult and continuing education, although it will be
recognised that the use of adult education in social
engineering is contrary to the philosophy of some
writers on the subject.
     Having thus outlined a number of perspectives
in social policy it is now necessary to use them
as a basis of discussion about adult and
continuing education, so that the next section of
this chapter will apply them.   However, it must
be recognised that the application will be brief
and illustrative, since a book could be written
on adult and continuing education and social
policy.

Application of Social Policy Models to Adult and
Continuing Education
A variety of approaches to social policy analysis
were examined above   and they constitute the
basis for the discussion in this section.   Clearly
none of them are discrete entities in themselves
nor does one alone provide an absolute and complete
explanation of any policy statement about adult
and continuing education, so that the division here
is drawn only in order to facilitate discussion
and to illustrate the approach.

The Welfare Approach: It is perhaps significant
that the concept of need appears as frequently in
the social work literature as it does in that of
adult education, so that the welfare approach may
be seen immediately to have significance for
analysis in this field.

The institutional model suggests that there
will always be a need for the social services and
as Russell (1973 para 58) states: 'needs change
as circumstances change and the satisfaction of
one need may lay the way open for others to appear'.
In other words, there are always needs and they
are relative to the situation. The Report goes
on to specify a variety of needs that exist which
can only be met by permanent education. Hence,
Russell advocated a state funded educational
service for adults:

> It must be a public service drawing upon
> public funds. The needs are such that few
> of our citizens could meet them by their
> own efforts, and large sections of the
> population could not afford to meet them
> at full cost or through commercial provision.
> The lead must come from central government,
> since it is a national system of uniform
> high quality that is required.
> (Russell 1973 para 63)

The Russell Report also advocated the establishment
of a development body for adult education (para
160.4) but that would have removed some of the
control from central government, so that what
ultimately transpired was the formation of the
Advisory Council for Adult and Continuing
Education which was funded for three years only
in the first instance, which left all control
with central government. However, during its
lifetime there was a change of government and the
new government to which it made its reports did
not subscribe to an institutional welfare policy
model but a residual one. Hence, fewer of its
recommendations probably found favour with the
Conservative government than they might have done
with the Labour one and as a consequence only
minority groups having special needs, e.g. the
unemployed, have been recipients for funded
projects in adult education. A few other areas
that might alleviate the need for provision have
also been funded but, to a considerable extent,
adult and continuing education has not been viewed

as falling within a needs meeting policy.

The Beneficiary Approach: Liberal adult education has traditionally been orientated to the individual and to the enrichment of the individual's life. This has clearly been specified in a number of places in the earlier discussion, e.g. Paterson (1979:17) writes that 'education is the development of persons as independent centres of value whose value is seen to be an intrinsically worthwhile undertaking'. Few people would actually deny the overall tenor of this, but it does not mean that the state should intervene and provide the service. This is contrary to the political ideology of liberalism, in which the state should remain neutral and passive. Paterson (1979:18) goes on to argue that by 'forming educated individuals, we are forming an educated society' which, by inference, must be beneficial to society as a whole. However, such an argument is far from convincing in terms of making available financial provision. Finch (1984:93:94) cites the case of the formation of the Open University, which clearly has a liberal adult education basis and which was promoted by the then prime minister, Harold Wilson, on the following four grounds:

> technological - the need to use all advanced technology, including broadcasting, to best advantage
> economic - the need to use hitherto untapped talent
> egalitarian - an opportunity for those who had not previously had the chance of higher education
> political - the need to maintain Britain's prestige abroad.

Of these, only the egalitarian one is individual-istic and to the benefit of individual learners, while the other three reasons are all directed to the benefit of the state . Finch (1984:94) draws the telling conclusions:

> In contrast with the more obviously individual's benefit recommendations of the Russell Report, proposals for the Open University were implemented, making it a most significant development in the field of adult education.

Perhaps even more significantly, however, even the
Open University's funding is being curtailed as it
has been seen to produce a great deal of individual
benefit that may be adjudged to outweigh any gain
to society.
   More recently, the State has placed considerable funding with the Manpower Services Commission,
which has itself promoted various educational
schemes with the unemployed, the young adult and
which has been concerned with adult training.   Its
discussion paper specifies a number of reasons why
a new approach is needed urgently:

   - to raise productivity and improve the
     flexibility and motivation of the labour
     force
   - to enable management and other employees
     to adjust quickly and effectively to new
     methods, processes, products, services
     and technologies
   - to help those starting up new firms to
     establish business successfully
   - to enable individuals to update and
     extend their skills, often on a quite
     radical basis, and to develop through-
     out their working lives.
     (M.S.C. 1983 para 11)

None of the above are about individual benefit and
the only time that individual benefit is mentioned
is within the context of the individual's working
life.   Hence, it may be seen that governmental
funding is much more likely when educational
projects are clearly designed to ensure that the
state is the main beneficiary in the process.

The Social Engineering Approach: It will be
recalled that Finch (1984:114-115) suggested three
aspects to this: change in education; change in
other areas of social policy; educational change
designed to produce social change.   Each of these
is now discussed separately here.
Change in education designed to change educational
outcomes: Finch suggested that the abolition of
the 'eleven plus' selection examination in order
to allow a greater opportunity to late developers
would be an example of this approach.   Clearly
adult and continuing education has been subjected
to a number of similar policy decisions: it might
be argued that the establishment of the Open
University and Open Tech Programme fall into this

category;   certainly the open college consortium
enabling adults to gain access to higher education
could be regarded as social engineering.   Clearly,
since the establishment of the Welfare State,
changes in education have usually been regarded as
state intervention to the benefit of those whose
previous educational opportunity has been limited
but recent governmental policy in reducing the
number of places in higher education may be
regarded as social engineering designed to change
educational outcomes by reducing the opportunity
for individuals to acquire higher education and in
this sense it produces a broader social effect of
reducing opportunity for social mobility (Halsey
et al 1980:218).

Changes in other areas of social policy, designed
to change educational outcomes: This is less
likely to occur with adults but it would be
possible for national or local government to provide
more funding for day nurseries so that women may
have greater opportunity to return to study;   it
would be possible for government to encourage
industry to allow paid, or assisted, educational
leave so that employees may follow non-vocational
education.

Changes in education designed to produce social
change outside of the educational system: It has
already been pointed out above that by reducing the
number of places in higher education the conservative government in the early 1980s has effectively
used education to prevent social mobility, so that
education may be seen to have some wider social
effect.   However, as an institution in the superstructure of society it might be argued that
education is more likely to be the recipient of
the forces of change rather than a change agent.
While this is true to some extent, it is possible
to see how communities have been developed by the
rise of education, especially in the Third World.
Hence, such schemes as those reported by Stone
(1983:297-304) in which a non-formal community
education is funded to help develop local
communities does indicate that the educational
institution can actually have an effect on the
social structures of local communities.

Social engineering does occur in all elements
of the implementation of social policy and, as noted
above, education can be used by a state intent on
offering opportunities for depressed groups to have
additional opportunities but it may also be used
to ensure that those who have social privileges

retain them.   It should not be assumed that
because education is 'good' that its use in social
policy terms is always or necessarily beneficial
to all people in a society.

Concluding Discussion
The above discussion has not been an exhaustive
attempt to analyse adult and continuing education
in social policy terms.   Nevertheless, it has
endeavoured to demonstrate the efficacy of such
an approach.   It has been suggested that
education may be regarded as an instrument of a
benign state or as Griffin (1983a) argues as an
instrument of social control.   Hence, it is
important for educators of adults to recognise that
not only may adult and continuing education be
analysed from this perspective, it is in any case
being used as an instrument in government policy.
Hence, this is an important perspective and from
the above discussions a number of conclusions may
be drawn in respect to the purpose, funding and
control of adult and continuing education.
     The purpose of adult education has been discu-
ssed by philosophers of adult education, such as
Paterson (1979), but it is clear that their
deliberations may be removed from those of the
policy makers.   Hence, it is important to
understand the process as they understand it.
Rivera (1982:11-12) sums this up neatly:

     Governmental and inter-governmental bodies
     tend to stress the role of adult education
     as a tool for economic (and "human resource")
     development, and that perspective has also
     permeated the profession's thinking.

Rivera goes on to argue that in America   the
government's role has gone almost unquestioned by
adult educators;   indeed, it has become regarded
as quite essential since support for the education
of the disadvantaged could only come from federal
funding.   However, for any professional group to
allow itself to become the handmaiden of government,
if its social policy is not benign, is dangerous
and, if Rivera is correct, his strictures should
act as an indication that both the philosophers of
the profession and the ideologies of the policy
makers have to be examined and analysed with great
care.
     However, the reason why government is
considered so important is that it controls by the

distribution of funds. It may be recalled that the Advisory Council for Adult and Continuing Education was initially funded for three years only and was then funded for another three years only before its activities were terminated. Funding does not only control activities, it also controls the direction of research and, therefore, the development of the knowledge of the discipline. Hence, the Department of Education and Science (1984) announced that it had set aside a sum of money to promote research and development for the adult unemployed. Thus, new knowledge in adult education terms will arise from these research projects. In this way, the development of new knowledge in the discipline is itself subject to the control and direction of those who control the funds.

Since central government is involved in adult and continuing education both through the implementation of social policy and legislation, then it is open to the pressures of interests groups. Perhaps this is an element of the education of adults in the United States that has developed to a greater degree than it has in the United Kingdom. Kazanjian (1982:38) argues that Federal involvement in the education of adults demands constant questioning and she suggests that consequently every educational interest is represented in Washington. She (1982:39) claims that the lobbying process can itself be educational in helping 'Members in sorting out the complexity of it all'. She (1982:41-42) goes on to note that lobbyists must understand the complexity of the whole process,/but that:

> There is no doubt that "lobbyists" do influence policy outcomes at the Federal level. Despite generic differences among lobbying groups, both public and private there is at least three common functions carried out to influence policy outcomes: 1) supplying facts and figures on the need for and/or impact of policy alternatives; 2) sifting out and utilizing political considerations, and 3) serving as a focal point for communication among all parties involved. Any one function can be carried out effectively only if a sense of trust has been built between the lobbyist and the party to be influenced.

Adult and Continuing Education and Social Policy

Since adult and continuing education is an object
of social policy, it is, therefore, one about which
there should be considerable public debate and one
in which all interested parties should be involved
in the interests of democracy.

PART IV

ADULT AND CONTINUING EDUCATION IN THE ORGANIZATIONAL
CONTEXT

Chapter Twelve

THE ORGANIZATION OF ADULT AND CONTINUING EDUCATION

Self-directed learning can occur at any time and in any place but the majority of teaching and learning transactions occur within an organizational context. In this sense, education may be regarded as institutionalized learning, a point to which further reference is made below. Organizations are, however, a common feature in contemporary society. Indeed, it has been described as an organization society. Hence, the study of organizations is quite fundamental to the comprehension of modern society. As a concept, however, organization has nearly as many definitions as it has had writers about it but, for the purposes of this chapter, Hall's (1972:9) definition is accepted here:

> An organization is a collectivity with
> relatively identifiable boundary, a
> normative ·order, authority ranks,
> communication systems, and membership
> co-ordinating systems; this collectivity
> exists on a relatively continuous basis
> in an environment and engages in
> activities that are usually related to a
> goal or set of goals.

This is a complex definition, as Hall himself admits, and yet there are features about it that are significant and which relate closely to the analysis of adult and continuing education organizations. The final section of this chapter, for instance, makes reference to the idea of 'a normative order' since this may be seen as an organizational subculture and as a hidden curriculum.
      Organizations are clearly of different types and, as Hall's definition suggests, exist for

different purposes.   Based upon the idea of who
actually benefits from the existence of the
organization, Blau and Scott (1963:43) suggest that
there are four types of organization: mutual
benefit organization, where the prime beneficiary
is the membership, i.e. a political party, a
religious sect;   business concerns, where the
owners are the prime beneficiaries;   service
organizations, where the client group is the prime
beneficiary, i.e. social service organizations;
commonweal   organizations, where the public at
large is the prime beneficiary, i.e. the fire
service.   It is an interesting exercise to try to
classify organizations of adult and continuing
education within this useful typology.   It could
be claimed, for instance, that they are commonweal
organizations offering a service to the whole
community within which they are situated as in
the case of distance education organizations offering a service to the public at large.   At its
most idealistic it might be claimed that the
universities, especially the Open University, does
offer a service to the public at large, although
there are sufficient restrictions on entry as to
make this claim dubious.   Community education
organizations, extra-mural departments and adult
education institutes might be seen in this respect
but even here it is doubtful whether they could
legitimately be classified as commonweal
organizations.   Most educational organizations have
specific client groups, so that it is maintained
here that most adult and continuing education
organizations are service organizations.   According
to Blau and Scott, one of the features of this
type of organization is that it is a professional
organization in as much as the employees are
professionals who seek to offer a service to a
specific group of people, based upon the professio-
na's own diagnosis of the real needs of the
client.   Without anticipating some of the
discussion that occurs in the final chapter of this
book, it is recognised that this is not necessarily
an adequate description of many adult and
continuing education organizations, especially in
liberal adult education, where the clients are
mature, know their own learning needs and choose
the class to which they come.   However, this will
be seen to be a quite contentious debate and one
which Blau and Scott (1963:53) anticipated in
relation to the universities where they wrote:

> To convert the university to a business
> concern that "gives the customers what
> they want" does not serve the best
> educational interests of the students;
> rather students are best served when
> professional educators determine what
> and how they are to be taught.

Clearly, Blau and Scott may not reflect an educationalist's perspective and they were also unaware of more recent debates in education about negotiated curricula. But the significant element about the above quotation is that it raises questions about the wisdom of trying to classify educational organizations within the second category, about expecting them to be organized on a self-financing or a financial profit basis, since this is to misconstrue the nature of education.

Hence, it is maintained here that adult and continuing education organizations are service organizations that are analysable from the perspectives of the organizational theorist. That it has not actually been undertaken, however, must make this chapter rather tentative, but its aim is to sketch some of the elements that such an analysis should include, although it does not endeavour to be exhaustive. The chapter itself has four main sections: the organization of the service; the bureaucratic organization; the centre-periphery model of organization; dilemmas of institutionalised education.

The Organization of the Service

Adult and continuing education has never been a single co-ordinated service and as its history reveals it had a multitude of different beginnings, so that it has evolved into a very complex system. This, Knowles (1980a:39) maintains gives it the flexibility to respond to whatever social needs may arise. By contrast, Griffith (1980:74) considers that this variety of providers and lack of centralised plan of provision is a fundamental weakness in the system. These views are also reflected in the publication by the Ministry of Education in Ontario (n.d.:42), which argues that:

> The variety of education agencies, the
> informality of courses, and the voluntary
> aspect of attendance, among other factors,
> require not control and regulation, but

co-ordination, co-operation and advocacy.

This Canadian statement at least suggests that in that country adult and continuing education is being institutionalised into a formal third educational system.   This is in contrast to what is appearing in the United Kingdom where, in addition to the variety of local authority provided adult education, college and university provided continuing education, industry's own provision, etc., there is also a great deal of provision by private suppliers of education.

Hence, two models of provision are evident here: central planned provision and free market provision. In the former, a central agency plans the provision and then makes it available and, despite what the Ministry of Education in Ontario claims, that usually results in a model of control; the latter is the classical model of the free market with its claims to consumer sovereignty. Since both models are appearing it is necessary to examine them carefully in order to detect their strengths and weaknesses.   However, it must be recognised that they are ideal types and that, as such, they may not be found in their 'pure' form in any social system.

Free Market Model: This model appears to have two variants;   that of neo-classical economics based on supply and demand and the one that appears to be emerging in the United Kingdom which reflects the position held by Knowles, that the adult and continuing education system has to be flexible enough to respond to need.   For the sake of clarity these two models are called the free market demand model and the free market need model.

The free market demand model has at its basis the classical, liberal ideology of free, rational man able to act in the pursuit of his own interests and desires.   Any needs in society are residual, so that while the needy should be helped it is only a temporary phenomenon.   Hence, this model assumes that education can be offered on the market and its supply will be regulated by the amount of demand and that the price of the commodity will also be fixed in response to what the purchasers of the commodity are prepared to pay. Hence, if potential students are prepared to pay a specific fee for the course then it will run but if another course cannot command sufficient enrolments at the marketable fee then it will not be organised.

Hence, this model assumes a considerable degree of flexibility and also it assumes consumer sovereignty, both of which may appear superficially attractive in the first instance. But there are a number of points in this model that demand further discussion and that cast doubts upon the apparent strength of the position. In the first instance, no prospectus of adult or continuing education ever offers the total number of possible courses that could be organized for the total population that might respond to that offer. Once there is any restriction placed upon the choice of courses, then the potential students do not make a sovereign choice in a free market. Secondly, the actual range of choices offered to the market is not determined by potential students but by the providers. Indeed, there is no way in logic that potential consumers can determine the production of a commodity before it is produced unless it is made to order and requests in prospectuses for suggestions for courses does not constitute such a situation. Hence, there is not actuality a response to market demand but a response to the selection of courses that the providers decide to offer. Indeed, it could be argued that the tastes of the potential students are being manipulated, albeit far less intensely than the manner in which mass media advertising is used to sell commercially produced commodities, by the choice that is offered and the advice that is provided about the best choices that meet potential students' interests. Finally, if the fee mechanism and the number of enrolments determines the actual curriculum of any adult and continuing education institution, then it favours the most popular courses and those able to pay for their education. Ideologically, this may not be very acceptable to most educators of adults but, clearly, it is favoured by the educational entrepreneurs who offer education as a commodity on the 'free' market and by governments having a liberal ideological perspective which try to convert service organizations into business concerns.

The free market needs model is one that has many similarities to the above in as much as it endeavours to respond to something of a market mechanism but it makes fewer claims for consumer sovereignty. In this instance, it would claim that the courses offered to the general public for selection have been chosen by the educators

either because they perceive a need in that
locality or because they consider the choice
educationally desirable. Hence, the rationale
for their inclusion in the prospectus is that they
endeavour to respond to individual, organizational,
community or societal needs or that they are
enriching to the potential students.   In other
words, the reason for their inclusion in the
prospectus is that they are considered to be
educationally worthwhile. Having made the offer
the adult and continuing education service will
try to help any potential students who desire it to
decide upon the best ways of meeting their needs
through an educational advisory service (ACACE
1979c). Because this approach is more welfare
orientated, it is much more likely to be flexible
in terms of level of fee and number of enrolments,
provided that the organization is able to balance
its finances at the end of each year.   Even so, the
model is open to the same criticisms, to a lesser
degree, as the free market demand model, even
though it is much more humanitarian.   Indeed, it
approximates to that which operates in some
liberal adult education provision in the United
Kingdom, although the financial stringency of the
present Conservative government appears to be
pushing it in the direction of the demand model but
this pressure appears contrary to the desires of
adult educators themselves.

Central Planning Provision Model: This model, while
it espouses a form of co-ordination, frequently
results in a method of control.   Yet this model
reflects the reformist ideology that people need
help to see their real needs or to achieve their
aspirations, so that it offers an institutional
welfare policy.   The educational planners, in this
instance, seek to ensure a balanced and co-ordinated provision through a given location.   The
Ministry of Education in Ontario (n.d.42-45)
suggests that local learning councils should be
established and that all providers of education
for adults in that locality should be members.
The councils would seek to meet the needs of
learners in the community, act as a liaison forum
for educational institutions and initiate new
provision.   While this might appear to be an
attractive method to plan provision and to ensure
efficient use of resources, central planning tends
to become totalitarian, slow to change to demands
or needs and the provision is that which the

providers deem possible or desirable. Hence,
central planning tends to be inefficient and
inflexible.

Thus it may be seen that the varying models of
provision examined above all have their strengths
and weaknesses. If there is total planning of
adult and continuing education, as the third model
suggests, then it would not overcome the problems
of the market, nor of need or demand. It would,
however, result in a very cumbersome and not very
efficient system. By contrast, the free market
demand model may be ideologically unacceptable to
many educators of adults whose own ideological
orientation may be more humanistic. Hence, a
compromise 'mixed economy' model may be a practical
solution to the problem of organizing the service.

Bureaucratic Organization
Adult and continuing education provision is made
by many different organizations, as indicated by
the above discussion. Indeed, even local
education authority provision of general education
for adults varies from one authority to another.
Mee (1980:31-32) suggests that three main linkages
occur: adult education as a separate organization,
even though it has to use other premises than its
own e.g. local schools when they are not in use;
adult education as a department within a
community school or college of further education,
etc.; adult education combined with another
service, such as the youth service, and organized
as a joint provision. Additionally, continuing
education is provided by colleges, polytechnics and
universities; sometimes in combination with adult
education but often separately, sometimes in an
academic department and sometimes as part of the
registry of the organization. Large industrial
and commercial companies also have their own
departments of continuing education, even though
they may not go under that name. Within this
diversity it is very clear that adult and continuing education is frequently provided in and by
large organizations that may be conceptualized as
bureaucracies. Yet there has been little academic
research in adult and continuing education that
reflects this perspective, so that it is necessary
to provide a broad overview of the bureaucratic
organization in order that some of the problems
of the discipline may be elaborated.
Bureaucracy has been the subject of numerous

investigations and Hall (1963) studied the work of
nine major writers about bureaucracy and none had
the same list of characteristics about it.   Since
Hall's work there have been many other pieces of
work about bureaucratic organizations but there are
still no agreement about the characteristics of
the phenomenon.   While it would be both tedious
and unnecessary to rehearse all of these analyses
here, it should be borne in mind that listing
characteristics of any phenomenon without a conceptual framework is an invalid procedure.   The
reason why this is so is because any other
characteristic may be added to or subtracted from
the list without reason, since there is no
theoretical foundation to the list.   However, one
approach that has been used widely in empirical
research, both of industrial and commercial
organizations and of ecclesiastical ones (Ransom
et al 1977) in recent years is that developed by
Pugh et al (1963) at Aston University.   The
characteristics that they suggest have been
found to be relevant in their research and are,
therefore, employed here.   They maintain that
there are six primary dimensions that comprise
the basis of organizational structure:

    specialization, i.e. division of labour
    standardization, i.e. of procedures and roles
    formalization, i.e. in terms of communication
        about role performance
    centralization, i.e. of authority
    configuration, i.e. the shape of the organi-
        zation in terms of span of control
    flexibility, i.e. the ability to change or
        respond to the forces of change.

While the last of the six dimensions was originally
called 'traditionalism', these six have gained some
support from scholars, such as Hall (1972) and
since it has formed the basis of some empirical
research it may be useful in the analysis of
organizations providing adult and continuing
education.   Unfortunately no such sociological
analysis has yet been undertaken and even recent
analyses of adult education centres (Small and
Tight 1983) are largely descriptive and have little
theoretical analytical base.   While they do not
set out to provide one, it is unfortunate that
even their organization chart is not really precise,
so that such an analysis is still awaited.   Even
so, the Aston group's model is one that would

allow a comparative organizational analysis of providers of adult and continuing education. It might be hypothesized, were such an analysis conducted, that compared with the small adult education institutes, such as that described by Small and Tight, that the larger colleges and universities have: greater specialization; more standardization and formalization; similar authority structures that are centralized in terms of administration and policy matters but decentralized in academic matters; have more administrative strata; less flexibility. Pugh et al (1969:98), for instance, found that:

> Large organizations tend to have more specialization, more standardization and more formalization than smaller organizations. The lack of relationship between size and the remaining structural dimensions, i.e. concentration of authority and line control of work flow ... was equally striking.

Hence, comparative structural analyses could be conducted in adult and continuing education and it would probably be discovered that certain aspects of structure are a function of size. Even so, the structure of the organization may not necessarily be the most appropriate to achieve the purpose of the organization itself. Whilst efficiency studies have been conducted within the study of organizations none have actually been conducted in adult and continuing education, so that this will not be pursued here. However, it is very evident that management studies need to be conducted; indeed, that management training needs to be undertaken in this field and further reference will be made to this in the final chapter.

Commencing any study of an organization from the structural perspective will, it will be recalled, influence the manner in which the individual actors within the organization are perceived. However, it would be possible to relate some of these studies to the role of the educator of adults, but since this constitutes the topic for the final chapter further discussion is deferred until then. By contrast, it is possible to study organizational behaviour from an interactionist perspective, in which the social order is seen as negotiated between the role players.

Studies exist in initial education of this nature, e.g. (Geer 1971), Becker (1971) and also studies by hospitals and mental institutions (Strauss et al 1973), Goffman (1961), but none exist in adult and continuing education. Nevertheless, it would be quite possible to use existing research in studying this area of education and some examples are discussed below. Geer and Becker, in differing ways, both discuss how the classroom is a negotiated order: Geer specifying how the teacher and the pupils create informal rules and that once they. are made how all the role players should conform to these expectations. In precisely the same way the emphasis that adult educators place upon the first class of a course may be interpreted as negotiating the order of the class and both tutor and students working out how they will perform their respective roles. From a wider organizational perspective, Strauss et al analyse the ways in which the main groups of actors in the hospital negotiate their roles with each. They (1973:315) specify that:

> there is a patterned variability of nego-
> tiating in the hospital pertaining to who
> contracts with whom, about what, as well
> as when these agreements are made. In-
> fluencing this variability are hierarchical
> positions and ideological commitments, as
> well as periodicies in the structure of
> ward relationships (for instance, because
> of a relational system that moves person -
> nel periodically on and off given wards).

A similar approach might be employed with all the personnel who interact regularly with each other in an adult education institute, a community college or a polytechnic or university involved in adult and continuing education. Such an approach, examining the patterns of negotiation would then throw considerable light upon the way that organizations providing adult and continuing education actually function. A similar approach to Goffman's study of the mental hospital might also be employed, in which he examined the world of the inmate, that of the staff, interaction ritual, the process of hospitalization and socialization, etc. It would be possible to examine the world of the adult student, the world of full-time educators of adults, the world of part-time staff, etc. and then to look carefully at the interaction ritual.

Thus it may be seen that there is a richness and diversity in the study of organizations that has not yet been utilised by scholars in adult and continuing education. However, as the sociology of adult and continuing education emerges, so some of these researches will probably be employed. At present, one major study or organizational theory has been employed in adult education and that must now be examined.

Centre-Periphery Model of Organization

The one model of organization theory which has been applied to adult and continuing education is the centre-periphery model devised by Schon (1973), which relates to the diffusion of innovations. The model was first used in adult education in U.K. by Elston (1975) and subsequently employed by Mee (1980). Reference is made below to the research on diffusion of innovation because the context in which this model arises is important to under-standing it. However, the model may best be described as that of a central organization with outreach agencies working away from the centre in order to spread the innovation with which the centre is concerned. It is basically an entre-preneurial or a missionary model. Schon (1973:77) specifies that there are three basic premises to the model: that the innovation to be diffused actually exists; diffusion is regarded as an innovation that moves from the centre outwards; directed diffusion is a centrally managed process of dissemination, training, provision of resources and incentives. Schon himself regarded the proto-type of the diffusion the agricultural extension agent, who is clearly a part of the adult and continuing education movement in America. Indeed, one of the early adaptations of the research into the diffusion of innovation by Rogers (1962) was by the agricultural extension agencies e.g. Fisher J.D., Wesselman R.A. et al (1968) Indeed, it was within the sphere of agriculture one of the earliest of all diffusion studies was undertaken when Ryan and Gross (1943) examined the process of adopting a new type of seed corn in two communities in Iowa. However, it is a model that has considerable similarities to that which occurs in some extra-mural departments and some forms of continuing education outreach, in which the department itself is at the centre and its tutors and other staff work away from the centre in the periphery. Where the staff actually

conduct courses in the region, Schon regards this
as a "Johnny Appleseed" model, whereas when the
staff seek to attract students from the pheriphery
to the centre it is a "magnet" model.   However,
some of the agents at the periphery may actually
create secondary centres in the vicinity where
they are teaching, so that a proliferation of
centres model emerges.   This model, as Mee (1980:
27) has suggested, typifies the structure of many
local education authority adult education institutes and, indeed, that of some extra-mural
departments.   In these instances, the department
itself remains as the main centre and the
outstations are secondary centres.   Schon suggests
that the primary centre actually assumes specialized functions, such as training, while the
secondary centres undertake the work of teaching,
etc.   However, the majority of adult education
institutes and extra-mural departments are
probably not quite large enough for the centre to
adopt a totally different programme to that of
its outstations and nor are the outstations quite
so independent;   for instance, the member of
academic staff responsible for the administration
of a secondary centre may have academic
responsibility for his discipline throughout the
whole institute.   Such a division of labour may
help to ensure the unity of the institute, whereas
independent secondary centres may create a
situation of instability, but the dual responsibility may cause role strain among academic staff.
     The diffusion of innovations perspective
adopted by Schon is quite significant in continuing education especially.   Hence, its
significance to the agricultural extension movement
in America.   Underlying this approach is the way
that new knowledge is disseminated to practitioners
in the field and Rogers (1962) suggested that
there is a patterned process of adoption in which
five different types of respondent appear:

> innovators, eager to adopt new ideas and
>   venturesome (2½%)
> early adopters, part of the professional
>   system and role models for
>   colleagues (13½%)
> early majority, rarely take the lead but
>   have high peer participation (34%)
> late majority, respondents to social
>   pressure (34%)
> laggards, traditional often professional

isolates, suspicious of new ideas (16%)

The percentages represent the proportion of the professional group which fall into each category. The significant group are the early adopters, who are the trend setters or the opinion leaders. They tend to be slightly younger, have higher status, more favourable financial position, more specialized work, more contacts with research centres, more sources of information and have a more cosmopolitan orientation than most other practitioners. Knowing the opinion leaders is an important strategy for extension agents since if they are to diffuse an innovation it is wise to know whom others will copy. Such a strategy may become more significant in the United Kingdom as continuing education becomes more institutionalised, but it may not be the whole strategy.

Schon, himself, was a little critical of this form of organization since large organizations frequently viewed adaptations by secondary centres as failures of primary centre control. Hence, he (1973:102) points out that the proliferation of centres system:

> suffered from the dependence of limited
> resources and competence at the primary
> centre, from the rigidity of central
> doctrine, and from a feedback loop within
> which information moved primarily between
> secondary and primary centres.

Thus he suggests that the new form that is emerging is the learning system or network, which is more flexible in the face of rapid social change. While there is a movement in the direction of the creation of learning networks (ACACE:1983b) it must be recognised that there are significant conceptual differences between the organization of education and the creation of learning networks, which entails recognition that education and learning are not essentially the same phenomenon.

Learning may be regarded as a part of the process of human living in which individuals acquire new knowledge, skills or attitudes by a variety of different means but education is a much later phenomenon in which specific forms of learning are incorporated. Education, then, is the institutionalization of human learning, so that learning networks may themselves institutionalize in the same way as other successful movements have

done in the past.   They may not institutionalize
into the same educational form as the present
education system, but if they do not, then it
raises the interesting possibility of education
and another institutionalized learning system
co-existing, hence making the future system even
more complex than the one which McCullough (1980)
found so complex to describe.   However, in a
time of declining resources the question must be
raised about the extent to which a new system will
be allowed to perpetuate itself if it competes for
students in a free market.   Nevertheless, the
theory of social change discussed earlier in this
text is one of social evolution, so that the
creation of learning networks would merely indicate
the direction in which the next phase of this
social phenomenon will take.

Dilemmas of Institutionalised Education of Adults
Once learning is institutionalised certain
dilemmas are created and in this section some of
these are explored but prior to undertaking this
task it is necessary to understand the process of
institutionalization.   Institutions, claims
Berger (1966:104) 'provide procedures through which
human conduct is patterned, compelled to go, in
grooves deemed desirable by society.   And this
trick is performed by making these grooves
appear to the individual as the only possible
ones'.   Education, then, is institutionalised
learning and, as was pointed out above, the
recognition that learning still exists outside of
the educational institution has resulted in the
idea that institutionalized learning networks
should be created.   However, implicit throughout
this study has been the paradox of institutionalization and in this brief section some of the
dilemmas of this paradox are discussed.
    Learning is the acquisition of knowledge,
skill or attitude and it does not matter how it is
acquired, it is still learning, so that an
individual can spend a lifetime reflecting upon
the nature of the universe and of the human beings
that live on this planet and can think some of
the profoundest thoughts and achieve some of the
greatest insights into human behaviour.   He can
read some of the best books and understand a wide
range of disciplines.   In short, he can be a
very learned person.   Yet if he has no General
Certificate of Education passes at Ordinary Level
he may appear on an application form for a job as

a person without education.   Hence, one of the
dilemmas of institutionalised education is simply
that the education process does not define a learned
person even though philosophers may seek to define
an educated man.

Hence a second dilemma arises, that of freedom
versus control.   The self-directed learner may
endeavour to master a wide variety of disciplines,
may work as his own pace and may link his studies
as he wishes.   Hence, some of the lifelong
learners described by Gross (1977) were free to
study disciplines in the way that they considered
right for them.   However a curriculum is
negotiated within the education system, the learning
of the student is controlled to some extent by the
teacher, the examination and the time limits
imposed by the academic year.   Hence, any
institutionalized learning follows the patterns
and parameters dictated by others and is, consequently, subject to control.   That education is
subject to considerable control has been a feature
of the analysis contained in this study.

Another problem of institutionalization is
that there arises a normative order within the
organization which seeks to provide the education.
All who wish to teach and learn, or both, within
that organization are expected to conform to that
order.   This normative order can be viewed as
an educational sub-culture which imposes a hidden
curriculum on those who seek to participate in
the organization.   Sociological studies of schools
in initial education have pointed to the fact
that they have a middle class, or a lower middle
class, sub-culture into which the children from
those social classes fit more easily than do the
children of working class origin.   Adult and
continuing education organizations likewise have
their own middle class, or lower middle class, sub-
culture in which adults from that background fit
easily enough.   However, adult and continuing
education organizations seek to attract students
from working class backgrounds as well.   Yet the
very existence of the organization creates a
barrier to people from working classes coming,
since their sub-culture is foreign to that of the
middle   classes.   Hence, many working class people
reject the educational organization and its sub-
culture but this does not mean that they reject
learning, only institutionalized learning.

One writer aware of the problems of institutionalization is Illich, who in a number of books

has sought to demonstrate some of its weaknesses in
medicine, in the professions, etc.   Illich and
Verne (1976:14) claim that: 'Medicine has made
life the subject of medical care; education makes
existence the subject of a study course'.   Hence,
while educational aims may be to produce independent adults, able to learn for themselves, in fact
it creates adults dependent on an educational
system for their learning.   Thus the nature of
adult education itself is called into question
according to Illich and Verne by this process
and the independent versus the dependent adult
becomes one of the dilemmas of institutionalization.

The final dilemma that is to be discussed
here is what of O'Dea (1966:91) calls the 'dilemma
of mixed motivation'.   Teachers of adults
frequently enter the occupation in order to be of
service to adults, often the motivation is very
high and based on the fact that they regard themselves as lucky to have received an education and
they want to be involved in helping others have
the same type of opportunities.   Yet the educational organization is a bureaucracy and a career is
open to the educators to rise up the bureaucratic
hierarchy.   In order to gain seniority the
teacher may have to put some ideals behind him and
to function as an administrator and organizer
within the constraints that the educational
organization imposes.   To provide education for
adults may be a time-consuming unsocial hours'
occupation, working in the evenings to ensure that
provision is made at the time when adults are
able to attend it.   But to be an administrator of
an organization may ensure that the working hours
are more social and the remunerative rewards
higher.   Hence, the educator of adults is faced
with a dilemma in respect of his vocation.   This
dilemma is perhaps exacerbated within the administrative framework because it is easy for
administrators to be more concerned with perpetuating the organizational structures than with the
goals of the organization.   Merton (1968:253)
regards this phenomena as displaced goals.

Hence, the institutionalization of learning
may be seen to be a social process, that like
the institutionalization of other movements,
creates problems and dilemmas.   These are in the
nature of the institutional organization itself
and are not easily resolvable.

Conclusion

Adult and continuing education is a highly organized activity and yet few studies have yet appeared which employ the insights of organizational analysis. This chapter has examined some of these perspectives and sought to apply them to adult and continuing education, but in the process it has raised issues that require further research and consideration. One area of organized education that has been quite fully researched is the participation of adults in education and this constitutes the subject for the next chapter.

Chapter Thirteen

ADULT PARTICIPANTS IN EDUCATION

Once learning is institutionalized and educational
organizations are created, a number of issues
arise immediately, as was apparent during the
discussion in the previous chapter, because of the
characteristics of the organization. One of the
dilemmas of institutionalization was shown to be
the fact that education may require organization in
order to make provision but the existence of
the organization itself inhibits some from taking
advantage of it. Hence, the intention in this
chapter is to examine this process in greater detail
and the chapter contains three sections: access,
participation and barriers to participation.

Access to Adult and Continuing Education
The significance of the term 'access' in adult and
continuing education is itself an interesting
phenomenon. Why should access be an important
concern? Clearly it is not merely a term that
has recently come to the fore out of a concern for
the survival of educational organizations threa-
tened by closure because of financial stringency,
although Mee and Wiltshire (1978:95) do point to
the fact that full-time adult educators are aware
of 'the political value of stressing work of a
compensatory kind in arguing a case for public
expenditure' so that terms like 'access' do have
ideological connotations. Clearly, it is
politically appropriate to be demonstrating that
access to the educational system is open to
everybody throughout their lives, so that an
appearance of egalitarianism occurs. Hence,
anybody can acquire access to one of the major
vehicles of social mobility, if they have either
the motivation or the ability, or both. Since
anyone can apparently do this, there appears to

exist an opportunity for any person to change his
position in the social structure by individual
effort, which suggests that those who are at the
apex of the social hierarchy have also got there
by the same methods. This gives society an
appearance of openness and consequently legitimates the social structures. It is perhaps this
legitimating function that is one of the major
reasons for the significance of the term. But,
like other functions, it may be interpreted
differently. Adult educators have continually
regarded adult education as a movement and their
role as a mission, so that the more that they can
make adult education accessible to more people the
more that they are fulfilling their mission. Hence,
to many adult educators, committed to the movement,
access is an element in their ideology and, as
such, is a rationale for being involved in the
movement. In this sense, participation has been a
concept rather like organization membership, with
the more members of the organization signifying
the success of the movement. This analysis can be
developed a little further in as much as the
more who participate in the movement, the more the
movement is seen to be useful to the wider society
which, in its turn, re-inforces the ideology of
the movement and of its members. Thus McKnight
(1977:78-79) accuses professionals of needing
deficiency so that they can solve the client's
problems.

Hence, it is suggested here that Griffin's
(1983:81-83) argument that adult educators think
about access in institutional terms is correct but
he does not really develop it sufficiently. He
claims that access 'can only be conceived in
simplistic and material terms unless some kind of
curricular dimension is attributed to it?' While
he is correct about the curricular dimension,
it is not correct to claim that without curriculum
access can be thought of only in simplistic and
material terms. Even without consideration of
the curriculum access is an ideology and participation the measure of success of a movement that
has few educational criteria, such as examinations,
by which to evaluate its contribution to society.

Griffin is, however, correct to draw
curriculum into consideration of the discussion of
access but it may be best discussed as a barrier to
access rather than in the context of access itself.
Curriculum, like the normative order of the
educational organization, has a middle class

orientation, and while it assists people with that social background, either by ascription or achievement, gaining the benefits of education it certainly inhibits those from a working class background. There is, however, one significant element about working class access to continuing education and that is one place of the Trades Union Movement. Killeen and Bird (1981:12-13) make the point that there is a long history of co-operation between liberal adult education and the trade unions, so that the latter have obtained educational opportunities for the working classes which helps them overcome the barriers that have already been mentioned. Hence, access has other connotations within this context.

Therefore, it is now important to examine participation in adult and continuing education before the barriers can be realistically discussed.

Participation in the Education of Adults

Since participation is so crucial to organized adult education it is hardly surprising that it has been thoroughly researched. Indeed, it would probably be true to claim that as much empirical data exist about this aspect of adult and continuing education as any other. Yet much of it has been gathered in a rather non-theoretical manner but one of the points that is argued here is that since the education of adults occurs in organizations, and that much of it is voluntary, it is a leisure time activity and its participants will be similar to those joining other voluntary organizations, e.g. churches, political parties. But education does have its own characteristics, so that participation will also relate to those special aspects, e.g. since older adults are supposed to be incapable of learning there will be a decline in participation amongst the elderly. However, this section does not endeavour to be an exercise in comparative organized leisure, so that comparative data are not produced here. Nevertheless, it should be noted that people who join religious organizations, with the exception of the sectarian movements, tend to be: middle or lower middle class; women rather than men, although men are more likely to be the organizers and leaders; have been brought up in a religious family, so that they have the religious cultural capital; older rather than younger. With the exception of the last characteristic, which has especial relevance to religion, all of these features will

be shown to be true of participants in organized
education. That older people join religious
organizations and younger ones join educational
organizations may itself have significance in a
variety of ways, such as younger people tending
still to endeavour to explore while older ones
seek to reflect, etc. and even this is to be
discovered in some of the education for the
elderly activities (Thorsen 1978) which is
expressive in nature.

This section examines reported statistics from
eight relatively concurrent recent studies, although
it would have been possible to discuss many more
these eight have been used because they reflect
recent research in the United Kingdom and North
America. The statistics are discussed in relation
to the demographic and cultural variables mentioned
above and while it is recognised that these are
restricting the amount of research data that exists
it is sufficient for the purposes of this chapter,
which is necessarily selective since it would
otherwise merely report the findings of the
publications to which reference is made. The
eight studies are as follows; Sidwell (1980) who
conducted a questionnaire survey of sixty-three
evening and nine day modern language classes in
Leicestershire in the academic year 1978-79 in
which he gained a 41.7 per cent response rate from
1,139 students; Jarvis (1982a) surveyed all the
students in a small village centre in the first
week of the academic year 1978-79 in which 368
students (77.1 per cent response rate) replied;
the Advisory Council for Adult and Continuing
Education (1982b) commissioned an interview survey
between 28 January and 20 February 1980 to which
2,460 responded from 3,613; Daines et al (1982)
report on two surveys in six Dernyshire centres in
1976 and 1981; Killeen and Bird (1981) report on
paid educational leave in England and Wales in
1976-1977; Bryant (1982) conducted similar
research in Scotland and his data are for 1978;
Cross (1981) records participation rates in the
USA in organized education in 1978; Boshier and
Collins (1983) report data from forty eight
different pieces of research, all using the
education participation scale devised by Boshier,
in North America, Ghana, Singapore, Malaysia,
Hong Kong and the Canadian Artic in which 12,191
students were involved. This section has four
main sub-sections followed by a concluding
discussion.

Socio-Economic Class: It will be recalled that one
of the features of voluntary organizations is that
they have a middle class bias, with certain notable
exceptions, and a similar feature has been noted
about initial education e.g. Entwistle 1978.
Already in this study it has been pointed out that
both the culture and the curriculum of adult
education organizations is based towards the
middle classes, so that Westwood (1980:43) could
claim that:

> Adult education with its middle class bias,
> its uniformity within the common core
> curriculum ... has a re-inforcing role.
> But in relation to the concept of hegemony,
> it can be said to have a much clearer role
> in maintaining the status quo, engendering
> a state of consensus and contributing
> positively to the mechanisms whereby
> hegemony is maintained.

Obviously there are different theoretical perspectives between those who claim that they are
offering a service to the wider public and those
who argue that they are re-inforcing the status quo
and acting as a state ideological apparatus. But
the facts remain, that adult education organizations have a middle class membership to a very
large degree, as the following data demonstrate.
Sidwell records 82.9 per cent were from non-manual
classes while Leicestershire, as a whole, had
33.9 per cent of its population in these classes in
1977: Jarvis records that the great majority of
the participants at Lingfield were from the middle
classes; the Advisory Council survey records only
60 per cent of the current students in the sample
were non-manual; Daines et al note that in 1976
there were 61 per cent of the participants from
non-manual classes but by 1981 that figure had
increased to 76 per cent although the 1971 census
data revealed only 36 per cent of the population
as non-manual; both Killeen and Bird and Bryant
show that paid educational leave is not equally
distributed between occupational groups and
that professional and managerial personnel are
over-represented in the continuing education
courses; Cross reports that in the United States
those earning the highest salareis, while collar
workers, were more likely to attend adult
education courses; Boshier and Collins suggest
that the occupational role was more likely
to be at a level between skilled manual and

clerical/sales (17.59 per cent), manager/
administrator (10.66 per cent) and technical
educational/professional (37.29 per cent).
    Hence it may be seen that all of these studies
provide conclusive empirical evidence that there
is a middle class bias in the composition of the
adult student body attending courses of all types.
Hence, it needs to be asked whether the middle
class ethos of adult education is a cause of the
middle class clientele or whether the latter is
a cause of the former.   It will be recalled that
Griffin (1983) argued that it is essential to
consider the nature of the curriculum is considerations such as this.   It must be recognised that
the mode of presentation of knowledge is biased
towards the middle classes both in terms of
language and content.   Hence, the curriculum
considerations imply that the middle class ethos
in education is a cause of the middle class
clientele.   Additionally, the school experiences
of adults whilst they were undertaking their
initial education also selected out those who were
labelled as successful in education and those who
saw themselves as failures within the organizational culture (Willis 1977:52-88).   Hence, the
individual biography is a constituent factor in
the middle class ethos of the adult education
organization.   This combination of factors is
such that it is hardly surprising that adult
educators have tried to reach out from the
organization into the community in order to offer
an educational service to the working class.
Lovett (1975:37) notes how an attempt was made to
interest parents in a dockland school in Liverpool
in the history of the area but, despite having a
well-known local historian, the project was
abortive.   But the venue was a school and the
curriculum was middle class!   A beetle drive was
successful there but a history course was not!
When the curriculum is adapted and relevant to
the immediate needs and experience of the learners,
then there may be more participation (Lambers and
Griffiths 1983).   Relevant is seen as useful in
an instrumental sense in the context of the work
reported by Lambers and Griffiths of adapting the
Open University materials for informal learning
groups.   Perhaps the instrumentality of the
subject is significant, since Boshier and Collins
note that the main reason for the enrolment of many
working class groups in education is professional
advancement while the higher occupational groups

enrol out of cognitive interest. Hence it may be
seen that the expressive bias of liberal adult
education, the idea of education for education's
sake and Dewey's (1916:50) claim 'that the educational process has no end beyond itself; it is its
own end' is a statement of middle class values and
if the middle classes seek to impose their values
on the working classes in adult education then the
working classes do not participate.

Sex of Participants: The stereotypical image of
liberal adult education is that it is a middle class
women's leisure pursuit and stereotypes rarely
emerge without some substance, so that it is not
surprising that the statistics recorded below give
some support for the stereotype. Sidwell records
that 54.9 per cent of the participants in his survey
of language classes were women; Jarvis discovered
that 87.8 per cent of the respondents to his survey
were women; the Advisory Council survey claimed
that 13 per cent of the women in its survey were
studying but only 11 per cent of the men but it also
specifies that the men's courses were more likely to
be work-related than were the women's; Daines et al
report that between 1976 and 1981 the proportion of
men attending local adult education in South East
Derbyshire declined from 28 per cent to 25 per cent;
Cross' statistics for the United States are very
similar to those discovered by the Advisory Council,
with 12.7 per cent of the women studying but only
10.7 per cent of the men. By contrast, Killeen and
Bird (1980:46) write that whereas 'two in five
workers are female, only one in six of those who
receive P.E.L. (paid educational leave provided in a
college is a woman and that men receive far more of
all educational leave than women! Bryant specifies
that in Scotland 80 per cent of the leave went to
men but he (1982:57) writes that employers claim
that women 'were reluctant to take up offers' of
paid educational leave. Boshier and Collins report
that 69.56 per cent of the 11,567 respondents who
revealed their sex in the surveys were women but
they note that men were much more likely to enrol
in courses for social contact, social stimulation,
professional advancement or community service
whereas women were more inclined to specify that
they enrolled out of cognitive interest. There is,
therefore, a total consistancy about these date:
men are more likely to have an instrumental
orientation to their education while women are

more likely to have an expressive orientation.
Thus it may be seen that the education of
adults merely reproduces the sexual division of
labour in society. Traditionally , the male role
has been instrumental and the female role
expressive, the male has been the leader and the
female has been concerned with the emotive, person-
orientated element of life. It is perhaps
significant here to note Parson's (1951:49)
discussion of these two concepts: he defines
instrumentality as goal-attainment whereas
expressiveness is not an orientation 'to the
attainment of a goal anticipated for the future'.
Hence, the traditional female role of expressiveness
is closer to the ideology of liberal adult
education than is the traditional male role. It
is perhaps hardly surprising that liberal adult
education may attract more women to it.
Even so, these orientations are themselves social
constructs, since they themselves reflect the
sexual division of labour. Nevertheless, by so
doing it may be seen that the education of adults
approaches and re-inforces the sexual division of
labour in society and, in effect, the division of
labour in society. Consequently, feminists have
discussed this function of the education of
adults in some detail. Thompson (1983:61-75),
for instance, argues that adult education is
patriarchal and in the sense that it is male
dominated and controlled with females playing a
subordinate role, she is totally correct. However,
it is possible to argue that the sexual division
of labour in the education of adults reproduces
the capitalist social system, so that Deem
(1978:53) claims that:

> Girls (in school) ... are treated and seen
> in quite separate ways from male pupils.
> Thus, on leaving school, most girls are
> prepared only or mainly for the traditional
> place of women in the sexual division of
> labour: the home and family.
> The results of this process of estab-
> lishing sex differences are entirely satis-
> factory for the capitalist labour market
> and society in general. Workers are cared
> for by women, new potential workers are
> borne and socialized within the family,
> and women are also available - either
> before or after marriage if economic neces-
> sity or culture dictates - for a variety

of unskilled, low paid, temporary or
part-time jobs.

Thus it may be seen that adult and continuing education reproduces the sexual division of labour in
society and the recent curtailment of liberal adult
education in order to increase vocational provision,
merely reflects that women's opportunities, even in
leisure, are still subject to male dominance and
are regarded as something that is dispensable when
it is claimed that it cannot be afforded.

Educational Background of Participants: It will be
recalled that Bourdieu (1973) argued that those
having cultural capital would benefit most from
education and he showed statistics that supported
his argument. Hence, it would be expected that
those voluntarily continuing their education would
be in possession of some educational capital
already. Sidwell showed 71.5. of those studying a
language in an adult education institute in
Leicestershire had studied a language at school,
8.1 per cent had done so in further education and
5.3 per cent at university. He also discovered that
38.7 per cent had attended a language class
previously. Similarly, Daines et al showed that in
their 1976 survey 60 per cent of the participants
had completed their full-time education by the age
of fifteen years but by 1981 that proportion had
declined to 38 per cent. In contrast, the proportion who had continued their education beyond
sixteen years had increased from 21 per cent to
35 per cent during the same period. Surprisingly,
they offer little comment or interpretation about
any of the statistics that they record so that they
are of limited value. No reference is made here to
the paid educational leave studies because the
element of voluntariness is less evident but Cross
showed that in the United States there is a relationship between the length of initial education as
a contributory factor in pursuing further. Of the
8.405 participants whose educational background were
recorded in Boshier's and Collin's study, 22 per
cent already had a university degree.
    The previous educational experiences of indivi-
duals is usually regarded as a good indicator of
future participation and as such it confirms
Bourdieu's thesis. Nevertheless, it has to be
recognised that logically just because individuals
have experienced education in the past is no reason
why they should desire it again in the future.

Hence, there must be at least one other factor in this relationship that would motivate people to continue to learn. Boviously, there are many factors, Aslanian and Brickell (1982) record life transitions, Jarvis (1983b) suggests disjuncture between a person's stock of knowledge and his socio-cultural environment, and a variety of others have been suggested. However, one other factor that is significant here is the fact that most individuals will seek to re-enact pleasant experiences and eschew unpleasant ones. Individuals who had a pleasant and successful initial education are more likely therefore, to seek to continue their education than those whose initial education was unpleasant and unsuccessful. Hence, the self-perception of the participant and his perception of education also act as factors in participation in further education.

Age of Participants: Earlier in this chapter it was noted that older people tend to join religious organizations and it was suggested that younger ones tend to join educational ones. This latter suggestion is actually what has been discovered. Sidwell reported that 40.8 per cent of his respondents were between 25-39 years of age; Jarvis found 62.0 per cent of his survey between 22-45 years; the Advisory Council survey discovered 71 per cent of those currently studying under 45 years old; Daines et al noted that between 1976 and 1981 there had been an increase from 38 per cent to 46 per cent of the student population under 35 years old and a disproportionately small proportion of the students over 55 years old in comparison with the census data, but once again there is insufficient statistical analysis to allow many conclusions to be drawn from these findings. Killeen and Bird (1980:42) claim that 'those under thirty years of age have a relatively high liability to receive P.E.L., and those over thirty years of age have a low liability'. Cross discovered an inverse rela-tionship between age and the likelihood of participation in adult education and she (1981:56) claims that this reflects 'certain socialized expectations about the role of education at various life states'. The mean age of the 11,684 students recording their age in all the research reported by Boshier and Collins was 35.34 years with a standard deviation of 14.70 years, so that once again all the statistics indicate similar findings.
    While Cross may be correct when she maintains

that people have been socialized into the expectation that education is for the young, she would
need to produce research evidence of this in order
to substantiate her claim. Obviously age is a
barrier to access and this will be noted in the
following section but the increasing amount of
emphasis on education for the elderly, e.g. pre-
retirement education, elder hostels, University of
the Third Age, etc. have all helped to begin to
destroy the myth that the elderly are incapable of
learning. Indeed, Boshier and Collins note that the
reason why older people enrol on courses is that
they are interested in learning for its own sake
whereas younger persons were more likely to suggest
professional advancement as a reason for continuing
their education. Hence, it may be seen once again
that the instrumental role is attributed to the
young and the expressive one to the elderly, so that
education also reproduces the age division of labour
in society. There is little need here to repeat the
type of argument discussed previously when the
sexual division of labour was the subject of the
deliberation, but this is quite a significant
element in this discussion since it could be argued
that instrumentality is clearly connected with work
and expressiveness with leisure. However, it could
be argued that as the amoung of leisure increases in
society so the opportunity will exist to study for
the sake of learning. While this may be true, it
will only be so with those who already have the
cultural capital to benefit from such an organized
leisure time pursuit. Indeed, as liberal adult
education is curtailed and the fees rise it may only
be those who have sufficient wealth to afford to pay
the fees who will be able to enjoy liberal adult
education.

Thus far it will be noted that basic education
has not been discussed apparent. Adult basic education has a perceived immediate relevance i.e. it
is instrumental and it is offered freely to those
who have neither and cultural capital nor the
finance to pay for the service. There is a sense
that this may be regarded as something that the
state can support as a residual need and once
initial education has been improved then adult
basic education will be no longer necessary.

From the above discussion it may be concluded
that educational participation is not merely a
matter of motive or intent by participants, but it
is something that is clearly related to both the
individual's position in the social system and

also to his position in the life cycle. Boshier
and Collins (1983:175) concluded that:

> All E.P.S. (educational participation scale)
> scores were variously related to the life
> cycle and the socio-economic variables
> employed. The result provides general
> support for the notion that motivational
> orientations are related to socio-economic
> and other attributes of the participant's
> 'life space'.

Such a conclusion is hardly surprising sociologically but it needed a large scale research undertaking to demonstrate what is self-evidently true
to those who practise adult education. One of the
significant points of this discussion has been
that psychological factors have hardly entered the
debate: this is not to deny the psychological
factors nor the relevance of the psychological
research that has been conducted that it is to
emphasize the significance of realizing that the
individual is not free of social constraints and
rational, etc. He may well be constrained by
social factors of which he is unaware, so that the
socialogical correlations are important.

One theoretical piece of work that has
endeavoured to take into account the social
pressures is that by Miller (1967) who endeavoured
to produce a model that showed that certain forces
operated upon the individual, depending upon his
position in the social structure, that either drove
him or prevented him from participating in adult
education. His work was a combination of Malsow's
hierarchy of needs and Lewin's field force
analysis. He claimed that for those people who
are in the lower-lower class there are four
positive forces: survival needs, changing technology, safety needs of the female culture and
governmental attempts to change the opportunity
structure. By contrast, the negative forces are:
action-excitement orientation of the male culture,
hostility to education and to middle class object
orientation, relative absence of specific immediate
job opportunities at the end of training, limited
access through organizational ties and weak family
structure. However, he maintained that lower
middle class individuals had no negative forces
in their culture and he listed the following
positive forces: satisfy survival and safety needs,
strong status need, changing technology, access
through organizational ties, acceptance of middle

class career drives and familiarity with educational
processes. It may be seen immediately that Miller
has listed many of the points that have become
apparent during the above discussion. Even so,
were there no negative forces in the lower middle
class sub-culture and system, he would have to
account why so many lower middle class people do
not attend adult and continuing education. Such
a model, while useful, is patently over-simple and
Long (1983:124-125) claims that it has one other
basic weakness and that is that it is based upon
a questionable conceptual foundation, i.e., Maslow's
hierarchy of needs. There have been other
conceptual approaches to participation and some of
these are cited in Cross (1981) and Long (1983)
but they do not raise the sociological issues in
quite this way, nor are they based on rigorous
empirical research. One reason for citing Miller
here is to indicate that there are negative social
forces that act as barriers to participation and
that constitute the subject of the final section of
this chapter.

Barriers To Access
Miller's (1967) rather simplistic model postulated
some negative forces to participation and,
obviously, these must exist or else everybody would
participate. The Advisory Council survey (1982b)
records some data about non-participants in adult
and continuing education and it delineates four
types:

- Did not wish to participate in the past
  and do not wish to do so in the future: 15%
  of the population fall into this category
  and this lack of interest is positively
  correlated with ageing but inversely related
  to economic class.
- Did not wish to participate in the past
  but would like to do so in the future: 14%
  of the population fall into this category,
  slightly more men that women but the
  difference is insignificant and there appears
  to be no relationship to age or class.
- Wished to participate in the past but did
  not and do not wish to do so in the future:
  6% of the population fall into this category, more women than men and this group
  are more likely to be older and from the
  lower classes.
- Wished to participate in the past and would

like to do so in the future: 15 per cent
of the population fall into this category,
slightly more women than men but the
difference is insignificant, they are
distributed quite evenly throughout the
population but with slightly more working
class people intending to participate in
the future.

Thus it may be seen that 50 per cent of the
population come into these four categories: in
actual fact the Advisory Council survey (1982b:84)
discovered 51 per cent who had not participated in
any form of post-initial education but in the break-
down the above statistics are reached. 47 per cent
had definitely participated (the remaining 2 per
cent were actually in full-time study during the
time of the survey) and of these 6 per cent had
participated in the past but had no intention of so
doing in the future. These tended to be older than
the remainder of the population.
From the survey it is possible to conclude
that ageing acts as a barrier to participation in
education, despite all the efforts to provide
education for the elderly. Whether these efforts
will change the current picture remains to be seen
in the fugure. Since 59 per cent (ACACE 1982b:95)
were also unaware of the local providers of adult
education there is sufficient reason for the
existence of an advisory service, but the added
impetus for the establishment of such a service
is to increase the amount of participation in an
educational service which is at present under
threat.
However, the Advisory Council survey made no
attempt to discover what barriers actually exist,
although it may be concluded from all the surveys
thus far reported that there are many. In
America, Carp, Peterson and Roelfs (1974)
discovered three sets of perceived barriers:
situational, institutional and dispositional.
Among the potential learners, the cost of the course
is the more prevalent situational barrier and
while Daines et al (1982) imply this, they do not
actually demonstrate that a relationship exists.
Among other significant barriers are time and
home and occupational responsibilities.
Institutional is taken here to refer specifically
to the barriers created by the organization and as
it was suggested earlier these constitute a
paradox of provision, the need to organize may

act as a barrier to some people.   This is
certainly the case in the findings of Carp et al.
They discovered that the inability to attend the
organization at the time that the course that
interested the potential learner was one of the
barriers.   Three other prevalent institutional
barriers were lack of information, the bureaucratic
procedure and the non-provision of relevant
courses.   It might be claimed that the last of
these could arise out of ignorance of what the
organization actually provides, thus providing a
reason for advertising the provision; but if it is
true then it indicates the failure of educational
organizations to discover the learning requirements
of its potential clientele and is, therefore,
merely an indictment of bad market research.
Among the dispositional factors are that the
potential learner is too old to learn, lacks
confidence and does not really enjoy studying.   The
last two of these may reflect the potential
learners' experiences at school and stereotype of
ageing again appears prevalent.   Obviously there
is need for a great deal more research into non-
participation in order to understand fully why
individuals do not wish to join in formal
education and to discover if individual learning
is related in any way to non-participation.

Conclusion

> It is ironic that those adults who are most
> advantaged in terms of education background,
> occupational status, and family income
> are more likely to participate in adult and
> continuing educational programs than are
> less advantaged adults who have most to
> gain from such programs.
> (Niemi and Nagel 1979:139-140)

Perhaps 'ironic' is the wrong word since the social
forces that advantage some people, disadvantage
others and those who are enabled to take advantage
of educational provision are already the advantaged.
Hence, it is a social reality but one that many
adult educators would seek to change, but to do so
necessitates social change of tremendous propor-
tions.   The alternative is to 'win' the occasional
individual and leave the system untouched and this,
it appears, is the more likely.
    Having examined the interface between the
educational organization and the wider society, it

213

is now necessary to analyse the processes that
occur in the organization itself.

Chapter Fourteen

INTERACTION WITHIN THE ORGANIZATION

Adult and continuing education studies have
concentrated upon teaching methods in respect
of interaction within the organization, so that
Legge (1971:83) produces some very familiar group
interaction diagrams but does so in the context
of the discussion method rather than the study of
the group. It is perhaps natural that the
practicalities of teaching and learning should
precede other theoretical elements in the
understanding of adult and continuing education.
Nevertheless, there is considerable body of
literature about interaction within the organization
and within the group that is relevant to adult
education and the intention of this chapter is to
begin to apply some of it.   Four aspects have been
selected here for study, although the body of
literature is far wider than this: interaction
and registration, the student role, classroom
interaction and group behaviour.

Interaction on Registration
Every bureaucratic organization requires a reception
staff, a primary function of that staff being to
ascertain the requirements of the potential clients
and to help them make contact with the appropriate
member of the staff of the organization.   This
appears, on the surface, to be a simple function,
and so it is, if this is all that the receptionist
is required to do.   However, studies in fields
other than adult and continuing education have
tended to suggest that this is not what actually
occurs.   It is also likely, consequently, that
this is also the case with the reception staff in
colleges of further and higher education and in
institutes of adult education, but no research has
been conducted about it, so that it is necessary

to examine research literature in other professional occupations.

Hall (1977:141) notes that because the function of the reception staff in a social service agency appears to be passive it is rarely examined. Yet he discovered that in the agency where he conducted his research, no precise outline of the duties and functions of the reception staff exist, although that seems to be general agreement among senior staff about what the receptionist should be doing. However, no training is provided and the parameters of the job are not defined. Hence, the receptionists use their common sense and just acquire their knowledge as they gain experience. But the lack of parameters results in the receptionists extending their roles, often with the tacit approval of the professional staff, into areas which should be the concern of the latter. For instance, among the receptionist's duties is the expectation that the clients' requirements will be ascertained by the receptionist. Hence, the receptionist actually conducts the initial interview with the client and, if untrained, may extend that interview by asking the client the reasons for their requirement. Knowing the reason, since most clients are most likely to provide it, the receptionist may make a suggestion in response to the situation and when the client actually sees the professional his request may have actually been formulated and narrowed by the receptionist. However, it is not far removed from ascertaining the reason for an interview, and even helping the client formulate his request, to actually providing advice and guidance. Hall (1977:145-146) is only too well aware of this:

> a second important 'reception service' is the provision of advice and guidance. Reception staff are constantly faced with the problem of dealing with clients when no officer is available to see them. The lack of any specific appointments system coupled with other factors such as high mobility of officers in the course of their work, result in a large number of 'wasted visits' by clients to the office. ... When a client 'has' explained her problems to the receptionist and (an officer) is unable to see her, the natural reaction of the receptionist is to advise as best she can in the absence of more professional assistance.

While the additional responsibility and feeling of
service may increase the job satisfaction of the
receptionist, it may not necessarily result in the
client receiving the best possible advice.

Clearly this a pattern that relates not only
to the reception staff in a social service agency
but to them in all organizational settings,
including adult and continuing education. As
educational organizations do not have full-time
advisers for enquiries of this nature it is often
difficult for the reception staff to find an
educator when an enquiry arises, so that much advice
may be provided by secretarial and administrative
staff. It is not hard to recognise either of the
situations described above in the context of adult
education. Firstly, a potential student seeking
advice about the best courses to follow to achieve
a specific qualification and the reception staff
making a specific suggestion. Hence, when the
enquirer sees an adult educator he merely asks
when the course suggested by the secretary is being
held. Neither is it difficult to imagine the
secretary actually providing the advice and
guidance, because there is no educator present.
Such advice and guidance may actually be given to
a potential student over the telephone, with the
enquirer being completely unaware that the person
providing it is only a secretary. The more that
adult and continuing education organizations
advertise their willingness to provide an educational counselling service, the more likelihood
that the above situations could occur, so that it
is most important that the actual mechanism of
advice and guidance in adult and continuing education is fully investigated.

The Adult Student Role

The student role is traditionally a role played by
a child or a young person but it is not usually a
role that it is expected that adults play. Hence,
the student role is not one that usually comes
within the stereotype of adulthood. The student
role, therefore, is not seen as an adult role and
there is a tendency for adults new to the role
to perform it in the same way that a younger
person would. Hence, the stereotype of the student
may actually be one of the barriers to participation and the difficulty that adults actually
discover in performing this role for the first time
is one of the reasons why adult educators place
such stress on the first meeting of any course since

they claim that they can put new students at their
ease, or define for them the way that they should
perform the role.

Ruddock (1972:18) highlights this problem for
the adult student thus:

> the student in Further and Adult education
> often expects the teacher to expect
> submissive behaviour. Further, when it
> becomes clear that the teacher welcomes
> self-assertion on the part of the student,
> a class may show their disapproval,
> because their role expectations have been
> upset.

This highlights the problem of adult student role
definition, since the traditional definition of the
student role is to sit passively and learn from the
teacher, who is the fount of wisdom. However,
teachers of adults may have to help adult students
redefine their student role and this may only
occur successfully if the student is at ease with
the teacher and the class. However, not all
teachers of adults have the role expectation
that Ruddock implies. Indeed, many of them have a
more traditional definition of the role, so that
they re-inforce the stereotype of the younger
student and this is especially true if they have
experienced nothing else.   Harries-Jenkins (1982:
20) points out that many of these tutors are
products of traditional adult education in which
the student role may be defined in the traditional
sense. He notes that the good student is
often defined by the tutor

> within a framework of educational criteria
> which value cohesion rather than conflict,
> excellence rather than equality and
> achievement rather than participation.

Yet students are at different stages of the life
cycle, do come from different socio-economic
backgrounds and do have different levels of
knowledge and experience, so he claims that the
good student role requires careful re-examination.
He recognises that role is a creative exercise
rather than a pre-determined one.   Hence, adults
are not actually involved in performing a role that
is determined for them by a tutor or by a stereotype, but this is not to claim that the tutor's
definition of the role is not taken into

consideration. Indeed, it may play a significant part in the way that the adult finally creates his role, but that the final product is a negotiation in which the students' 'different and often conflicting interests and capacities' (Harries-Jenkins 1982:27) have a part to play. Hence, the adult student role is a creative exercise rather than a prescribed performance and since the student is only part-time in many instances his perception of his role will be re-inforced from his wider social and cultural experiences as well as by the organizational climate. Hence, Harries-Jenkins (1982:29-37) suggests that these wider experiences which interrelate in each student may be classified as: social, personal, and institutional. Thus , he concludes that a definition of the good student in adult education that rests only on educational criteria is of limited value and that the wider conceptual framework is necessary in order to understand the role more fully.

Harries-Jenkins has, therefore, offered a conceptual framework that encourages educators of adults to recognise the whole field in which the adult functions and to break away from the rather limited traditional perspective. He has suggested that interactionism offers a better theoretical basis to understand the way that students perform and that educators should comprehend these factors on entering such a negotiation. Indeed, interactionism forms the basis for much of the analysis in this chapter, although not all interactionists have attempted to place the actor in as wide a social context as Harries-Jenkins does.

Classroom Interaction
Interactionism is perhaps the best theoretical perspective from which to analyse classroom behaviour in an adult class, in which the negotiated order to the classroom is discussed. Perhaps the approach adopted by Strauss et al (1973) in which they examined the way in which the patterns of behaviour were negotiated in accordance with the differing positions of the actors in the social hierarchy. They showed how professionals interacted with non-professionals and showed how taken-for-granted order was negotiated between the actors which resulted in stability. However, with the change in personnel a new order had to be negotiated and they demonstrate how the actors can themselves break unwritten contracts which lead to

new negotiations of order.   Such an approach is
very relevant to interaction in the classroom and
many studies of interaction in the classroom in
initial education exist.   One study that highlights
the idea of negotiated order and the respect for
unwritten roles, etc. is that by Werthman (1971)
who showed how young people from gangs in San
Francisco responded to different teachers in the
classroom, respecting some and rejecting others.
Obviously, but perhaps unfortunately, a great deal
of adult and continuing education will be much more
restricted in its clientele than this but the
same perspective is highly relevant.
     Another important interactionist approach is
that of Goffman (1971) whose study of the way
individuals present themselves in everyday life is
a most enlightening undertaking.   The way in which
adult students perform in the classroom and the
way that the teacher of adults performs would be an
interesting study.   Goffman liken social interaction to a drama in which individuals perform their
roles, even to the extent of preparing the stage
on which the performance is to be played.   Hence,
it is possible to see how the teacher of adults
prepares the classroom for the students e.g. the
arrangement of the furniture in the classroom
and where he places himself.   Hence, if the
teacher wishes to perform a didactic teaching role
all the desks and chairs will be in serried ranks
facing the stage on which he is to perform but if
the teacher wishes the students to participate
then the tables and chairs are arranged accordingly.
In precisely the same manner the way that the
adult student acts his part may be demonstrated
in his facial expressions, his mannerisms and even
the act of confidence presented when he arrives in
the classroom for the first time.   Students may
be seeking to manage the impressions that they
create in precisely the same way as   the teacher
of adults at the same time .   As teacher and
students each perform their roles, so the classroom
becomes an arena in which the order is negotiated
and the unwritten rules learned.   But once that
sub-culture has been created it is difficult for
a newcomer to enter into the complexity of the
order that has been negotiated.   The newcomer
is rather like Schutz's (1971) stranger who has
not participated in the history of the creation
in the classroom culture, so that it does not have
the authority of a tested system for him.   Until
he can acquire that culture and internalize it,

until he has learned the way that the class say
things and what the hidden meanings are, he is still
outside of the group. The greater the group
cohesiveness, the harder it is for a stranger to
become a member of the in-group and learn to
perform a role within it. Hence, it may be seen
that interactionist theory and research offer a
way of analysing adult behaviour in the classroom
that would highlight many aspects of the teaching
and learning transaction. Indeed, it is suggested
here that some of the basic elements of interactionism might be employed with understanding to
enhance teaching and learning, since according to
Brundage and Mackeracher (1980) adults learn best
in social situations in which they feel at ease
and esteemed.

Another approach that has been devised as
a theoretical model of group facilitation by Heron
(1977) could also prove the basis for research into
teacher interaction with the class is the six
dimensions of the facilitator style. Heron
(1977:3) suggests that the facilitator may act
along any of the following six dimensions:
directive-nondirective ; interpretative-
noninterpretative; confronting-nonconfronting;
cathartic-noncathartic; structuring-nonstructuring;
disclosing-nondisclosing. While these categories
have been devised to train group leaders, they do
provide a basis upon which classroom interaction
may be analysed since they analyse and interpret
the mode of interaction between the teacher
and the class.

In all of these approaches thus far mentioned
the place of language has not been explicit and this
is because the language of the adult classroom is
another unresearched area. Considerable work has
been undertaken into the language of school
children in the classroom and even the social class
language differences. For instance, Bernstein's
(1973) well known distinction between elaborated
and restrictive speech codes has demonstrated the
problems that working class children have in a
middle class educational organization. Since
Bernstein discovered that the elaborated speech
code in absent to a considerable extent from
working class adults attending middle class
educational organizations will be as deprived as
they were as children attending initial education.

Flanders (1970) discovered that in initial
education teachers talk for 68 per cent of the time,
children contribute 20 per cent of the time and the

remainder is either silence or confusion. This is
an interesting approach to the analysis of classroom interaction since it uses a category analysis
similar to the approach that could be devised
from Heron's (1977) work. However, Flanders uses
seven categories of teacher talk: accepting
feelings, praising or encouraging, accepting or
using pupil's ideas, asking questions, lecturing,
giving directions and criticizing or justifying
authority. He has only two categories of pupil-
talk: imitation and response. Finally, he has
the category of confusion or silence. Flanders
claimed that teaching and talking were synonymous
in his findings. But such a finding would almost
certainly be unfounded in adult and continuing
education. It is suggested here that adult student
talk would have to be extended into a number of
additional categories, such as: questioning each
other, responding to each other, contributing
observations, making affective/conciliatory
statements. In this way it would be possible to
analyse the complex modes of interaction, since
sometimes the class may operate as a single unit
and other times it may be sub-divided. Silence,
however, may be less significant.

This very brief section has examined some of
the approaches to classroom interaction that have
been utilised successfully in schools and other
interactionist approaches that might form the
basis of research in adult education. As yet
little or no data exist about interaction in the
classroom in adult and continuing education but
it is necessary to discover and analyse the process
so that it can contribute to the discussion about
teaching adults being similar to or different from
teaching children. It is suggested that this is
an area in which research will occur in the near
future, especially as the training of adult
educators is becoming more prevalent. Indeed, it
is necessary to have such evidence in order to
enrich the training process itself. However,
before examining adult education as an occupation
one other important element of interaction remains
to be discussed.

Group Behaviour
Small group discussion is a common occurrence in
adult and continuing learners to express and
exchange experiences etc. about a specific topic.
Yet this is frequently undertaken without
understanding the dynamics of small groups,

despite the fact that the literature on the topic
is voluminious. This section cannot hope to
reproduce it all, but three relevant areas are
selected out for discussion: leadership roles,
group decisions and social influence.

Leadership: Often some of the research about
leadership is referred to in discussions about
teaching styles, e.g. Rogers (1977), Jarvis (1983b).
However, it is less frequently referred to in
respect to the discussions that occur in the small
groups and yet once the teacher of adults has
created a tutor-less group students begin to
play leadership roles. Two major types of role
emerge in small groups of this nature: authoritarian and democratic. The authoritarian leader
wields considerable power in the group, he tends
to determine group policies and tasks and he also
often attempts to prevent other people participating
in the decision making process. Groups that have
an authoritarian leader tend to become dependent
upon him and the group's survival is at risk if
he is not present. Authoritarian leaders,
according to Krech et al (1962:434), encourage a
segregated group structure in which the development
of close interpersonal relationships between
members is inhibited. This lessens the attracti-
veness of the group for its members and may make
the adult education class less enjoyable for its
members. This is especially true when there
are more than one person in the group who would
like to be the authoritarian leader because it
results in frustration and conflict between the
potential leaders and, often, other members of
the group playing a less significant role than
they would have done otherwise. Once, however,
there is a leader, the group may appear to function
smoothly and in the plenary reporting sessions
it may appear that the group has reached a
conclusion but what may have occurred is that the
authoritarian leader had imposed his solution/
interpretation/response upon the group. In
this case, the small group has defeated the
purpose for which it was established and instead
of having the teacher's interpretation a student's
interpretation is substituted.
    By contrast, democratic leadership is the type
that seeks to evoke the maximum involvement and
participation in the activities of the group by
all its members. The democratic leader endeavours
to spread responsibility rather than concentrate

it and he is concerned with the interpersonal relationships within the group. Hence, he will seek to diffuse any tension and potential conflict and he seeks always to carry out the mandate of the group. Unlike the authoritarian leader, the democratic leader seeks to create a group that can survive without him. However, for this group to survive and function effectively there needs to be greater task motivation from the members and in adult and continuing education, especially when it is voluntary attendance, it may be assumed that this motivation exists. Hence, the group may enjoy its interpersonal relationships, seek to ensure that the task is done. However, it must be noted that if the motivation does not exist the group may not function as effectively as the authoritarian-led group. Nevertheless, at the plenary report back session the democratic group may not have reached a decision and this is reported, since in this instance the group leader does not seek to impose his solution upon the group.

It is possible, therefore, to see these two types of leadership within the context of instrumentality and expressiveness and, in this instance, the expressive type of leadership may be seen to be truer to the ideology of adult education. Indeed, the authoritarian leader in the group is simply imposing an 'education from above' even though 'the above' in this case, is still at the student level. Nevertheless, the types of leadership that emerge in the small group discussion is an important consideration in the analysis of interaction within the classroom.

Group Decisions: Much of the early work on leadership was conducted by Lewin (1952) who was also responsible for studying the mechanics of group decision making and the effects that it had upon behaviour. Two studies were conducted that sought to investigate the effectiveness of different methods of changing attitudes and behaviour. In the first, groups of American housewives were encouraged to eat beefhearts, sweetbreads and kidneys, foods that were generally absent from American diets. Some of the groups were lectured to, during which time they were told of the health and economic advantages their diets accordingly. Other groups were presented with precisely the same information but were encouraged to discuss it among themselves and at the end of the session were asked to indicate by a show of hands if they intended to serve the foods. A follow-up study showed that 3 per cent of those who attended the lectures but 32 per cent of those who participated in the discussion groups actually, served the foods. A similar study amongst farmers' wives in Iowa was conducted at the time of the birth of their child. Tehy were informed either by lecture or group discussion about the advantage of giving their children orange juice and cod liver oil and a follow-up study revealed similar results. The reason for this may be that group pressure acts upon the individual to produce conformity, to which the individual then adheres after having left the group.

This clearly has significant implications for teaching because the group discussion may provide the opportunity for adult students to exchange ideas and experiences with each other but at the same time if it operates in such a way as to reach decisions it may produce conformity to the group, something that may be contrary to the aims and objectives of the process of educating adults. Indeed, some adult educators suggest that the process of reflection can occur within the group but such a claim remains completely unsubstantiated in this type of group.

Social Influence: However, research has shown that the group acts in an even more significant manner upon individuals, producing conformity for a variety of reasons. Asch (1955) has showed in a series of experiments that under group pressure some individuals conform, while others remain independent. However, of those that conform there are three different types of conformity:

> Distortion of Perception - a few people actually yield totally to the pressure of the group and have their perception changed, so that they report perceiving an event in the same manner as the group pressure suggests that they should.
> Distortion of judgment - more individuals actually consider that their perception was incorrect and judged the group to be correct, so that they adjusted their judgment to the group pressure.
> Distortion of Action - these individuals neither doubted their perception nor

their judgment but they did not wish to
appear different from the majority of
the group, so they acted in a conformist
manner.

Crutchfield (cited Krech et al 1962) subsequently
replicated Asch's work in a totally different
setting, this time exposing the individual only to
the group results without actually being in the
small group.   Hence, it may be concluded that
some types of individual are more likely to yield
to the pressure of the group than are others.
Both Asch and Crutchfield report that those who
remained independent of the group tended to be
more intelligent, self-confident, leaders and were
less conventional in respect of rules and
regulations.   But those more likely to conform
were more anxious, conventional, authoritarian and
unable to tolerate ambiguity.
   Thus it may be seen that the small group is a
teaching method that needs considerable research
since these researches suggest that the group
method may create social conformity rather than
independent thinkers.   It should be recalled that
Lifton (1961) showed the effectiveness of the
group in though reform in Chinese prisons.
Obviously the conditions were totally different
but the group effects were not insignificant.

Conclusion
Interactionism is an important theoretical and
research method in the study of individuals in
organizations.   Obviously it only describes the on-
going process rather than the ideological or
specifically educational elements.   Even so, it
has been employed with considerable benefit in
initial education.   Harries-Jenkins (1982)
correctly suggested that it could also be employed
beneficially in adult and continuing education,
although it has not been so employed.   However,
this chapter has outlined four areas of interaction:
in reception, in perception of the student role,
in interaction in the classroom and in the small
group.   Each is relevant to the education of
adults and since much adult education is part time
it is important to recognise, as does Harries-
Jenkins, that the reference groups of the individual
as well as his other membership groups all play
a sginificant part in the way that adults perform
their student role in the educational
organization.

Chapter Fifteen

THE EDUCATOR OF ADULTS

Educators of adults, like most other employed
people, work within an organization and like them,
adult educators suffer similar satisfactions,
constraints and problems.   Because adult education
is organized it is significant to note that
unless there is an existential relationship between
the organization and educator, the individual is
not actually an educator;   it is having a contrac-
tual relationship that enables a social definition
of an occupation to occur.   The educator of
adults has been subject to more research and more
literature than almost any other area of adult
education although some of it is not based upon a
firm or a wide theoretical base.   Even so, the
basic research findings can be used to construct
a more thorough theoretical understanding, so that
this chapter, in contrast to the preceding one,
utilises much more empirical research and seeks to
construct a sociological understanding of the
occupation of adult educator.   Since some of these
ideas have been published elsewhere (Jarvis 1983b:
179-209) there will be some overlapping between
that chapter and this one.   However, the
theoretical perspective here is more specifically
sociological, so that the intention of the two
chapters is totally different.   This chapter has
three main sections: the occupation of educator
of adults;   occupations within organizations;   the
professionalization of the education of adults.

The Occupation of Educator of Adults
It is extremely difficult to determine how many
people are actually employed to teach adults since
it is almost impossible to draw parameters around
this occupational group and delimit it.   Obviously,
a salesman teaching his client how to use a

complicated piece of machinery that he has just
sold him may be teaching his client but he is not
employed as an educator of adults.   But a
lecturer in a college of further education who
spends the majority of his time teaching sixteen
year olds and two hours a week teaching adults may
be considered an adult educator, although he spends
less time per week actually teaching adults than
does the salesman.   Hence, the fact that an
individual is employed by an educational organization is quite fundamental to the definition of
the occupation.   Hall (1969:5-6) actually defines
an occupation as:

> a social role performed by adult members
> of society that directly and/or indirectly
> yields social and financial consequences
> and that constitutes a major focus in the
> life of an adult.

Hall's definition contains four basic components:
social role, social consequences, remuneration and
a major life focus.   Whilst it is possible to
dispute the validity of this definition, it does
reflect a considerable amount of research into
occupations so that it is proposed to adopt it
here and once it is adopted it is realized that
each of these four elements can be discussed in
detail, although there is no reason here to discuss
remuneration.

Social Role: The social role of many full-time
adult educators may be that of organizer,
administrator and manager rather than teacher.
They may be tutor-organizers but they are more
likely to be organizers than tutors.   Yet others
who teach adults may see themselves as engineers,
dentists, sociologists, etc. rather than adult
educators.   By contrast, a part-time employee
who teaches adults for six hours a week, and is a
housewife for the remainder of the time, may well
see herself as a teacher of adults.   Hence, it is
very difficult to restrict the social role of the
adult educator and, indeed, Newman (1979) suggests
that it includes: entrepreneur, wheeler-dealer,
administrator, manager, animateur, trouble-shooter,
expert on method and trouble shooter - nowhere does
he specify teacher!

Social Consequences: The consequences of any
occupation are obviously far wider than merely

financial and Hall stresses this in his discussion.
It is clear that from many studies of occupations
that these include: social identity, personal
identity, social contacts, use of time, etc. etc.
However, one of the problems with adult education
is that many who teach adults may not define
themselves as adult educators while some who teach
adults but little may so define themselves and also
a head of an adult education centre whose work is
totally administrative may be defined by others as
an adult educator.

Major Life Focus: A housewife who teaches for two
hours a week may not see her main focus in life to
be adult education, nor may an accountant who
conducts a class one evening a week. By contrast,
another housewife who teaches four classes a week
may regard her adult teaching as a major focus
in her life. Hence, it is difficult to decide
precisely at what point the major life focus
constitutes the basis for an occupation.

From this brief discussion it is clear that a
major difficulty is defining the occupation of
adult education lies in the fact that it has only
a comparatively few full-time staff and many part-
time staff. Indeed, the Russell Report (1973:131)
indicated that there were about 1,300 full-time
and 100,000 part-time staff employed in adult
education. But since many professions and other
sectors of education employ staff who teach
adults in their continuing education programmes it
is extremely difficult to specify the exact ratio
of full-time to part-time staff. However, it is
obvious that the great majority of individuals
who are employed to teach adults do so on a part-
time basis. Another important factor that
emerges from this discussion is that the majority
of full-time staff in adult education spend much
of their time in organization and administration
within the educational organization whereas few
part-time staff are employed in this capacity and
far more are employed specifically in the role of
teacher of adults. Herein lies the nub of the
problem raised above: that the actual role of many
of the full-time adult educators is not actually
the practice of teaching adults but it is the
practice of management. Mee and Wiltshire (1978:
64), for instance, record how one principal of an
adult education institute who maintained that the
'next group of principals will be accountants not

educationalists'.   The significant factor here is
basically that if full-time adult education staff
are not actually teachers of adults any longer,
then they are managers and the management role is
not the same as the teaching role.   Hence, even
those full-time staff in adult education, who have
been trained in adult education, are not performing
the roles for which they have been trained and they
have not been prepared.   This is no new phenomenon,
and indeed it is relatively common in some other
occupations e.g. the clergy are trained in
theology but spend their time in organizing the
parish church and social work!   However, the point
is clear and needs not be laboured here though it
will be recalled that among the recommendations by
the Haycocks Committee was one which suggested
that adult educators required training in management.   However, as it will be shown later in
this chapter, almost every attempt to define a
profession has included within it the idea of
the practice of an occupation based upon an
academic discipline and at present it is difficult
to see that management is based upon such a
foundation.   Indeed, there is a considerable body
of literature that seeks to contrast the
professional and the bureaucrat and which suggests
that the two forms of occupation are fundamentally
different.   While it will be argued later that
there are similarities between the two types it
must be recognised here that sociologically it is
difficult to reach any other conclusion than that
for the greater part of the time the full-time
adult educator's work is bureaucratic rather than
professional.   A similar conclusion cannot be
reached, however, with the part-time staff whose
occupation is the practice of teaching adults and
whose job may actually have an academic basis in
education.

      The part-time staff in adult education come
from a variety of backgrounds and have different
employment patterns.   Mee and Wiltshire
(1978:20-21) specify two types of non-full-time
employment: the part-timer and the spare-timer.
While their distinction is perfectly valid, it is
a pity that they employ the term 'spare-timer'
with all its connotations to refer to the category
of adult education employment that is most
frequently referred to as part-timer.   Their
use of 'part-timer' refers to an educator who gives
part of his occupational time to the education of
adults and the remainder to the youth service,

school teaching, etc.   However, this distinction
is not retained here, although Mee and Wiltshire's
part-timer is a category of employment which Morris
and Murphy (1959) postulated would sub-divide as it
evolved because it was spread over more than one
situs. The category part-timer will be used here
for those employed in a part-time capacity in
adult education.   Newman (1979) depicted these as:
the professionals - who spend their leisure teaching
about their full-time jobs;   the horses' mouth -
who teach about their experience rather than any
academic discipline that they have studied;   the
passionate amateurs - who teach their hobbies;
the school-teachers - who teach the discipline
that they teach at school or college.   Like
Newman, Graham et al (1982:59-63)classify the
part-timers as: gratified school teachers, subject
specialists, professionals and apprentices.
Their 'professionals' is the same as Newman's and
neither relate in any way to the idea of adult
education being a profession, while apprentices
are those who began by attending adult education
classes as a student in the subject that they now
teach and who have worked their way from student
to teacher.
     One significant factor about adult educators
is the sex difference between the full-time and the
part-time staff.   Mee and Wiltshire (1978:59)
claim that 'there are probably nine male organizers
to every female' in the United Kingdom.   Similarly,
in the higher status adult teaching, 87 per cent of
responsible body tutors were male (university
extension teaching) but in local authority teaching
57 per cent were female (Hutchinson 1970). Similarly
findings are recorded from other research into local
authority adult education: Graham et al (1982:51)
report 64 per cent of their sample were women;
Handley (1981:82) noted that 73 per cent of her
respondents were women;   Jarvis (1982a) recorded 79
per cent of the tutors in a small village adult
education prospectus were women; Martin's (1981:122)
research revealed that two thirds of her respondents
were women.   Thus it may be seen that the managerial
and high status areas of adult education are male
dominated and the female domination is in the
actual teaching in the lower status areas of adult
educations.   This is not an unsurprising finding
since it was claimed earlier that adult education
is a patriarchal occupation.   However, it must
be pointed out that it is the part-time women
teachers who are the reserve army of labour in

adult education; Hetherington (1980:327) writes

> If a course doesn't continue or even start
> for lack of support, it is the tutor, not
> the centre, who carries the financial loss,
> even though weeks and months of preparation
> may have gone into it. It may also be that
> a principal requests a specific course to
> suit his overall strategy for his centre,
> and yet if it fails he has lost nothing.
> The tacit assumption is inherent in this
> situation that courses do not succeed or
> fail according to the estimated market for
> them, but that somehow the tutor is
> inadequate or at fault.

Hetherington is right, of course, when she claims
that the tutor suffers but there is no tacit
assumption that the tutor is at fault: the fact
is that the part-time tutor is used as a reserve
army of labour to be dispensed with if the market
conditions are unfavourable to the sale of the
commodity. It is possible to do this because
the majority of part-time tutors are women and in
the sexual division of labour the women's primary
responsibility is defined as being domestic. In
the same way, those male part-time staff who are
also part of the reserve army of labour may be so
treated since adult education is not their primary
responsibility. This is an assumption that Mee
and Wiltshire (1978:21) make when they suggest:

> The spare-time adult educator may seem
> the least committed of all, and so no
> doubt he generally is. But he may feel
> another kind of commitment: he may be
> doing this job in his leisure because he
> likes doing it rather than simply for the
> financial reward; he may to some extent
> be a volunteer and this voluntary element
> may sometimes give his work a supererogatory
> zest and quality.

Among the major problems with this assumption
are that the part-time adult educator is less
committed, is male and is a willing volunteer to a
welfare type movement. All of which would need
careful argument in order to be substantiated.
Thus it may be concluded that the adult
educator's occupation is a very complex one which,
upon analysis, demands a reconsideration of some

of the basic assumptions about the approach to the occupation. But at the same time it must be recognised that these issues are ones that have been examined within other occupations.

The Occupation Within the Organization

It is clear from the above discussion that adult educators are a diverse group of individuals so that it would be difficult to prescribe their role, whether it is part-time or full-time employment. Hence, it is maintained here that each educator of adults creates his own role and that the role concepts should be understood from the interactionist perspective, in precisely the same way as Harries-Jenkins (1982) suggested for the role of the adult student. However, there are a number of ways of analysing that role and one is within the conceptual framework of the adult educator's role set. The role set is defined by Merton (1968:423) as 'the complement of role relationships which persons have by virtue of occupying a particular social status'. Hence, the role player creates his role in relation to colleagues, students, visitors, administrative staff, local education authority representatives, managers, the inspectorate, etc. Every role play will be predetermined by the tutor's own perception of how the role should be played but the actual performance will be negotiated with each person within the role set. Role conflict will occur when the tutor wishes to perform the role in one way and the principal, for example, desires that it should be played in a different manner. Obviously too much role conflict can result in a decline in job satisfaction. In addition, the tutor may experience role strain when conflicting procedures demand that the role should be played in different ways at the same time or whether the tutor role or the organizer role should take priority. The creation of the role of the adult educator is a unique and individual performance, one which demands an interactionist analysis.

Among the pressures that act upon the role player in the educational organization are the pressures that the organization exerts upon him to conform both to its normative order and to its goals. Clearly the organizational pressure if the pressure that is created either by the principal of the organization or by the local or national governmental policies that affect the organization

itself, will affect his role performance.   Merton
(1968:193-211) has suggested that individuals
adapt to the organization in different ways, so
that they then perform their role differently.
He produced a typology of modes of adaptation
to organization and the following diagram
reproduces and extends Merton's analysis.

Table 15.1   A Typology of Modes of Individual
               Adaptation - an extension of
               Merton (1968:194)

Modes of Adaptation	Cultural Goals	Institutionalized Means
Conformity	+	+
Innovation	+	-
Ritualism	-	+
Retreatism	-	-
Rebellion	±	±
....		
Goal innovation	±	+
Radicalism	±	-
Means innovation	+	±
Revolutionary	-	±

Key: + accept   - reject   ±   substitute new
                                   values

Merton actually produced only the first five types
and as such he did not complete the typology.   The
latter four are an attempt to demonstrate the
possibilities of the typology that he created.
Some adult educators may perform their role in a
conformist manner, and it would be expected that
this would be the case, or else the organization
would be unstable.   Others may be innovators and
in varying ways they wish to change some aspect
of the life of the organization, e.g. some may wish
the adult education to assume a greater community
orientation but still retain the normal means of
operating so their own role may be goal innovation.

Other adult educators may be disillusioned with all
the pressures that are constantly being placed
upon them and either become retreatists or
ritualists.   Others may play their roles in
different ways and be seen as radicals, rebellious
and even revolutionaries.   The point about this
typology is that it does provide the analyst with
a conceptual framework into which to fit the role
performance of adult educators employed within
the organization.
    An important study of teachers in organizations
was published by Gouldner (1957-58) who suggested
that teachers responded to the organization in
terms of whether it was their reference group or
whether the wider occupation was their reference.
He called those whose reference was the educational
organization the 'locals' and those whose
reference was the wider occupation he called
'cosmopolitans'.   Four groups of locals emerged:

Dedicated - those committed to the organiza-
            tion and its smooth-functioning
True Bureaucrat - loyalty to the place itself,
            seek security within the
            organization
Homeguard - has little occupational specialism,
            middle management and their
            reference group within the
            organization
Elders - committed to the organization,
            intending to remain in it
            indefinitely

By contrast, Gouldner recognised two groups of
cosmopolitans:

Outsiders - hardly integrated into the
            organization, highly committed
            to specialist skills, looks
            widely afield for intellectual
            stimulation and influence but
            has little loyalty to the local
            organization
Empire Builders - feel that their place in
            the employment market is secure,
            interested in their own specialism,
            having little loyalty to the
            organization itself they seek to
            exercise power within it.

Gouldner considered that his study could provide
clues for the analysis of role performance in
bureaucratic organizations. Clearly it is
important and may be applied to educators in
adult and continuing education organizations.
Those adult educators whose occupational specialism
is administration and organization are the locals
while those who are committed to an occupational
discipline are the cosmopolitans. However,
this raises a significant issue within adult and
continuing education and that is the extent to
which there exists an occupational discipline.
It will be argued later in this chapter that no
such discipline yet exists in adult and continuing
education although it is in the process of
formation. Hence, the occupational discipline to
which adult educators have shown loyalty in the
past has been the subject that they have taught,
e.g. sociology, so that as a sociologist they have
acted as cosmopolitans.
    Perhaps the most significant element about
Gouldner's local-cosmopolitan distinction is that
it paved the way for the studies which distin-
guished the bureaucrats from the professionals.
Many different occupations were studied in the
following two decades, with a tremendous emphasis
on the professional employed in a bureaucracy and
the distinction between professionals and bureaucrats. In a theoretical paper Scott (1966:269)
postulated that four quite distinct areas of
conflict would arise for professionals employed
in a bureaucracy - the professional: would resist
bureaucratic rules; reject bureaucratic standards;
resist bureaucratic supervision, would have only
conditional loyalty to the organization. However,
Clark (1966), among others, pointed out that not
all organizations were totally bureaucratic and
some, like universities, were able to incorporate
professionals into organizational structures.
Hence, the discussion about the professional or
organizational base of the occupation has been a
rigorous one in which many elements have been
explored but it is one in which the professional-
bureaucratic distinction has been maintained and
it is into this context that it is now necessary
to fit the discussion about the occupation of
adult education.

Professionalization of the Education of Adults
From the above discussion it is clear that a
distinction may be made at this point between those

who actually teach and those whose role is
administrative.   The latter group will be discussed
first because it is clear that these are the full-
time tutor organizers in the adult education
institutes.   Their work is clearly administrative,
except where they teach.   Yet teaching is a small
part of their role.   Hence, they must be
regarded in the bureaucratic mode rather than the
professional.   But are they educators?   Technically
they are involved in the provision of organized
education but unless they are performing a
teaching role they are not teachers;   although that
may have been their training, it is not now their
occupation.   This does not deny their commitment
to adult education, since it must be recognised
that the efficient provision of adult education
is an important element.   Does this make the full-
time adult educator a bureaucrat?   There is
perhaps an important difference between the
bureaucrat in Gouldner's sense of a 'local',
committed to an organization and the adult educator.   Since adult education has some of the
characteristics of a voluntary movement, with its
long history in the churches and other voluntary
organizations, the adult educator tends to be
committed to the movement, so that Mee and
Wiltshire (1978:105) can conclude that:

> Adult educators are on the whole deeply and
> personally committed to the service of
> adult education.   A consequence is that
> they tend to overwork themselves and to be
> overworked.   This tendency can be found
> in all types of institutional setting and
> among spare-time, part-time and full-time
> practitioners.

Hence, full-time adult educators tend to have a
cosmopolitan outlook in the field of adult
education, to know about the varieties of
provision and other innovations in the work, but
they still undertake a basically administrative
role within the organization of the education
of adults.

It now remains to discuss those whose
occupation it is to teach adults and they fall
into two categories: those who do so within the
context of colleges of adult, further and higher
education full time and those who undertake the role
in a part-time basis and are among the 100,000
referred to by Russell (1973).   The initial

problem that needs to be clarified is how they
define themselves: for many it may be as college
lecturer, sociologist, etc. and consequently
discussion about those occupations falls outside
the sphere of this chapter. However, many of
those who are employed to teach adults may define
their occupation as adult educator. It is this
category that requires consideration here.

The majority of part-time staff have classroom
contact with adults but spend but little time
performing a management role. Nevertheless, their
academic qualifications in adult education tend to
be very low or non-existent. Hence, they may be
professionals in as much as they are experts in
a discipline, although since many teach crafts and
hobbies this may be a minority of those who teach
part-time, but few have the theoretical expertise
in adult education which would allow them to be
regarded as professionals in this sphere.
Theoretical expertise is significant in analysing
the extent to which any occupation might be
regarded as a profession since, although there is
no agreement among sociologists as to what constitutes a profession, there is general agreement
that it is an occupation based upon some sphere
of learning, a body of abstract knowledge and this
does not at present exist for adult education.
Hence, there can be little justification for
claiming that adult education is a profession, but
this is a point that is discussed further later in
this section.

The concept of profession itself has provided
considerable difficulty for scholars working in
this field and many have tried to specify a set
of characteristics that would satisfy all the
empirical evidence. Mee (1980:105) does just
this. But Millerson (1964:5) showed the problem
of this approach when, reviewing the work of
twenty-five writers on the professions, he listed
twenty-three different occupational traits that
they attributed to them. This approach has
dubious validity in any case, since characteristics
may be added to or subtracted from any existing
list by any author or any occupational group
without any theoretical rationale. Such is the
confusion in and profusion of definition that
Vollmer and Mills (1966:vii) suggest that the
term 'profession' should be used only as an
ideal type, rather than to arbitrate about the
extent to which an occupation is a profession.
Vollmer and Mills (1966:vii-viii) prefer to use

the term 'professionalization' which is:

> the dynamic process whereby many occupations
> can be observed to change crucial character-
> istics in the direction of a "profession"
> even though some of these may not move very
> far in this direction.

A number of writers have sought to isolate and
describe this movement towards professional status,
including Caplow (1954), Greenwood (1957) and
Wilensky (1964).   Caplow was perhaps the first to
demonstrate the process and Greenwood highlighted
it for social work, but Wilensky's work has been
the most widely cited, in which he claimed that all
occupations could begin the process, even though
They need not progress very far along it.   He
suggested that, while the sequence is not invariant,
there is some form of progression:

   i   to start doing full-time the thing
          that needs doing
  ii   establishing a training school, which
             if not at the outset, later seeks
             to integrate with universities
 iii   forming a professional association which
          seeks -
          a.   a self-conscious definition of
                 the core tasks of the occupation
          b.   a cosmopolitan perspective to
                 the practice of the occupation
          c.   to compete with the neighbouring
                 occupations in order to
                 establish an area of exclusive
                 competence
  iv   seeking legal support for the protec-
             tion of the job territory
   v   publishing a code of ethics to indicate
             the commitment of the practitioner
  vi controlling licensing and certification.

It may thus be seen that the process of professionalization involves changes in the occupational
structure, so that it reflects whatever professional model the elite of the occupation espouse.
This process, whatever goal is adopted, certainly
reflects the social reality of occupations seeking
to have the status 'profession' attributed to them,
as well as ascribing it to themselves.
     Hetherington (1980) actually argues that there
is a need for part-time adult education to

professionalize and while she is clearly concerned
about the students the thrust of her argument
is that part-time adult education will only
professionalize when there is greater status and
security attached to the role.   In other words
she is suggesting that either a more permanent
form of part-time employment should be introduced
or that there should be more full-time posts.
In the former instance, a new concept of occupation
emerges that Wilensky did not consider and yet
there appears to be no reason why permanent part-
time employment might not constitute an occupation
since it could constitute both the main source of
financial income and the main focus of self and
social identity.   Hence, there appears to be no
reason why permanent part-time occupations should
not professionalize.

Wilensky's second stage is to establish a
training school and while a number of universities
offer Diplomas in Adult Education and some institutions of higher education offer certificates in
the education of adults, the process has begun at
the foundations of the part-time occupation.   The
Advisory Committee on the Supply and Training of
Teachers (Haycocks 1978) recommended a scheme of
training in three stages for adult educators.
The first stage is a single module of training
designed as an induction module initiating the new
recruits to the occupation into basic teaching
skills.   By contrast, the second stage consists
of sixty hours of theory and thirty hours of
supervised teaching and the third stage is
designed for both full-time and part-time adult
educators and should lead to full certification.
Hence, the initiative of introducing schemes of
preparation for part-time and full-time adult
educators is clearly one more stage along the
process of professionalization, according to the
model produced by Wilensky.

However, there is a significant development
that is occurring as a result of the introduction
of these courses in the preparation of adult
educators, it is resulting in the growth in the
amount of teaching of adult education as a subject.
These courses are forcing the trainers of adult
educators to systematise their knowledge about
adult education, so that there is now an emerging
sub-discipline which is becoming more widely
studied, which may gradually be called andragogy,
the name given to the area of academic study in
Eastern Europe (Kulich 1984:128) rather than a

technique of teaching (Knowles 1980). Hence, the growth in training part-time and full-time adult educators may help to develop a body of knowledge upon which the occupation is based, which is a fundamental prerequisite for any occupation to gain professional status. Thus it may be seen that the first stages in Wilensky's model have been approached and adult education is still only in the early stages of professionalization.

This approach to adult education has examined the structure of an occupation and debates about whether an occupation is a profession tend to be rather sterile. A more significant concept is perhaps that of professionalism, the ideology of professional practice. At its least professionalism is an ideology that demands that the practitioner keep abreast with the new development in the discipline(s) upon which his occupation is based so that he can render the best possible service to the client (Jarvis 1983a). It was shown earlier (Rogers 1962) that research into different high status occupations suggest that this does not occur evenly throughout the occupation, but as yet no research has been conducted to investigate the professionalism of those who are adult educators, full-time or part-time so that this remains another area to be investigated as adult education professionalizes.

Conclusion

Not everything about the process of professionalization is necessarily beneficial either to the occupation or to the clients of the occupation. The term is a word that, like Janus, has two faces: for some, professions are good, while for others, they are imperious and less than good. Illich (1977) has constantly criticised those high status occupations, like medicine, for being too imperious to offer the best possible service and it behoves all who are members of occupations which are professionalizing to take note of his strictures, even though they are often made without sufficient empirical evidence to support the claims he makes!

This chapter has, therefore, endeavoured to place the occupation of adult education within the wider context of the sociology of professions and occupations and in so doing demonstrates that the research in occupations other than adult education is relevant to what is currently occurring in this field. But then this has been one of the main aims of the whole of this book, since the education of adults cannot be understood totally in isolation from all the other social forces that help to make it what it has become.

Advisory Council of Adult and Continuing Education,
    Towards Continuing Education, Leicester
    ACACE   1979a
Advisory Council of Adult and Continuing Education,
    A Strategy for the Basic Education of Adults,
    Leicester   ACACE   1979b
Advisory Council of Adult and Continuing Education,
    Links to Learning, Leicester   ACACE   1979c
Advisory Council of Adult and Continuing Education,
    Protecting the Future for Adults Education,
    Leicester   ACACE   1981
Advisory Council of Adult and Continuing Education,
    Continuing Education: From Policies to
    Practice, Leicester   ACACE   1982
Advisory Council of Adult and Continuing Education,
    Adults: Their Educational Experience and
    Needs, Leicester   ACACE   1982b
Advisory Council of Adult and Continuing Education,
    Distance Learning and Adult Students
    Leicester   ACACE   1983a
Advisory Council of Adult and Continuing Education,
    Continuing Education: Local Learning Centres
    Leicester   ACACE   1983b
Althusser   L   Ideology and Ideological State
    Apparatuses reprinted in Cosin B R (1972)
    op cit   1972
Archambault R D (ed) 1965   Philosophical Analysis
    and Education, London   Routledge and Kegan Paul
    1965
Asch S E   Opinions and Social Pressure in
    Scientific American   Vol 193   1955
Aslanian C and Brickell H "Passages" of Adulthood
    and Triggers to Learning reprinted in Gross
    R (ed) op cit   1982
Becker H S Social Class Variations in the Teacher-
    Pupil Relationship in Cosin et al (eds) 1971 op cit

Belbin E and Belbin R M Problems in Adult
    Retraining London Heinmann 1972
Bellah R Beyond Belief, New York Harper and
    Row 1970
Berg I Education and Jobs: The Great Training
    Robbery, Harmondsworth Penguin 1966
Berger P L Invitation to Sociology, Harmondsworth
    Pelican 1966
Berger P L The Social Reality of Religion
    London Faber and Faber 1969
Berger P L and Luckmann T The Social Construction
    of Reality London Allen Lane, the Penguin
    Press 1967
Berger P L, Berger B and Kellner H The Homeless
    Mind Harmondsworth Penguin Books 1974
Bergevin P A Philosophy for Adult Education
    New York The Seabury Press 1967
Bergsten U Adult Education in Relation to Work and
    Leisure Stockholm Almqvist and Wiksell 1977
Bernstein B On the Classification and Framing of
    Educational Knowledge in Young M F D (ed)
    1971 op cit 1971
Bernstein B Class, Codes and Control (vol 1)
    St Albans Paladin 1973
Blamire J and Dawkins P n.d. Recruitment and
    Publicity for Rural Adult and Basic Education
    Kent County Council Education Committee
Blau P M and Scott W R Formal Organizations
    London Routledge and Kegan Paul 1963
Blum A The Corpus of Knowledge as a Normative
    Order in Young (ed) 1971 op cit
Bocock R, Hamilton P, Thompson K and Waton A (eds)
    An Introduction to Sociology Fontana
    Paperback in association with the Open
    University Press 1980
Boshier R and Collins J B Education Participation
    Scale Factor Structure and Socio-Demographic
    Correlates for 12000 Leaners in International
    Journal of Lifelong Education Vol 2 No 2 1983
Bottomore T B Elites in Society Harmondsworth
    Pelican 1966
Bottomore T B and Rubel M (eds) Karl Marx:
    Selected Writings in Sociology and Social
    Philosophy Harmondsworth Pelican Books 1963
Boucouvales M Interface: Lifelong Learning and
    Community Education Charlotteville
    Mid-Atlantic Center for Community Education
    1979
Bourdieu P Cultural Reproduction and Social
    Reproduction in Brown (ed) 1973 op cit 1973

Bibliography

Bourdieu P and Passeron J C Reproduction - in
    Education, Society and Culture   London
    Sage Publications   1977
Bowles S and Gintis H   Schooling in Capitalist
    America   London and Henley   Routledge and
    Kegan Paul   1976
Boyd R D, and Apps J W   Redefining and Discipline
    of Adult Education   San Francisco
    Jossey Bass Publishers 1980
Bradshaw J The Concept of Social Need in
    Fitzgerald M et al (eds) 1977 op cit
Brookfield S Adult Learners, Adult Education and
    the Community   Milton Keynes   Open Universit y
    Press   1983
Brown R (ed) Knowledge, Education and Cultural
    Change   London   Tavistock Publications   1973
Brundage D H and Mackeracher D   Adult Learning
    Principles and Their Application to Program
    Planning   Ontario Ministry of Education 1980
Bryant J Paid Educational Leave in Scotland in
    International Journal of Lifelong Education
    Vol 2   No. 1   1983
Business and Technical Education Council
    Continuing Education for Business and Industry
    London   B/TEC   1983
Business and Technical Education Council
    Continuing Education for Business and Industry
    London   B/TEC   1983
Butler L   Adult External Candidates for G.C.E.
    Examinations   Leicester   ACACE   1981
Cantor L M and Roberts I F   Further Education in
    England and Wales   London and Boston
    Routledge and Kegan Paul   1972 (2nd Ed)
Caplow T   The Sociology of Work   Minneapolis
    University of Minnesota Press   1954
Carlson R A   The Foundation of Adult Education:
    Analyzing the Boyd-Apps Model Published in
    Boyd and Apps (1980) op cit   1980
Carlson R et al Recreation in American Life
    Belmont   Wadsworth   1972
Carp A, Peterson R and Roelfs P   Adult Learning
    Interests and Experiences cited in Cross
    (1981) op cit   1974
Carr E H What is History? Harmondsworth Penguin
    1964
Charters A N et al Comparing Adult Education
    Worldwide   San Francisco Jossey Bass Inc.
    1981
Chickering A W et al   The Modern American College
    San Francisco Jossey Bass Publishers   1981

Bibliography

Clark B Organizational Adaptation to Professionals
    in Vollmer H and Mills D (eds) 1966 op cit
Cohen P Modern Social Theory London Heinemann
    1968
Coleman A Preparation for Retirement in England
    and Wales Leicester National Institute of
    Adult Education 1982
Cookson P S The Boyd and Apps Conceptual Model
    of Adult Education: A critical Examination in
    Adult Education Quarterly Vol 34 No. 1 1983
Cooper C L (ed) Theories of Group Processes
    London John Wiley and Sons 1975
Cosin B R Education, Structure and Society
    Harmondsworth Penguin Books 1972
Cosin B R, Dale I R, Esland G H and Swift D F (eds)
    School and Society London Routledge and
    Kegan Paul in association with The Open
    University Press 1971
Cross K P Adults as Learners San Francisco
    Jossey Bass Inc. 1981
Cunningham P M Review of 'Adult Education for a
    Change' in Adult Education Quarterly Vol 33
    No 4 1983
Daines J, Elsey B and Gibbs M Changes in Student
    Participation in Adult Education University of
    Department of Nottingham Adult Education
    1982
Dale R, Esland G and MacDonald H (eds) Schooling
    and Capitalism London Routledge and Kegan
    Paul in association with The Open University
    Press 1976
Dave R H Foundations of Lifelong Education
    Oxford Pergamon Press for Unesco Institute of
    Education 1976
Davies I K Objectives in Curriculum Design
    London McGraw Hill Book Co. 1978
Dawe A The Two Sociologies British Journal of
    Sociology Vol 21 pp 207-218 reprinted in
    Thompson K and Tunstall J (eds) 1971 op cit
    1970
Day C and Baskett H K Discrepancies between
    Intentions and Practice: Re-examining Some
    Basic Assumptions about Adult and Continuing
    Professional Education in International
    Journal of Lifelong Education Vol 1 No 2 1982
Dearden R F Needs in Education in Dearden R F
    et al (eds) 1972 op cit 1972
Dearden R F, Hirst P H and Peters R S (eds)
    Education in the Development of Reason Part
    London Routledge and Kegan Paul 1972

246

Bibliography

Deem R Women and Schooling London Routledge and
    Kegan Paul 1978
Department of Education and Science Programme for
    the Adult Unemployed London DES 1984
Dewey J Education and Democracy London and
    New York The Free Press 1916
Dewey J Experience and Education London
    Collier-Macmillan Publishers 1938
Douglas J D Understanding Everyday Life: Towards
    the Reconstruction of Sociological Knowledge
    London Routledge and Kegan Paul 1971
Douglas M Natural Symbols: Explorations in
    Cosmology London The Cresset Press 1970
Durkheim E The Elementary Forms of Religious Life
    translated by J W Swain London George Allen
    and Unwin Ltd. 1915
Durkheim E Education and Sociology translated
    by S D Fox New York The Free Press 1956
Durkheim E The Division of Labour in Society
    New York The Free Press 1964
Eisner E W Instructural and Expressive Educational
    Objectives: Their Formulation and Rise in
    Curriculum in Popham W J et al 1969 op cit
Elias J L Andragogy Revisited in Adult Education
    Vol 29 pp 252-256 Washington 1979
Elliott P The Sociology of the Professions London
    Macmillan 1972
Ellis J F and Mugridge I The Open Learning
    Institute of British Columbia Milton Keynes
    The Open University 1983
Elsdon K Training for Adult Education Nottingham
    Dept of Adult Education University of
    Nottingham in association with NIAE 1975
Entwistle H Class, Culture and Education
    London Methuen 1978
Entwistle H Antonio Gramsci: Conservative
    Schooling for Radical Politics London
    Routledge and Kegan Paul 1979
Esland G, Salaman G and Speakman M (eds)
    People and Work Edingburgh Holmes McDougall
    in association with Open University Press,
    Milton Keynes 1975
Evans N The Knowledge Revolution London
    Grant McIntyre 1981
Finch J Education as Social Policy London
    Longman 1984
Fisher J D, Wesselman R A et al Agricultural
    Extension Training: a course manual for
    extension training programs
    Nairobi, Kenya United States Agency for
    International Development 1968

Fitzgerald H, Halmos P, Muncie J and Zeldin D (eds)
    Welfare in Action London Routledge and Kegan
    Paul 1977
Flanders N A Analysing Teacher Behaviour
    New York Addison-Wesley 1970
Flew A Sociology, Equality and Education
    London and Basingstoke Macmillan 1976
Freire P Pedagogy of the Oppressed
    Harmondsworth Penguin 1972a
Freire P Cultural Action for Freedom
    Harmondsworth Penguin 1972b
Freire P By Learning They can Teach in Convergence
    Vol 6 No 1 1973
Freire P Education: The Practice of Freedom
    London Writers and Readers Publishing
    Cooperative 1974
Freire P A Few Notions about the Word
    'Conscientization' reprinted in Dale et al
    (eds) 1976 op cit
Garfinkel H 1956 Conditions of Successful
    Degradation Ceremonies in American Journal of
    Sociology Vol LXI (March) 1956
Garfinkel H The Origins of the Term 'Ethnometho-
    dology' reprinted in Turner R (ed) 1974
    opcit
Geer B Teaching in Cosin et al (eds) 1971 op cit
Gelpi E A future for Lifelong Education (2 vols)
    Manchester Monographs No 13 1979
Gelpi E Lifelong Education: Opportunities and
    Obstacles in International Journal of
    Lifelong Education Vol 3 No 2 1984
Gerth H H and Wright Mills C (eds) From Max Weber
    London Routledge and Kegan Paul Ltd. 1948
Giddens A Capitalism and Modern Social Theory
    Cambridge University Press 1971
Giddens A Central Problems in Social Theory:
    Action, Structure and Contradictions in Social
    Analysis London Macmillan 1979
Giroux H A Ideology, Culture and the Process of
    Schooling Lewes The Falmer Press 1981
Goffman E Asylums Harmondsworth Penguin 1968
Goffman E The Presentation of Self in Everyday
    Life Harmondsworth Pelican Books 1971
Goldthorpe J H (in collaboration with
    C M Llewellyn and C Payne) Social Mobility
    and Class Structure in Modern Britain
    Oxford Clarendon Press 1980
Goode W E The Librarian: From Occupation to
    Profession in the Library Quarterly Vol 31 No4
    1961

Bibliography

Goode W E Exploration in Social Theory New York
    Oxford University Press   1973
Gorz A   Technical Intelligence and the Capitalist
    Division of Labour in Bocock et al (eds) 1980
    op cit
Gouldner A W Cosmopolitans and Locals: Towards an
    Analysis of Latent Social Roles (1-2) in
    Administrative Science Quarterly Vol 2
    1957-58
Graham T B, Daines J H, Sullivan T, Harris P and
    Baum F E The Training of Part-Time Teachers
    of Adults   University of Nottingham
    Department of Adult Education   1982
Greenwood E   Attributes of a Profession in
    Social Work Vol 2   1957
Griffin C   Recurrent and Continuing Education - a
    curriculum model approach   University of
    Nottingham School of Education
    1978
Griffin C   Social Control, Social Policy and
    Adult Education in International Journal of
    Lifelong Education Vol 2   No 3   1983a
Griffin C   Curriculum Theory in Adult and Lifelong
    Education   London   Croom Helm 1983b
Griffith W S Co-ordination of Personnel, Programs
    and Services in Peters J M ET AL (1980)
    op cit   1980
Gross R   The Lifelong Learner   New York
    Touchstone Book   1977
Gross R (ed) Invitation of Lifelong Learning
    Chicago Follett Publishing Co.   1982
Hall A S Client Reception in a Social Service
    Agency in Fitzgerald et al (eds) 1977
    op cit 1977
Hall R H The Concept of Bureaucracy: An Empirical
    Assessment in The Americal Journal of
    Sociology Vol 69 No 1
Hall R H Occupations and the Social Structure
    Englewood Cliffs, New Jersey Prentice Hall
    Inc.   1969
Hall R H Organizations: Structure and Process
    Englewood Cliffs, New Jersey Prentice Hall
    Inc.   1972
Halmos P The Concept of Social Problem in Social
    Work and Community Work block 1   Milton
    Keynes Open University 1978
Halsey A H, Heath A F, Ridge J H Origins and
    Destination Oxford Clarendon Press 1980
Handley J An Investigation into the Training
    Needs of Part-Time Tutors, with particular
    reference to the development of courses

at ACSET Stage II Level   University of Surrey
Unpublished MSc dissertation   1981
Harries-Jenkins G   The Role of the Adult Student
in International Journal of Lifelong Education
Vol 1   No 1   1982
Harris N   Beliefs in Society   London C P Watts &
Co Ltd.   1968
Hartree A   Malcolm Knowles' Theory of Andragogy: a
Critique in International Journal of Lifelong
Education   Vol 3   No 2   1984
Haycocks J N (Chairman)   The Training of Adult
Education and Part-Time Further Education
Teachers   London   Advisory Committee for
the Supply and Training of Teachers   1978
Heron J   Dimensions of Facilitator Style
University of Surrey and   University of London
Dept of Educational   British Postgraduate
Studies   Medical Federation
1977
Heron J   Education of the Affect
University of Surrey and   University of London
Human Potential   British Postgraduate
Reseach Project   Medical Federation
1982
Hetherington J   Professionalism and Part-time Staff
in Adult Education in Adult Education
Vol 52 No 5   Leicester   NIAE   1980
Hirst P H   Liberal Education and the Nature of
Knowledge reprinted in Archambault K   (ed)
1965 op cit
Hirst P H and Peters R S   The Logic of Education
London   Routledge and Kegan Paul   1970
Hoare Q (ed)   Marx: Early Writings
Harmondsworth   Penguin 1975
Hollins T H B (ed) Aims in Education   Manchester
University Press   1964
Hopper E (ed)   Readings in the Theory of Educational
Systems   London   Hutchinson   1961
Hostler J   The Aims of Adult Education
Manchester Monographs 17   1981
Houle C O   Continuing Learning in the Professions
San Francisco   Jossey Bass   1980
Hoyle E and Megarry J (eds)   Professional
Development of Teachers   London   Kogan Page
1980
Hutchinson E N (ed) 1970   Adult Education - Adequacy
of Provision in Adult Education Vol 42 No 6
London NIAE   1970
Hutchinson E and E M   Learning Later   London
Routledge and Kegan Paul   1978
Illich I   Disabling Professions in Illich et al

(1977) op cit
Illich I and Verne E   Imprisoned in the Global
    Classroom   London Writers and Readers
    Publishing Cooperative   1976
Illich I, Zole I K, McKnight J, Caplan J and
    Shaiken H   Disabling Professions   London
    Marion Boyars   1977
Jackson K   Foreword to Thompson J (ed) 1980
    op cit
Janne H   Theoretical Foundations of Lifelong
    Education: A sociological Perspective in
    Dave R G (ed) 1976 op cit
Jarvis P   A Sociological Analysis of the Doctrine
    of Ministry and Ordination in Contact No 2
    1976
Jarvis P   District Nurse Examiners - How They
    Score? in Nursing Times (March) 1978
Jarvis P   Towards a Sociological Understanding of
    Superstition in Social compass Vol XXVIII
    pp 285-295   1980
Jarvis P   The Open University Unit: andragogy or
    pedagogy? in Teaching at a Distance No 20
    Milton Keynes   Open University   1981
Jarvis P   What's the Value of Adult Education ? in
    Adult Education Vol 54 No 4   Liecester NIACE
    1982
Jarvis P   Adult Education in a Small Centre: a
    case study in the village of Lingfield
    University of Surrey, Dept of Educational
    Studies   1982a
Jarvis P   Professional Education   London and
    Canberra   Oroom Helm 1983a
Jarvis P   Adult and Continuing Education: Theory
    and Practice London and Canberra Croom Helm
    New York Nichols   1983b
Jarvis P   Religiosity: A Theoretical Analysis of
    the Human Response to the Problem of Meaning,
    in Research Bulletin
    University of Birmingham, Institute for the
    Study of Worship and Religious Architecture
    1983c
Jarvis P   The Lifelong Religious Development of
    the Individual and the Place of Adult
    Education, in Lifelong Learning: The Adult
    Years Vol 6 and 9 1983d
Johnstone J W C   Leisure and Education in
    Contemporary American Life: Notes and Essays
    on Education for Adults No 43
    Boston Centre for the Study of Liberal Education
    for Adults   1964
Joll J   Gramsci   Glasgow   Fontana   1977

Bibliography

Kazanjian M A   Policy Development and the Lobbying
      Process for education of Adults in Wharples G
      and Rivera W(eds) 1982 op cit
Keddie N   Adult Education: an ideology of
      individualism in Thompson J (ed) 1980 op cit
Kelly T A History of Adult Education in Great
      Britain Liverpool University Press 1970
Kerr C, Dunlop J T, Habison F, Myers C A
      Industrialism and Industrial Man
      Harmondsworth Pelican 1973(ed)
Killeen J and Bird M Education and Work
      Leicester NIAE 1981
Knowles M S The Modern Practice of Adult Education
      Chicago Association Press 1970
Knowles M S The Adult Learners: a neglected
      species Houston Gulf Publishing Co. 1978
      (2nd Ed)
Knowles M S The Modern Practice of Adult
      Education Chicago Association Press
      1980 (Rev Ed)
Knowles M S The Growth and Development in Adult
      Education in Peters J M et al (1980)
      op cit 1980a
Kolb D A Learning Styles and Disciplinary
      Differences in Chickering et al (1981) op cit
Kolb D A and Fry R Towards an Applied Theory of
      Experiential Learning in Cooper C L (ed)
      1975 op cit   1975
Krech D, Crutchfield R S and Ballachey E L
      Individual in Society New York McGraw-Hill
      Book Co Inc. 1982
Kulich J Approaches to Theory Building and
      Research in Adult Education in East Europe in
      International Journal of Lifelong Education
      Vol 3 No 2   1984
Kumar K Prophecy and Progress Harmondsworth
      Pelican 1978
Lambers K and Griffiths M Adapting Materials for
      Informal Learning Groups in Teaching at a
      Distance No 23   Milton Keynes Open University
      1983
Langerman P D and Smith D H Managing Adult and
      Continuing Education Programs and Staff
      Washington National Association for Public
      Continuing and Adult Education 1979
Lawson K H Philosophical Concepts and Values
      in Adult Education University of Nottingham,
      Department of Adult Education 1975
Lawson K H Community Education: a critical
      assessment in Adult Education Vol 50 No 1
      Leicester NIAE   1977

Lawson K H Analysis and Ideology: Conceptual
    Essays on the Education of Adults
    University of Nottingham, Dept of Adult
    Education 1982
Lawson D Social Change, Educational Theory and
    Curriculum Planning London Hodder and
    Stoughton 1973
Legge D Discussion Methods in Stephen M D and
    Roderick G W (eds) 1971 op cit 1971
Legge D Review of Adult Education for a Change
    in Adult Education Vol 53 No 2 1981
Lester-Smith W O Education - an Introductory
    Survey Harmondsworth Penguin 1960
Levi-Strauss C Structural Anthropology
    Harmondsworth Penguin Books 1972
Lewin K Group Decision and Social Change in
    Swansson G E et al (eds) 1952 op cit 1952
Lifton R J Thought Reform and the Psychology of
    Totalism Harmondsworth Pelican 1961
Long H B Adult Learning: Research and Practice
    New York Cambridge Adult Education Co. 1983
Lovett T Adult Education, Community Development
    and the Working Class London Ward Lock
    Education 1975
Lovett T, Clark C and Kilmurray A Adult Education
    and Community Action London Croom Helm 1983
Lukes S Fact and Theory in the Social Sciences in
    Potter D (ed) 1981 op cit
Lynch J Policy and Practice in Lifelong Education
    Driffield Nefferton Books 1982
Mackenzie G World Images and the World of Work
    in Esland et al (eds) 1975 op cit 1975
McCullough K Owen Analyzing the Evolving Structure
    of Adult Education in Peters J M et al 1980
    op cit 1980
McKnight J Professionalized Service and
    Disabling Help in Illich et al 1977 op cit
Mannheim K Ideology and Utopia London Routledge
    and Kegan Paul Ltd 1936
Mannheim K and Stewart W A C An Introduction to
    the Sociology of Education London, Routledge
    and Kegan Paul Ltd 1962
Manpower Services Commission Towards an Adult
    Training Strategy: a discussion paper
    Sheffield MSC 1983
Marcuse H Industrialization and Capitalism in
    Stammer (ed) 1971 op cit 1971
Martin B A Sociology of Contemporary Cultural
    Change Oxford Basil Blackwell 1981
Martin L C A Survey of the Training Needs of
    Part-Time Tutors in a Region in Studies in

Adult Education Vol 13 No 2 Leicester NIAE 1981

Marx K *Early Writings* (Introduced by L Collelti) Harmondsworth Pelican 1975 (ed)

Marx K and Engels F *The Communist Manifesto* Harmondsworth Penguin Books 1967 (ed)

Maslow A H *Motivation and Personality* New York Harper 1954

Mead G H *Mind, Self and Society* University of Chicago Press 1934

Mee G *Organization of Adult Education* London Longman 1980

Mee G and Wiltshire H *Structure and Performance in Adult Education* London Longman 1978

Meighan R *A Sociology of Educating* London Holt, Rinehart and Winston 1981

Meltzer B N, Petras J W and Reynolds L T *Symbolic Interactionism: Genesis, Varieties and Criticism* London and Boston Routledge and Kegan Paul 1975

Merton R K *Social Theory and Social Structure* New York The Free Press 1968 (ed)

Mezirow J A Critical Theory of Adult Learning and Education in *Adult Education* Vol 32 No 1 Fall Washington USA 1981

Miller H L *Participation of Adults in Education: A Force Field Analysis* Boston University Center for the Study of Liberal Education for Adults 1967

Millerson G *The Qualifying Association - a Study in Professionalization* London Routledge and Kegan Paul 1964

Mills C Wright *The Power Elite* Galaxy Books New York 1959

Ministry of Education *Continuing Education: The Third System* Ontario Ministry of Education n.d.

Morris R T and Murphy R J The Situs Dimension in Occupational Structure in *American Sociological Review* Vol XXIV No 2 1959

Morsy Z (ed) *Learning and Working* Paris Unesco 1979

Musgrove F Curriculum, Culture and Ideology in Taylor P H (ed) 1979 *op cit* 1979

Nagel E *The Structure of Science* (extracts reprinted in Potter et al (eds) 1981 *op cit* London Routledge and Kegan Paul 1961

Newman M *The Poor Cousin* London George Allen and Unwin 1970

Niemi J and Nagel J Learners, Agencies and Program Development in Adult and Continuing Education in Langerman and Smith (eds) 1979 *op cit*

Bibliography

O'Dea T F   The Sociology of Religion
     New Jersey   Prentice Hall Inc.   Englewood
     Cliffs 1966
Ontario Ministry of Education   Continuing
     Education: The Third System - a discussion
     paper Ontario   n.d.
Parker S   The Sociology of Leisure   London
     George Allen and Unwin   1976
Parsons T   The Social System   London Routledge
     and Kegan Paul Ltd.   1079
Paterson R W K   1984 Objectivity as an Educational
     Imperative in International Journal of
     Lifelong Education Vol 3 No 1   1984
Peters J M et al Building an Effective Adult
     Education Enterprise   San Francisco   Jossey
     Bass Inc. 1980
Peters R S   Ethics and Education   London George
     allen and Unwin Ltd.   1966
Pinker R   Social Theory and Social Policy
     London   Heinemann   1971
Popham W J, Eisner E W, Sullivan H J and Tyler LL
     Instructional Objectives   Chicago Rand
     McNally   1969
Potter D et al (eds) Society and the Social
     Sciences London Routledge and Kegan Paul Ltd.
     1981
Pugh D S, Hickson D J, Hinings C R, MacDonald K M,
     Turner C and Lupton T   A Conceptual Scheme
     for Organizational Analysis in Administrative
     Science Quarterly   Vol 8 No 3   1963
Pugh D J, Hickson D J, Hinings C R and Turner C
     The Context of Organizational Structures
     in Administrative Science Quarterly Vol 14
     No 1   1969
Ransom S, Bryman a and Hindings C R Clergy,
     Ministers and Priests London Routledge and
     Kegan Paul 1977
Riesman D   The Lonely Crowd: a Study of Changing
     American Character New Haven Yale University
     Press   1950
Rivera W M   Reflections on Policy Issues in
     Adult Education in Wharples E and Rivera W
     (eds) 1982 op cit
Robinson J J and Taylor D   Behavioural Objectives
     in Training for Adult Education in Interna-
     tional Journal of Lifelong Education Vol 2
     No 4   1983
Rogers C R Freedom to Learn Columbus, Charles E
     Ohio Merrill Publishing Co.   1969
Rogers E H   Diffusion of Innovations   Glencoe
     The Free Press   1962

Rogers J   Adults Learning   Milton Keynes
    Open University Press   1977 (ed)
Rowntree D   Assessing Students - How Shall We
    Know Them?   London   Harper and Row Ltd   1977
Ruddock R   Sociological Perspectives on Educational
    Manchester Monographs No 2   1972
Russell L (Chairman)   Adult Education: a Plan for
    Development   London   Her Majesty's
    Stationery Office   1973
Ryan B and Gross N C   The Diffusion of Hybrid
    Seed Corn in Two Iowa communities in Rural
    Society No 8   1943
Salaman G and Thompson K (eds)   People and
    Organizations   London   Longmans   1973
Scheffler I   Conditions of Knowledge   Chicago
    University of Chicago Press   1965
Scheler M   Problems of a Sociology of Knowledge
    translated by Frings M S   London   Routledge
    and Kegan Paul   1980
Schon D A   Beyond the Stable State
    Harmondsworth   Penguin Books   1973
Schutz A   The Stronger: an essay in social
    psychology in Cosin B R et al (eds) 1971
    op cit   1971
Schutz A   The Phenomenology of the Social World
    London   Heinemann   1972
Schutz A and Luckmann T   The Structures of the
    Life World   London   Heinemann   1974
Scott W R   Professionals in Bureaucracies -
    Areas of Conflict in Vollmer H M and Mills D L
    (eds) 1966 op cit   1966
Sennett R   Distructive Gemeinschaft reprinted in
    Bocock   et al (eds) 1980 op cit
Sherron R H and Lumsden D.B.   Introduction to
    Educational Gerontology   Washington
    Hemisphere   Publishing co.   1978
Sidwell D   A Survey of Modern Language Classes in
    Adult Education Vol 52   No 5 1980
Silver H   Education and the Social Condition
    London   Methuan   1980
Simmel G   The Metropolis and Mental Life
    reprinted in Thompson K and Tunstall J (eds)
    1971 op cit   1971
Skilbeck M   Curriculum Development: the nature of
    the task cited in Lawton (1973) op cit   1969
Small N and Tight M   A Local Centre for the
    Education of Adults in tight M(ed) 1983
    op cit
Stammer O   Max Weber and Sociology Today
    Oxford   Basil Blackwell   1971

Bibliography

Stephens M D and Roderick G W (eds)   Teaching
    Techniques in Adult Education   Newton Abbot
    David and Charles   1971
Stock A   Review of Adult Education for a Change
    in Teaching at a Distance Vol 19 (Summer) 1981
Stock A   Adult Education in the United Kingdom
    Leicester   NIAE   1982(ed)
Stone H S   Non Formal Adult Education;   Case
    Studies from India in The International
    Journal of Lifelong Education Vol 2 No 3
    1983
Strauss A, Schatzman L, Ehrlich D, Bucher R and
    Sabsin M   The Hospital and its Negotiated
    Order in Salaman G and Thompson K (eds) 1973
    op cit
Stringer M   Lifting the Course Team Curse in
    Teaching at a Distance no 20   1980
Swanson G E, Newcomb T M   Hartley E L   Readings
    in Social Psychology New York   Holt
    1952 (ed)
Taylor P H (ed)   New Directions in Curriculum
    Studies Lewes The Falmer Press 1979
Taylor W   Professional Development or Personal
    Development? in Hoyle and Megarry (eds)
    1980 op cit
Thomas J E Radical Adult Education: Theory and
    Practice   Nottingham Dept of Adult
    Education University of Nottingham 1982
Thompson J L(ed) Adult Education for a Change
    London   Hutchinson   1980
Thompson J   Learning Liberation: Women's
    Response to Men's Education London   Croom Helm
    1983
Thompson K and Tunstall J (eds) Sociological
    Perspectives Harmondsworth Penguin Books in
    association with Open University Press 1971
Thorsen J A   Future Trends in Education for Older
    Adults in Sherron R H and Lumsdon D B (eds)
    1978 op cit
Tight M   Part-Time Degree Level Study in the
    United Kingdom   Leicester ACACE   1982
Tight M (ed) Opportunities for Adult Education
    London   Croom Helm 1983
Timasheff N S Sociological Theory: In Nature and
    Growth New York   Random House   1957
Titmus C J and Pardoen A R The Function of Adult
    Education Legislation in Charters A N et al
    1981 op cit   1981
Titmuss R Social Policy: An Introduction
    London   Allen and Unwin   1974

Toennies F Community and Society New York
    Harper and Row   1957
Tough A   The Adult's Learning Projects
    Toronto The Ontario Institute for Studies in
    Education   1979 (2nd ed)
Townsend P   Sociology and Social Policy
    Harmondsworth Penguin   1976
Turnbull C H The Human Cycle London Jonathan
    Cape   1984
Turner R   Sponsors and Contest Mobility in the
    School System reprinted in Hopper E (ed)
    1971 op cit
Turner R (ed) Ethnomethodology Harmondsworth
    Penguin   1974
Turner V W The Ritual Process Harmondsworth
    Penguin Books 1969
Venables P (Chairman) Report of the Committee on
    Continuing Education Open University   1976
Visaberghi A Education and the Division of Labour
    in Morsy Z (ed) 1979 op cit
Vollmer H M and Mills D L (eds) Professionalization
    Prentice Hall Inc. Englewood Cliffs,
    New Jersey 1966
Weber M   The Protestant Ethic and the Spirit of
    Capitalism London Unwin University Books
    1930
Weber M The Theory of Social and Economic
    Organization translated by Henderson A M and
    Parsons T New York The Free Press   1947
Weber M Class, Status and Party reprinted in
    Gerth and Wright Mills (eds) op cit 1948
Wedemeyer C A   Learning at the Back Door
    University of Wisconsin Press   1981
Werthman C Delinquents in Schools: a test for
    the legitimacy of authority in Cosin et al
    (eds) 1971 op cit
Westwood S Adult Education and the Sociology of
    Education: an exploration in Thompson J L
    (ed) 1980 op cit
Wharples G C and Rivera W H (eds) Policy Issues
    and Process University of Maryland Dept of
    Agricultural and Extension Education 1982
Wilensky H A L The Professionalization of
    Everyone? in American Journal of Sociology
    Vol LXX 1964
Williams R The Long Resolution Harmondsworth
    Penguin 1961
Williams R Base and Superstructure in Marxist
    Cultural Theory reprinted in Dale et al (eds)
    1976 op cit 1976

Bibliography

Willis P   Learning to Labour   Farnborough Saxon
    House   1977
Wilson J   Education and Indoctrination in Hollins
    (ed) 1964 op cit   1964
Wiltshire H   The Concepts of Learning and Need
    in Adult Education in Studies in Adult
    Education Vol 5 No 1 Leicester NIAE   1973
Woolfe R   Education, Inequality and the Role
    of the Open University in Adult Education
    Vol 50 No 2   Leicester NIAE   1977
Worsley P et al   Introducing Sociology
    Harmondsworth Penguin   1970
Wrong D H   The Oversocialized Conception of Man
    in Modern Sociology American Sociological
    Review   Vol 26   pp 183-193   reprinted in
    Wrong D H (1976) op cit
Wrong D H Skeptical Sociology   London
    Heinemann   1976
Yarnit M   Second Chance to Learn, Liverpool:
    Class and adult education in Thompson J L (ed)
    1980 op cit
Young M F D (ed) Knowledge and Control
    London Collier-Macmillan Publishers   1971

Index

boundary, 135, 162, 181
see also social
structures
grid, 52-55
group, 52-55
maintenance, 5, 52-55,
62, 161-163
Bourdieu P, 95, 96, 138-
139, 145, 146, 163,
207
bourgeoisie, 9
Bowles S, 121, 137
Boyd R D, 26-27
Bradshaw J, 64
Brickell H, 67, 208
British Post Graduate
Medical Federation,
152
broadcasting, 173
Brookfield S, 156
Brundage D H, 126, 221
Bryant J, 202-211
bureaucracy, 136, 140,
148, 152-153, 155,
161-162, 163, 187-191,
196, 213, 215, 235-236
bureaucrat, 230, 235, 237
bureaucratization, 29,
83, 151
business, 59, 109, 174,
182, 183, 185, 187
Business and Technical
Education Council, 59
businessmen, 36
Butler L, 118

Cambridge University, 22
Cantor L, 22
capital cultural 39
capitalism, 20, 81, 84-
85, 89, 151, 157, 163,
206-207
Caplow T, 239
Carlson R, 145
Carlson R A, 27
Carp A, 212-213
Carr E H, 76
catechism, 21
central planning 4, 183,
186-187, 191
centre-periphery model

of organization, 191-
194
ceremony, 128
certificate, 117-118, 120,
121, 122, 124-126, 129,
137, 240
children, 76, 100, 105,
110, 121, 140, 152, 168,
171, 195, 217, 221-222
Christ, 112
Christian-Marxism, 111, 114
church, 201
Clark B, 236
class
bias, 251
conflict, 17
middle, 21, 35, 39, 64,
71-72, 86, 88, 123, 136,
139-140, 195, 200-201,
203-205, 210, 221
ruling, 78-79, 138, 144
social, 9, 10, 25, 26,
67, 75, 76, 78, 81,
123, 144, 146, 166, 195,
203-205, 210, 211, 221
upper, 21, 81
working, 37, 71, 86-87,
136, 143, 145, 146, 163,
195, 201, 210, 211-212,
221
classroom, 96, 109, 190,
219-222
clergy, 230
Cohen P, 9
Coleman A, 23
college, 46, 148, 184, 189,
228, 231
adult, 143, 237
further education, 136,
187, 215, 237
Collins J B, 202-211
colonizer, 81
communication, 13, 94, 95,
124, 177, 181, 188
communist, 157
communitas, 153-155
community, 18, 26, 57, 70,
102, 151-164, 182, 186,
234
college, 158, 187, 190
education, 111, 149,

Index

Index

Index

Index